How to
TAKE
MONEY
from the
MARKETS

CREATING PROFITABLE STRATEGIES

Plus Six Ready-to-Use Systems

Steve Palmquist

Marketplace Books
Glenelg, Maryland

Publisher: Chris Myers
VP/General Manager: John Boyer
Executive Editor: Jody Costa
Senior Editor: Courtney Jenkins
Editorial Coordinator: Danielle Hainsey
Editorial Intern: Andrea Racine
Art Director: Larry Strauss
Graphic Designer: Jennifer Marin
Production Design Intern: Jessica Weedlun

This publication is designed to provide accurate and authoritative information in regard to the subject matter covered. It is sold with the understanding that neither the author nor the publisher is engaged in rendering legal, accounting, or other professional service. If legal advice or other expert assistance is required, the services of a competent professional person should be sought.

From a Declaration of Principles jointly adopted by a Committee of the American Bar Association and a Committee of Publishers.

ISBN: 1-59280-412-8
ISBN 13: 978-1-59280-412-2

Printed in the United States of America.

TERMS OF USE & DISCLAIMER

ACKNOWLEDGEMENTS

This book provides an opportunity to share more of my research into trading techniques. My first book, *Money-Making Candlestick Patterns*, focused on developing and testing trading techniques using popular candlestick patterns. This book investigates new trading techniques and strategies that were not covered in *Money-Making Candlestick Patterns*.

No man is an island; this research would not have been possible without those who have shared trading ideas and developed backtesting software that allows testing ideas to see which ones produce results, and which are just interesting techniques that cannot demonstrate results.

Thanks to Jody, Courtney, and Jennifer at Marketplace Books for their help and support during this project.

Thanks to Steve Hill, President of AIQ systems, and all the good folks there who developed Trading Expert Pro. The charts in this book are screen shots made on AIQ Systems Trading Expert Pro and used with permission.

Mary, I am a much better man for knowing you. You are always there for me in good times and bad. You have blessed my life.

Herb, I appreciate your emails, and the times we have spent discussing trading techniques at the annual Tahoe trading conferences.

Kevin, thanks for the lunchtime conversations exploring trading techniques and ideas.

Charles, thanks for introducing me to technical analysis.

Aaron, Brenna, Anna, and Liz, children are a blessing from God. You have brightened my life.

Thanks to the subscribers of my newsletter, *The Timely Trades Letter*. Some of your questions have led to interesting areas of research that I will continue to share in the Letter.

TABLE OF CONTENTS

FOREWORD

With *How to Take Money From the Markets: Creating Profitable Strategies plus Six Ready-to-Use Systems*, Steve Palmquist has written a highly informative and easy to read book that makes its critical point in the early part of the preface: "Most trading tools work in some market conditions and do not perform well in others."

The six trading systems that Steve shares in this book are all very logical, well researched, and the test data suggest that they might actually work. However, Steve goes an important step further than most authors and carefully describes the market conditions that are necessary for the systems to perform their best. Steve uses his knowledge and experience to avoid the common trap of proposing systems that supposedly work all the time. Each of Steve's systems has its place and the reader is carefully instructed as to when each system should be applied or avoided.

I hope that other authors will follow Steve's example and pay more attention to fitting systems to particular market conditions. I believe that thoroughly understanding a system and knowing when it will work best can be the difference between success and failure. Steve has written a wonderful book that was obviously intended to help the reader succeed.

– Charles LeBeau

Founder and Director, SmartStops.net

PREFACE

This book covers the design, development, and testing of six trading systems. The performance of each system is analyzed in different time periods and market conditions so that traders have some idea of how and when it is best used. The six tools developed here cover long and short techniques for:

- overbought and oversold stocks,
- pullbacks and retracements in trending stocks,
- and volume accumulation and distribution patterns.

Taken together, they provide a tool set for addressing most market conditions. The development and testing of each tool not only illustrates how and when they are effective, it also illustrates a number of valuable lessons in how stocks and the market behave. For example, the lessons learned about how stocks behave around the Bollinger bands in chapters one and two provide insights into trade management techniques that I use every day with many other trading systems.

Most trading tools work in some market conditions and do not perform well in others. Using the same tool all the time can lead to a run up in the account followed by a series of drawdowns. Just as a carpenter uses a number of different tools when building a house, or a doctor uses several different tools during surgery, traders need a variety of tools to adapt to changing market conditions. In order to know when to use the different tools, traders can test them in different time periods and market conditions.

Testing a tool does not guarantee its future performance, but it does give traders an idea of how the tool has performed during different periods and can provide an indication of when the tool should be used, and when another tool may be more appropriate. A carpenter is not born with the knowledge of when to use each of the different tools available; he develops the knowledge and skill by studying the capabilities of each tool and learning what type of results can be expected when using them. In the same way, traders need to study several different trading tools and learn how and when to use them. Note that just studying the tool does not turn a carpenter into a craftsman; he spends time practicing and developing the skill. It is the same for traders. It takes time and practice to learn and master all the necessary skills.

Trading is a statistical business; traders focus on risk management using systems that have been shown to provide an edge. Trading stock tips, news stories, stocks you are familiar with, and similar approaches can lead to mixed results. No one guesses right all the time. Trading is not about guessing or hoping. Traders need tools that are well understood, like an old friend. You usually know how a friend will react in a given situation. Sometimes you may be surprised, but more often than not you have a good idea of their reaction to things. Trading needs to be the same way. No system reacts as expected all the time; if it did, everyone would be driving BMWs to their yachts. A trader's job is to find a system that has an edge, learn how it behaves in different market conditions, and then be positioned to profit if the system does the normal thing.

A SYSTEM WITH AN EDGE

The trading systems in this book are analyzed using backtesting techniques. Backtesting does not guarantee future performance. Nothing guarantees future events. Trading always involves risk and those who cannot accept the risk, or loss of capital, should not be trading. Period. To illustrate it, imagine walking down the street every day for a month and passing two houses with dogs in the yard. The first dog runs up to the fence, wagging his tail every day. The second dog rushes the fence barking every day. Based on this past experience, you might draw conclusions about which dog you would rather pet. The past experience doesn't guarantee you are right, but it would seem more logical to pet the friendly dog that has been wagging its tail every day.

We draw conclusions based on what we have seen in the past. We act on these conclusions, and while frequently right, there is the possibility that they will be wrong. Backtesting can give us an idea of how a system has behaved in a variety of conditions in the past. I would rather trade a system that I have seen perform in the past than one for which there is no information.

Some trading systems will generate more trading candidates during certain market periods than a trader is willing or able to take. Traders need to have a clear strategy for picking among multiple opportunities. This book shows how different price and volume filters can affect trading system results, and hence be used for prioritizing among multiple trading opportunities. Traders do not guess; they take risks based on informed judgments, which are based on an extensive understanding of how the system has performed during similar market conditions in the past. This does not eliminate risk, but it does allow the trader to manage risk using informed decision-making.

This book also develops tools for analyzing the market, both by direct observation and through the use of custom developed tools. Few people can consistently predict where the market is going. Picking targets for the market is guesswork, and trading based on guesswork can lead to mixed results.

> The focus here is not on predicting the market, but observing the market; and then based on the current market conditions, selecting appropriate trading tools. When the market conditions change, traders should change with it and pick the most appropriate tool for what the market is currently doing.

Instead of guessing market direction, traders need to adapt to what the market is doing. This is a process I call Market Adaptive Trading, and it is one of the keys to trading.

This research will give you a start in Market Adaptive Trading. Trading, like most professions, is not something that is learned by reading one book or going to a weekend seminar. Few people would go to a surgeon who learned brain surgery after reading one book. It is amazing how many people will trade their life savings based on tips from friends or after reading a couple of books. This book will not turn you into an instant millionaire, nor is it intended to. The systems provided here, and the research behind them, is the beginning of a journey that requires time, effort, and continued study. However, each journey begins with the first step. 1:50 PM Feb. 13, 2013

The six systems researched in this book are different types of tools for use in different market environments. There is no magic system that wins all the time, and works in all market conditions. Traders need a variety of tools and the knowledge of how to select the appropriate ones for the current market conditions. The research in each chapter helps to determine the most appropriate times to use each system.

As part of the Market Adaptive Trading process, I analyze each system described in the book in different market conditions. I do not know what the market will do over the next few years, but it always will be made of bullish, bearish, and trading range periods. I want to understand how trading systems perform in these three types of market conditions, and then when I see one of these market conditions in the future, I will use the systems that performed the best during those conditions.

The first two chapters focus on trading techniques for overbought and oversold stocks based on their relationship to the Bollinger bands. These systems usually do not generate trading candidates every day because in general the market needs to be moving for awhile to generate overbought or oversold conditions. The reason for starting with these systems is that a great deal of information is uncovered about how stocks behave around the bands, and this information is useful in the management of trades using many other trading systems.

If one can construct a reasonable system for shorting stocks that have run up above the upper band, then it makes sense to close existing long positions as they move above the upper band. One of the great things about backtesting is that traders not only learn how a specific trading system works, they gain valuable insights into how stocks behave that can be used to improve results and manage trades taken with other techniques. The information developed in the design of the overbought and oversold systems described in chapters one and two has been an invaluable asset to me, and I use it constantly in determining whether or not to hold or exit existing positions.

The bread and butter systems that I use every day are described in chapters three and four, and are based on trading pullbacks and retracements in trending stocks. These systems are the "general purpose" trading tools, whereas the Bollinger band and accumulation tools described in the other chapters are "special purpose" tools. The Bollinger band and accumulation/distribution patterns are interesting and useful tools by themselves, but they also provide valuable insights on money management strategies for the other tools I use—which is why I start with them.

Many new traders follow one or more of the many indicators that are available in popular charting packages. I am amazed at how many people do this without any knowledge of how well these indicators do, or do not, produce results. Many of the indicators are simply not suitable for timing the market or for stock purchases. A lot of traders use the Stochastic indicator and so I have provided some test results for Stochastic in the Appendix. Rather than using the prepackaged indicators, I trade systems based on price and volume patterns that I have researched and that have shown promising results in testing. This book shares the design and test results of these six different systems.

There are no perfect trading systems, no matter what those slick brochures we all get in the mail say. Trading is a statistical business where it is important to manage risk. Every trading system has a certain percentage of winners and losers. If you bet big, or leverage the account with margin or options, you can see large profits when the natural statistics give you a number of winners in a row. However, the opposite is also true. Leverage in an account can hurt you when the natural statistics give you a number of losers in a row.

Trading involves more than just picking a stock and entering a position. You don't have a profit until you are back in cash. Exit strategies and money management techniques are important aspects of trading. Traders need to vary their position sizes and the number of trading positions used based on the current market conditions. In order to do this, traders need to know how their trading systems perform in different market conditions. <u>We cannot control what the market is doing, but we can react to it</u>. During conditions that result in lower success rates for a trading system, we need to either switch to a different trading system, or reduce position sizes as a way of reducing risk.

In addition to understanding the effectiveness of the different trading patterns in the trader's tool box, there are <u>a number of lessons about trading I have learned during the last 20 years.</u> Some of the more important ones are:

- There is no magic to trading. It is about putting the odds on your side and not trading unless they are. This sounds simple, but it takes a few years to get good at it. And like most things, while you are learning, it is best to work with someone. The learning time is long because traders have to see how things behave in different markets, and learn to trade the odds and not their feelings. See www.daisydogger.com for more information on my trading experiences.

- The market will not adapt to us, we must adapt to it. Active trading in a narrow range presents higher than average risk. Traders can compensate for higher risk market conditions by trading fewer positions and using smaller position sizes. Failure to do this can be costly.

- Successful traders adjust their trading style, trading system, holding period, and exit strategies based on the current market conditions. This is the process I refer to as Market Adaptive Trading. It is better to learn how to adapt to the market rather than running from one trading idea to the next looking for the next super system.

- As a trader, I do not care which way the market moves; I can make money either way. It is important to be able to quickly react to whatever the market does and not be emotionally attached to any particular choice.

- I cannot control what the market does, so I have a plan for whichever path it picks, and then I trade the plan.

- Successful trading is not about predicting what the market is going to do. It is about knowing how to react to whatever it does.

- Always be thinking about taking and protecting profits.

- If you are not sure what to do, exit the position. There will be others.

- You do not need to trade every day. Let the setups come to you and take the best ones. When the market is moving, there are lots of good setups to trade. If there are few setups, or most are failing, then listen to the message of the market.

- Do not rush in; there is plenty of time to get into a tradable move when the market changes. If a trend is worth trading, then by definition you do not have to be in on the first day.

- Never enter a position without a plan for exiting.

- Do not count your chickens before they hatch. You do not have a profit until you are back in cash.

- Never trade with money you cannot afford to lose.

- Trading is not a team sport. Stay away from chat rooms and financial TV. Seek the truth, not support from others with your point of view.

Finally, recognize that this book is the beginning of a journey, not the end. It takes time, expense, and effort to learn trading, but the results can be well worth it. As you go through the process, share what you learn with your trading friends. There are no colleges where you can go to get a degree in trading. Traders need to stick together and share the things they learn. When you have some financial success, celebrate it by sharing some of the proceeds, without asking anything in return, with someone in need and asking them to do the same when things improve for them.

—Steve Palmquist

founder of DaisyDogger.com, author of the
Timely Trades Letter and *Money-Making Candlestick Patterns*,
and presenter of *Proven Candlestick Patterns* and
New Money-Making Trading Systems.

Author's note: Please refer to my first book, *Money-Making Candlestick Patterns*, for additional information on my backtesting methodology and how to create calendar and market condition testing environments on your own. One does not have to be an expert on backtesting techniques to take advantage of the results any more than one has to understand the internal combustion engine in order to drive a car. Readers interested in backtesting techniques and the test results for a variety of candlestick patterns will find the material in *Money-Making Candlestick Patterns* to be of interest.

CHAPTER 1

BOLLINGER BAND STRATEGY FOR OVERBOUGHT STOCKS

Many traders use indicators to determine when to enter and exit trades. Most charting programs include dozens of different indicators that can be displayed on the charts. Popular indicators such as the Stochastic and MACD (Moving Average Convergence-Divergence) are frequently discussed when traders get together. I have listened to countless numbers of these discussions. The interesting thing is that people typically explain why they use a particular indicator by citing a number of examples of when it has worked for them. When they do, another trader will say something like, "well it did not work for me, so I use the XYZ indicator, which is much more reliable." When I ask the second trader why his XYZ indicator is more reliable, the explanation usually involves a few more examples of good trades.

This is how trading myths are born. Listen to me closely: a few examples do not prove anything. It is possible to flip a coin and have it come up heads five times in a row. Few traders would observe this and then think that when you flip a coin, it always comes up heads. Yet, for some reason, people will read an article about an indicator that produced four or five examples of good trades, and then they will go and risk their money trading the technique. They typically trade the new technique until it produces several losses in a row and then they start looking for another article that describes a "better" technique and the process repeats itself in an endless search for a better trading system.

Myth: One or two examples are enough to prove a winning trading system.

Fact: Trading is a statistical business. Traders need to understand how a potential system has performed over a large number of trades and in different market conditions.

Adopting a trading technique because it was recommended by someone, or written about in an article that showed a few working examples, is a high-risk endeavor. Trading is a statistical business. Traders need to understand how a potential system has performed over a large number of trades and in different market conditions.

If you flip a coin three times, there is a one in eight chance of it coming up heads three times in a row. If you observed three heads in three flips and then drew conclusions about the probability of heads coming up, you would be wrong; just like seeing three examples of when an indicator produced favorable results could also be wrong.

If you flip the coin ten times, there is less than one chance in a thousand that the coin will come up ten heads in a row. If you flip it a thousand times, the chances that it will come up heads every time are essentially zero. The more times you flip the coin, the more likely you will see the number of heads and tails balance out. The more trials you run, the closer you get to the true probability. The same idea applies to analyzing trading techniques. A few examples can lead you astray. A large number of tests gives you a clearer picture of what to expect.

Trading techniques are more complex than a coin flip, but since there is no system that works all the time, trading systems do have a win-loss percentage associated with them. The winning percentage of a trading system is affected by the system itself and also the specific market conditions in which it is used. Using a trading technique that has not been tested over a large number of trades and in different market conditions will expose you to an unknown risk. Trading is about risk management; trading without knowing the risks, or odds, of a trading system producing favorable results can quickly lead to ruin.

BOLLINGER BANDS

Bollinger bands measure the volatility of a stock around a simple moving average. The volatility is measured as the standard deviation from the average. The standard settings for the Bollinger bands are the 20-day simple moving average and two standard deviations around that average. The standard deviation measures the dispersion of the stock prices around the 20-day moving average. A low standard deviation means the stock prices are clustered near the moving average. A high standard deviation implies the stock prices are widely spread around the 20-day moving average.

It is not necessary to go into a long discussion of the math behind standard deviations; the key point is that two standard deviations typically contain about 95 percent of the data points. In the case of a stock chart, we could expect that 95 percent of the time, the prices will be contained within the Bollinger bands. It is unusual for prices to move outside the Bollinger bands, and this fact leads to a number of interesting trading systems based on the Bollinger bands.

Successful trading systems provide an "edge." They typically show winning trades more often than random chance. Based on this you can expect that, over a large number of trades, you should see the number of winning trades clearly out-numbering losing trades; which leads to profits. Since stock prices are rarely outside the bands, we can use this knowledge to build a trading system.

Courtesy of AIQ

Figure 1.1 shows a chart of the NASDAQ during 2008. Most of the time the price action, as expected, is contained within the Bollinger bands; which are the lines above and below the price action. A few times during the year, as marked on the price chart in Figure 1.1, the price moves outside the upper or lower Bollinger band. Note that the price is rarely outside the bands for more than a couple of days. Also note that when the price is outside the bands, it quickly snaps back inside them, and then often moves sideways or reverses direction.

Since movements outside the Bollinger bands typically do not last long, I look to take profits on positions when the stock moves outside the bands. Another interesting idea is to short positions that move significantly above the upper Bollinger band. In order to test this idea, I backtested a simple system (the AboveBB system) that used the following rules.

The AboveBB system:

- If today's high is more than four percent above the upper band, and
- The close is greater than $10, and
- The average volume is at least 300,000 shares, then
- Enter a short position at the opening tomorrow, then
- Hold the position for three days, then
- Close the position on the next open.

INITIAL TEST RESULTS FOR ABOVEBB

I used AIQ Systems Trading Expert Pro to evaluate this AboveBB system using my trading database of about 2,500 stocks. I found that during the calendar year 2008, there would have been more than 2,600 trades, and that 62 percent of them were winners. The results of this test are shown in Figure 1.2.

FIGURE 1.2:
INITIAL TEST RESULTS FOR ABOVEBB

AboveBB		Winners	Losers	Neutral
Number of trades in test:	2628	1650	973	5
Average periods per trade:	4.19	4.08	4.37	4.40
Maximum Profit/Loss:		45.62%	(55.64)%	
Average Drawdown:	(2.47)%	(0.80)%	(5.30)%	
Average Profit/Loss:	2.40%	6.63%	(4.75)%	
Average SPX Profit/Loss:	1.23%	1.94%	0.03%	
Probability:		62.79%	37.02%	
Average Annual ROI:	209.14%	592.51%	(396.78)%	
Annual SPX (Buy & Hold):	(36.32)%			
Reward/Risk Ratio:	2.36			
Start test date:	01/01/08			
End test date:	12/31/08			

Interval:Daily
Pricing Summary
      Entry price: [Open]
      Exit price: [Open]
Exit Summary
      Hold for 3 periods

Courtesy of AIQ

Notice that during the test period, this technique showed an interesting and positive annualized ROI during a period when the market was down by about 36 percent. The system had winning trades about 62 percent of the time, and there were plenty of available trades during the test period. Now, one test period does not prove anything, but these results are clearly the kind of thing that I would want to investigate further.

Most backtesting software provides a lot more data than the average trader is going to use. The people selling backtesting software may feel that more is better, but not all of the information is necessarily valuable.

The four key things I look for in backtesting results are:

1. Does the annualized ROI number beat buy and hold? If it does not, then why trade the system? Also, remember that the annualized ROI is not the number you would see in your account if you traded the system; it is more like a figure of merit with a higher number being better. In this case, the annualized ROI of 209 percent is obviously better than a 36 percent loss for holding the index during the test period. New traders will often use the annualized ROI as their only criteria for selecting a system. This can lead to a lot of problems in the real world because the percentage of winning trades affects position sizes and drawdowns. Systems that show large returns but only win once in awhile can lead to strong drawdowns, which may cause people to stop trading them before they show profits.

2. Does the percentage of winning trades clearly beat random chance? If it does not, then in most cases I am not interested in the technique. In this case, the test results for calendar 2008 indicate that about 62 percent of the trades were profitable. In trading, anything over 60 percent is clearly interesting. This does not imply that for every ten trades six will be winners. It is an average across a lot of trades. Some new traders think that if they make ten trades a week, then they should get paid every Friday just like they do in their job. Trading is not like that. You can easily have several weeks when you do not get paid. The percentages are calculated across all the trades in the test period and cannot be expected to hold up each and every week.

3. Does the average winning trade gain more than the average losing trade loses? In this case, the average winning trade shows a 6.6 percent profit and the average losing trade shows a 4.7 percent loss. If the system is winning more often that it loses, and the average winning trade is larger than the average losing trade, then it is easier to follow the system. Systems that show average losing trades equal to or greater than the average winning trade do not provide much room for slippage, commissions, and the other factors that happen in real world trading.

4. Is the tested system showing enough trades during the time period to be a valid test, and are there enough trades during the period to make the system practical to use? This system shows more than 2,600 trades during the year, and they are spread throughout the year rather than just in narrow clusters. A system that just shows a few trades a year, or one in which the trades are clustered in time may be event-driven. A system that shows hundreds of trades a year may be more likely due to the nature of the trading pattern repeating than just a few events during the year.

FIGURE 1.3:
EARLY JANUARY 2008 TRADES FOR ABOVEBB

Ticker	Held	Entry Date	Entry Price	Exit Date	Exit Price	Profit	D
DNR	5	01/04/08	33.0800	01/09/08	29.9200	3.1600	
FTI	5	01/04/08	63.6100	01/09/08	61.6500	1.9600	
GG	5	01/04/08	37.2500	01/09/08	37.0300	0.2200	
NEM	5	01/04/08	53.1800	01/09/08	52.4800	0.7000	
NG	5	01/04/08	10.3900	01/09/08	11.5500	-1.1600	
SPN	5	01/04/08	41.7000	01/09/08	44.4100	-2.7100	
GB	3	01/07/08	22.0700	01/10/08	22.1800	-0.1100	
SATS	3	01/07/08	36.4400	01/10/08	30.7100	5.7300	
ITMN	3	01/08/08	17.4900	01/11/08	17.7200	-0.2300	
MATK	3	01/08/08	33.7900	01/11/08	32.5100	1.2800	
QID	3	01/08/08	42.4200	01/11/08	43.5100	-1.0900	
SRS	3	01/08/08	124.4900	01/11/08	129.8700	-5.3800	
BG	5	01/09/08	127.3000	01/14/08	131.3600	-4.0600	
BRP	5	01/09/08	79.0700	01/14/08	70.6300	8.4400	
CVH	5	01/09/08	61.0600	01/14/08	61.6800	-0.6200	
HMY	5	01/09/08	12.3300	01/14/08	13.0200	-0.6900	
HWAY	5	01/09/08	66.7900	01/14/08	68.3900	-1.6000	
ISIS	5	01/09/08	18.5700	01/14/08	17.3700	1.2000	
KG	5	01/09/08	12.0500	01/14/08	11.7800	0.2700	
KGC	5	01/09/08	21.2400	01/14/08	24.0000	-2.7600	
RPM	5	01/09/08	21.0300	01/14/08	21.4000	-0.3700	
WBSN	5	01/09/08	17.4375	01/14/08	17.2500	0.1875	
CZZ	5	01/10/08	14.1400	01/15/08	13.9000	0.2400	
MZZ	5	01/10/08	63.6400	01/15/08	63.6900	-0.0500	
PPDI	5	01/10/08	45.1700	01/15/08	47.7400	-2.5700	
RAI	5	01/10/08	69.6700	01/15/08	66.5000	3.1700	
SKF	5	01/10/08	117.4500	01/15/08	113.7400	3.7100	
TNE	5	01/10/08	24.1500	01/15/08	24.2500	-0.1000	
TWM	5	01/10/08	82.4800	01/15/08	82.9100	-0.4300	
HS	5	01/11/08	21.2200	01/16/08	21.3700	-0.1500	
IBN	5	01/11/08	73.1600	01/16/08	68.2500	4.9100	
ILMN	5	01/11/08	35.9800	01/16/08	35.1100	0.8700	
VIVO	5	01/11/08	35.4000	01/16/08	33.8600	1.5400	

Courtesy of AIQ

When testing a trading system, it is important to look at the actual trades, not just the statistical summary information. If the test results are due to an event rather than the trading pattern itself, the results may be clustered around one or more dates, rather than distributed evenly through time. Figure 1.3 shows trades the basic AboveBB system took in early January of 2008. There were a number of trades between January 4, 2008 and January 11, 2008, which is the type of behavior I am looking for throughout the year. In scrolling through all the trades for 2008, I found that the trades occurred frequently and were not clustered around certain dates.

Examining the trades produced by a system can also give traders a better idea of what to expect when trading. New traders often just focus on the annualized ROI or winning percentage and assume that that is what they will see every week. Trading does not work that way.

If you only focus on one aspect of trading, it is like buying a business and just looking at last month's revenue. You might get a good deal, and you may get a business with only one good month. You may get a business with supply problems, or one that has been made obsolete by technology, or a host of other issues. If you are going to buy a business, you want to check it all out. If you are going to trade, you need to fully understand all the parameters associated with your trading technique. This requires time and effort, which is why many people do not do it. Those people are driving blind, and blind drivers eventually crash.

Traders do not get paid for clicking the mouse, or because it is Friday. They get paid if they find a well-researched system that they fully understand, has the odds on their side, and is traded when the current market conditions are favorable. And, here's the most important part—traders get paid if, and only if, they use prudent money management techniques. All these things play a role in whether or not your trading is profitable; skipping over any of them can lead to trouble.

EARLY JANUARY 2008 TRADES FOR BASIC ABOVEBB
SORTED BY PROFIT

Ticker	Held	Entry Date	Entry Price	Exit Date	Exit Price	Profit
SRS	5	11/20/08	232.9500	11/25/08	133.2400	99.7100
SKF	5	11/20/08	230.8000	11/25/08	160.8000	70.0000
FAZ	5	11/21/08	143.4000	11/26/08	77.9800	65.4200
SKF	5	07/16/08	190.9100	07/21/08	132.5200	58.3900
SRS	5	10/24/08	194.9600	10/29/08	137.9600	57.0000
SKF	3	01/22/08	143.9300	01/25/08	102.8000	41.1300
TWM	5	10/10/08	139.5700	10/15/08	103.5800	35.9900
TWM	5	11/21/08	161.6500	11/26/08	129.7300	31.9200
SMN	5	11/21/08	120.8000	11/26/08	89.7100	31.0900
RTP	3	02/04/08	440.0000	02/07/08	409.2700	30.7300
MZZ	5	11/21/08	144.4800	11/26/08	114.5100	29.9700
SMN	3	10/27/08	100.3500	10/30/08	71.0200	29.3300
SKF	5	09/17/08	125.6300	09/22/08	97.1500	28.4800
MZZ	5	10/10/08	119.9300	10/15/08	92.6900	27.2400
MZZ	3	10/27/08	125.5500	10/30/08	98.5700	26.9800
SKF	5	10/09/08	140.7000	10/14/08	114.5500	26.1500
FSLR	6	02/14/08	231.5100	02/20/08	205.4300	26.0800
TWM	3	10/27/08	135.3500	10/30/08	109.9900	25.3600
MOS	3	01/15/08	107.5900	01/18/08	82.7900	24.8000
SRS	5	01/23/08	136.7000	01/28/08	113.9900	22.7100
BLK	3	03/25/08	222.1100	03/28/08	200.0100	22.1000
CME	3	09/22/08	400.0200	09/25/08	378.0000	22.0200
TNH	3	04/22/08	166.9900	04/25/08	145.0200	21.9700
SDS	5	11/21/08	122.3800	11/26/08	100.7700	21.6100
SMN	5	10/10/08	99.1100	10/15/08	78.8100	20.3000
QID	3	10/27/08	85.2200	10/30/08	64.9300	20.2900
ANR	6	07/01/08	105.2200	07/07/08	85.0100	20.2100
ISRG	5	07/24/08	330.1000	07/29/08	310.0000	20.1000
GHL	5	09/19/08	91.9300	09/24/08	72.0700	19.8600
SKF	6	03/18/08	125.0200	03/24/08	105.1900	19.8300
WABC	5	09/19/08	76.3200	09/24/08	57.7200	18.6000
FSLR	5	11/05/08	168.2300	11/10/08	149.8500	18.3800
TTES	6	07/02/08	83.0000	07/08/08	65.5300	17.4700
FSLR	3	04/07/08	286.5600	04/10/08	269.4700	17.0900
SPW	5	07/31/08	133.2000	08/05/08	117.0300	16.1700
HBHC	5	09/19/08	67.3900	09/24/08	52.0000	15.3900

Courtesy of AIQ

Figure 1.4 also shows trades made during the 2008 test period, but in this case they are sorted by profit rather than by date (as shown in Figure 1.3). Sorting the trades during a test period by profit allows us to see if the profits of the system are coming from a few trades, or if the profits are more evenly distributed over a large number of trades. Figure 1.4 shows that there were ten trades that had profits of $30 or more. Scrolling to the bottom of the list (something hard to do in a book) showed that there were four trades with losses of $30 or more.

The big winners and losers are small in number, and fairly evenly balanced considering there were more than 2,000 trades during the test period. Watch out for a system in which most of the profits come from a very small number of trades. In this case, the vast majority of the trades had profits of plus or minus a few dollars. There were significantly fewer big winners and losers than there were trades that just picked up a couple of dollars here and there. This is what we want to see.

ABOVEBB TEST RESULTS
IN DIFFERENT TIME PERIODS

After examining the data shown in Figure 1.2, I found the results interesting and felt the AboveBB trading system was worth investigating further. The next step is to investigate how the system performed in other test periods. One test period proves nothing; the results may have been due to market conditions, major news events, or other factors that may not repeat from year to year. Figure 1.5 shows the results of running the same system, AboveBB, during calendar 2007.

Once again the test results are interesting. The annualized ROI clearly beats buy and hold during the test period with more than 55 percent winners, and there were plenty of trades during the test period. The spread between the

FIGURE 1.5:
TEST RESULTS FOR ABOVEBB DURING 2007

AboveBB		Winners	Losers	Neutral
Number of trades in test:	2272	1260	999	13
Average periods per trade:	4.38	4.39	4.38	4.62
Maximum Profit/Loss:		73.92%	(37.42)%	
Average Drawdown:	(1.99)%	(0.62)%	(3.74)%	
Average Profit/Loss:	0.66%	3.84%	(3.35)%	
Average SPX Profit/Loss:	0.28%	0.62%	(0.15)%	
Probability:		55.46%	43.97%	
Average Annual ROI:	54.65%	319.77%	(279.80)%	
Annual SPX (Buy & Hold):	2.05%			
Reward/Risk Ratio:	1.44			
Start test date:	01/01/07			
End test date:	12/31/07			

Interval:Daily
Pricing Summary
        Entry price: [Open]
        Exit price: [Open]
Exit Summary
        Hold for 3 periods

Courtesy of AIQ

average winning trade and the average losing trade narrowed considerably, so I would want to look at further testing to see if this could be improved. At this point, we know that the AboveBB system shows interesting results in two completely different test periods.

Some traders and investors get caught looking for "the hot hand." They want to put their money in what worked well last year, or the mutual fund that had the best performance last year. Many trading systems have results that can vary strongly from year to year, as we have seen in this example. During 2008, a trader using this system might be described by his friends as "someone who really knows how to trade," when in fact it was only a good year due to the natural ebb and flow of results from a single system in particular market conditions. This will become clearer as we look at the test results for the 2005 and 2006 test periods.

The test results for AboveBB during 2006 are shown in Figure 1.6 and the results for the 2005 test period are shown in Figure 1.7. During 2006, the percentage of winning trades dropped to 525 and the system showed a small net loss during a period when the market had a small gain. The results during

FIGURE 1.6:
TEST RESULTS FOR ABOVEBB DURING 2006

AboveBB		Winners	Losers	Neutral
Number of trades in test:	1836	959	862	15
Average periods per trade:	4.46	4.46	4.45	4.73
Maximum Profit/Loss:		29.33%	(111.18)%	
Average Drawdown:	(2.16)%	(0.60)%	(3.93)%	
Average Profit/Loss:	(0.02)%	3.24%	(3.65)%	
Average SPX Profit/Loss	(0.06)%	0.12%	(0.27)%	
Probability:		52.23%	52.23%	
Average Annual ROI:	(1.68)%	265.04%	(265.04)%	
Annual SPX (Buy & Hold):	13.45%			
Reward/Risk Ratio:	0.99			
Start test date:	01/02/06			
End test date:	12/29/06			

Interval:Daily
Pricing Summary
       Entry price: [Open]
       Exit price: [Open]
Exit Summary
       Hold for 3 periods

Courtesy of AIQ

FIGURE 1.7:
TEST RESULTS FOR ABOVEBB DURING 2005

AboveBB		Winners	Losers	Neutral
Number of trades in test:	1570	781	771	18
Average periods per trade:	4.39	4.35	4.42	4.72
Maximum Profit/Loss:		68.64%	(30.94)%	
Average Drawdown:	(2.19)%	(0.4805	(3.97)%	
Average Profit/Loss:	(0.05)%	3.51%	(3.66)%	
Average SPX Profit/Loss:	(0.08)%	0.14%	(0.31)%	
Probability:		49.75%	49.11%	
Average Annual ROI:	(4.31)%	294.44%	(302.21)%	
Annual SPX (Buy & Hold):	4.68%			
Reward/Risk Ratio:	0.97			
Start test date:	01/03/05			
End test date:	12/30/05			

Interval:Daily
Pricing Summary
       Entry price: [Open]
       Exit price: [Open]
Exit Summary
       Hold for 3 periods

Courtesy of AIQ

the 2005 test period were similar. The percentage of winning trades dropped to about 50 percent and once again the trading system showed a small annualized loss when the market showed a small gain.

If you show someone the test results for the AboveBB system during 2008, when the system had 62 percent winning trades and a very strong annualized ROI, they will be quite interested. If you show them the results from 2005 and 2006, when the system lost money, they won't care. This is the same as looking for the "hot hand," which is not necessarily how you become a successful trader.

Instead of looking at how a trading system (note that mutual funds are a form of trading system) performed during several individual years, some people look at how a system performed during the last year, and also during the last several years. Figure 1.8 shows the performance of the AboveBB system during the four-year period from January 3, 2005 to December 31, 2008. During this period, our trading system showed 56 percent winning trades and an annualized ROI of 78 percent, which compares quite favorably to a small loss in the index during this same time.

TEST RESULTS FOR ABOVEBB FROM 2005 THROUGH 2008

AboveBB		Winners	Losers	Neutral
Number of trades in test:	8324	4662	3611	51
Average periods per trade:	4.34	4.29	4.41	4.67
Maximum Profit/Loss:		73.92%	(111.18)%	
Average Drawdown:	(2.21)%	(0.66)%	(4.25)%	
Average Profit/Loss:	0.93%	4.65%	(3.86)%	
Average SPX Profit.Loss:	0.44%	0.90%	(0.16)%	
Probability:		56.01%	43.38%	
Average Annual ROI:	78.20%	395.88%	(320.05)%	
Annual SPX (Buy & Hold):	(5.77)%			
Reward/Risk Ratio:	1.56			
Start test date:	01/03/05			
End test date:	12/31/08			

Interval:Daily
Pricing Summary
 Entry price: [Open]
 Exit price: [Open]
Exit Summary
 Hold for 3 periods

Courtesy of AIQ

Many people looking at the test data for AboveBB during the last year, and the last four years, would find this trading system attractive. The system showed market-beating results over a four-year period and very strong results during 2008. Many people tend to assume that the overall statistics will apply over smaller time periods. They tend to think that because the system had great results last year, and strong results during the last four-year period, that these are the type of results they would get every week or month or year. As we have seen from the test results above, that is not the case.

Myth: Statistics for a trading system from a long period of time or by individual years will fully demonstrate a system's profitability on smaller time frames.

Fact: A system's winning percentage over a long period of time does not necessarily imply what the winning percentage will be over much shorter time periods. The winning percentage of the trading system is not necessarily evenly distributed over different time periods.

People looking at the trading data for each individual year during the last four years would find that it performed well in 2008 and 2007 but lost money in 2005 and 2006. They might feel that since the system lost money half the time, it would not be something they would want to trade. People looking at the results for the entire four-year period see statistics that are more interesting and may be attracted to the system. The second group are looking at the same trading system, during the same time periods, but are led to a different conclusion. Favorable statistics during a particular time period do not imply that the results are evenly distributed or that the winning percentages will be the same during smaller sections of the overall test period. One of the reasons for this is that the market goes through different periods of bullish, bearish, and trading range environments during longer test periods. As we will see later, it is important to analyze a trading system during specific market conditions and not just different calendar periods.

This phenomenon is why statistics can be so misleading: the same data presented in different ways can lead to different conclusions. Remember this the next time you look at mutual fund data or a national opinion poll, or the next time you listen to a politician justifying a new program. Traders need to fully analyze and understand a trading system and not just jump onto something because it worked well last year, someone recommended it, or it showed great results during a specific time period.

When you first meet someone, you have no database or background information, and thus cannot predict how he might react in a given situation. After you have been friends for awhile, you have a pretty good idea of how he will react to things. Analyze a trading system until it becomes an old friend, and you know what to expect. You will be surprised from time to time, but you will have a good idea of what to expect most of the time.

Testing trading systems during calendar year periods can be very helpful, but, as shown above, drawing conclusions from one or two tests can lead to trouble. Traders need to carefully analyze system performance in a variety of different time frames. They need to work with a trading system to understand how it has performed in a variety of different conditions.

ADDING A VOLUME FILTER TO THE ABOVEBB SYSTEM

So far all the testing has used the basic AboveBB trading system with the following rules:

- If today's high was more than four percent above the upper band, and
- The close is greater than $10, and
- The average volume is at least 300,000 shares, then
- Enter a short position at the opening tomorrow, then
- Hold the position for three days, then
- Close the position on the next open.

These rules are based on the price pattern of the stock and do not include any rules related to the stock's volume pattern. Volume measures the interest in a move; it shows how many traders are interested in purchasing a stock at the current price. The volume pattern also can play a strong role in the effectiveness of stock trading patterns, so it needs to be tested and examined in conjunction with the basic price pattern.

The test results for the basic AboveBB system during 2005, as shown in Figure 1.7, showed that the percentage of winning trades was a coin flip, and the system showed a slight loss for the period while the market showed a slight gain. Figure 1.9 shows the test results during 2005 that result from using the basic AboveBB system with one additional rule.

The new rule is that trades are only taken if the volume on the day the stock moves above the upper Bollinger band is below the 21-day simple moving average.

Figure 1.9 indicates that during the 2005 test period, the annualized ROI and the percentage of winning trades were significantly improved by adding the new rule that the volume must be below the 21-day moving average. The low volume on the move above the band indicates that fewer traders are willing to pay the higher price for the stock. When fewer people are willing to pay higher prices for something, the price often comes down.

I went to a high school football game to watch my oldest daughter play in the band. After a while, I walked over to the refreshment stand to get something to drink. As I was walking toward the stand, the crowd noise greatly increased, and people were cheering loudly. I knew from the increased noise level that something important had happened, so I turned around and saw the end of a long yardage play. Stock volume is a similar indicator; when stocks are moving on volume, there is a lot of interest in the play and traders should turn and pay attention.

If Sears had been selling a hammer for $30 and then suddenly raised the price to $40, they would expect to sell fewer of them. Sears would see the volume drop off and conclude that the price may not be sustainable. The same idea applies to stocks; when the price moves up on declining volume, the price change may not be sustainable.

FIGURE 1.9:
ABOVEBB TEST DURING 2005 WITH
BELOW AVERAGE VOLUME REQUIREMENT

AboveBB		Winners	Losers	Neutral
Number of trades in test:	116	66	47	3
Average periods per trade:	3.97	3.82	4.21	3.67
Maximum Profit/Loss:		68.64%	(18.54)%	
Average Drawdown:	(1.91)%	(0.41)%	(4.13)%	
Average Profit/Loss:	1.43%	5.38%	(4.00)%	
Average SPX Profit/Loss:	(0.01)%	0.15%	(0.22)%	
Probability:		56.90%	40.52%	
Average Annual ROI:	131.72%	513.42%	(346.77)%	
Annual SPX (Buy & Hold):	4.48%			
Reward/Risk Ratio:	1.88			
Start test date:	01/03/05			
End test date:	12/30/05			
Interval:Daily				
Pricing Summary				
Entry price: [Open]				
Exit price: [Open]				
Exit Summary				
Hold for 3 periods				

Courtesy of AIQ

FIGURE 1.10:
ABOVEBB TEST DURING 2005 WITH
"VOLUME LESS THAN YESTERDAY'S VOLUME"

AboveBB		Winners	Losers	Neutral
Number of trades in test:	608	301	301	6
Average periods per trade:	4.24	4.24	4.23	5.00
Maximum Profit/Loss:		68.64%	(51.74)%	
Average Drawdown:	(2.31)%	(0.51)%	(4.16)%	
Average Profit/Loss:	(0.05)%	3.63%	(3.73)%	
Average SPX Profit/Loss	(0.10)%	0.13%	(0.33)%	
Probability:		49.51%	49.51%	
Average Annual ROI:	(3.92)%	312.58%	(321.76)%	
Annual SPX (Buy & Hold):	4.68%			
Reward/Risk Ratio:	0.98			
Start test date:	01/03/05			
End test date:	12/30/05			
Interval:Daily				
Pricing Summary				
Entry price: [Open]				
Exit price: [Open]				
Exit Summary				
Hold for 3 periods				

Courtesy of AIQ

Another way to look at declining volume is to compare the volume on the day the stock moves above the band to the previous day's volume. Running the basic AboveBB system during 2005 using the single additional requirement that the volume must be less than the previous day's volume yields the results shown in Figure 1.10. Measuring a volume decline in this way leads to about the same results as the original test for the 2005 test period. It appears that during this test period, traders would be better off trading the pattern on days when the volume is below the 21-day simple moving average than trading either the basic system or one that looked for trades on volume below the previous day's volume.

Shorting stocks that move above the upper Bollinger band on below average volume shows a significant improvement in the 2005 test period over shorting moves above the band without the volume requirement. The question now is: "How does the new requirement affect results in the other test periods?" The results of each of the annual test periods using the low volume requirement are shown in Table 1.1.

TABLE 1.1
ABOVEBB WITH BELOW AVERAGE VOLUME TEST RESULTS

SPX ROI	TEST YEAR	% WINNING TRADES	ANNUALIZED ROI
4.7%	2005	57%	131%
13.4	2006	49	-40
1.6	2007	57	72
-36	2008	63	196

The test results shown in Table 1.1 are interesting. Adding the below average volume requirement improved the results during 2005 and 2007. The positive results for 2008 were about the same. The test results for 2006 show negative annualized ROI with or without the additional volume rule, but the results with the new volume rule during 2006 are more negative than they were without the requirement. The low volume rule resulted in about the same or better results in three of the four years, and worse results during 2006, which already had a negative annualized ROI. Running the test for all four years showed an improvement in annualized ROI from 78 percent (see Figure 1.8) to 124 percent and an improvement in the percentage of winning trades from 56 percent to 59 percent as shown in Figure 1.11.

Figure 1.12 shows the trades made by the AboveBB system with the below average volume rule. Scrolling through the results, I find that the trades occur regularly throughout the month and also during the full four-year test period. If the trades came in bunches with long periods of few or no trades in between, then I would be concerned that the trades might be due to one or more events that may or may not repeat in the future. Since the trades occur regularly, it is likely that they are just part of the normal ebb and flow of stock prices.

Another interesting thing you can learn by scrolling through the actual trades during the test period is how often the system produces multiple con-

ABOVEBB WITH BELOW AVERAGE VOLUME RESULTS FOR 2005 THROUGH 2008

AboveBB		Winners	Losers	Neutral
Number of trades in test:	778	459	313	6
Average periods per trade:	4.01	3.94	4.10	4.17
Maximum Profit/Loss:		68.64%	(37.33)%	
Average Drawdown:	(2.45)%	(0.74)%	(5.00)5	
Average Profit/Loss:	1.36%	5.42%	(4.55)%	
Average SPX Profit/Loss:	0.49%	0.91%	(0.11)%	
Probability:		59.00%	40.23%	
Average Annual ROI:	124.26%	501.69%	(405.89)%	
Annual SPX (Buy & Hold):	(5.79)%			
Reward/Risk Ratio:	1.74			
Start test date:	12/31/04			
End test date:	12/31/08			

Interval:Daily
Pricing Summary
      Entry price: [Open]
      Exit price: [Open]
Exit Summary

Courtesy of AIQ

secutive losing trades. In the middle of Figure 1.12, the data shows that six out of seven trades lost money. Near the top of Figure 1.12, there are a series of 12 winning trades in a row. Trading systems that average 60 percent winning trades do not usually show four losing positions in ten consecutive trades. This is the long-term average, and in the short run the system may show six or eight losing trades in a row. Traders should consider position-sizing strategies that allow them to see at least eight or ten losing trades in a row without any problematic drawdowns.

The AboveBB system, with the additional below average volume rule, has shown interesting results during several different periods. During this development process, we have shown that you get a better picture of a trading system by looking at results in several different consecutive time periods, rather than just one long time period. In addition to testing trading systems in different time periods, I test them in different market conditions. Time periods may or may not look similar in the future; however, they always will be made up of a combination of bullish, bearish, and trading range periods.

DECEMBER 2008 TRADES FOR ABOVEBB WITH VOLUME FILTER

Ticker	Held	Entry Date	Entry Price	Exit Date	Exit Price	Profit
JNK	4	12/29/08	30.1300	01/02/09	31.3400	-1.2100
OTEX	5	12/26/08	30.3125	12/31/08	30.5625	-0.2500
MAC	6	12/23/08	21.4400	12/29/08	20.3300	1.1100
RCL	4	12/22/08	12.4400	12/26/08	12.2600	0.1800
ISIS	5	12/19/08	13.6000	12/24/08	13.4100	0.1900
LMDIA	5	12/19/08	17.9000	12/24/08	16.6300	1.2700
MGLN	5	12/19/08	37.4700	12/24/08	37.3000	0.1700
MGM	5	12/19/08	13.6900	12/24/08	12.7600	0.9300
SPW	5	12/19/08	37.4800	12/24/08	35.7400	1.7400
AIV	5	12/18/08	14.4600	12/23/08	13.3000	1.1600
ARE	5	12/18/08	54.9000	12/23/08	54.0300	0.8700
CLI	5	12/18/08	23.9200	12/23/08	21.9500	1.9700
CNI	5	12/18/08	37.9600	12/23/08	35.0000	2.9600
HCP	5	12/18/08	27.0000	12/23/08	25.8000	1.2000
MAC	5	12/17/08	17.1800	12/22/08	21.2000	-4.0200
AMLN	3	12/16/08	10.9200	12/19/08	11.3300	-0.4100
BG	5	12/12/08	40.0700	12/17/08	47.1800	-7.1100
BID	5	12/12/08	10.2100	12/17/08	9.4100	0.8000
CLF	5	12/12/08	23.0600	12/17/08	26.6400	-3.5800
KGC	5	12/12/08	15.3000	12/17/08	18.4000	-3.1000
CTV	5	12/11/08	13.6000	12/16/08	13.6900	-0.0900
ITRI	5	12/11/08	57.0100	12/16/08	55.3500	1.6600
MELI	5	12/11/08	15.4500	12/16/08	15.4100	0.0400
NILE	5	12/11/08	27.3900	12/16/08	24.8600	2.5300
PKX	5	12/11/08	73.0100	12/16/08	70.7500	2.2600
SCHN	5	12/11/08	35.2600	12/16/08	34.2200	1.0400
ACH	5	12/10/08	14.7200	12/15/08	14.0000	0.7200
BAS	5	12/10/08	12.3400	12/15/08	12.0000	0.3400
BGG	5	12/10/08	16.2000	12/15/08	14.3200	1.8800
DECK	5	12/10/08	73.8200	12/15/08	66.9000	6.9200
MW	5	12/10/08	14.3400	12/15/08	13.1000	1.2400
RRGB	5	12/10/08	15.0900	12/15/08	15.3600	-0.2700
SRX	5	12/10/08	15.8800	12/15/08	15.4000	0.4800
TIF	5	12/10/08	23.6000	12/15/08	22.8800	0.7200
ITG	3	12/09/08	18.5900	12/12/08	19.5000	-0.9100
MIR	5	12/05/08	19.0200	12/10/08	20.0500	-1.0300
ITMN	5	12/04/08	13.2200	12/09/08	13.1700	0.0500
ASTE	3	12/01/08	29.5800	12/04/08	30.8000	-1.2200
BVN	3	12/01/08	15.7400	12/04/08	15.5600	0.1800
EXP	3	12/01/08	20.6000	12/04/08	19.4500	1.1500
FLR	3	12/01/08	44.5000	12/04/08	43.7000	0.8000
PCLN	3	12/01/08	66.0000	12/04/08	58.6800	7.3200

Courtesy of AIQ

TESTING ABOVEBB WITH BELOW AVERAGE VOLUME FILTER IN DIFFERENT MARKET CONDITIONS

The market has three basic modes. It can go up, down, or sideways. Over time, the market's movement is made up of combinations of these three different behaviors. None of these behaviors lasts for long because the market is always switching between them. This is one of the keys to trading. Traders need to recognize that the market moves between these three modes, and then have the ability to recognize that the change has arrived and be able to switch to trading tools suitable for the new environment. This is a process I call Market Adaptive Trading (MAT). We will discuss this more in Chapter 7.

As market conditions change, the next year may not look like the last, and the last five years may not provide any clues about next year. Therefore, testing a trading system over the previous year, or four-year, period may have little bearing on how it performs next year because the market conditions may be dramatically different. Take a look at Figure 1.13, which shows the market action between late 1998 and early 2009. The rapid rise of 1999 was unprecedented, as was the drop of 2000; however, both periods represented one of the three basic market modes.

Testing a system between 2000 and 2002 is unlikely to give you a good expectation of how it would perform during the bull market of 2003. Testing a system during the trading range of 2004 to 2007 is unlikely to tell you how it would behave during the steep decline of 2008. Annual periods may not repeat going forward, but whatever the market does next, it will be made up of a series of bullish, bearish, and trading range environments of differing lengths. This is why I want to know how a trading system performs in different market conditions, rather than just in different time periods.

FIGURE 1.13:
MARKET ACTION DURING A TEN-YEAR PERIOD

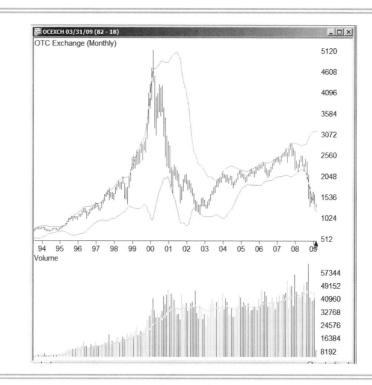

Courtesy of AIQ

FINDING BULLISH, BEARISH, AND
TRADING RANGE CONDITIONS

In order to test a trading system in different market conditions, I look at a chart of the NASDAQ and mark off bullish, bearish, and trading range conditions. Bullish market conditions are when the market is consistently moving up and typically forms a pattern of higher highs and higher lows. Usually, it is possible to draw a trend line under the lows of a bullish pattern, and as long as the market trades above the trend line, it is a bullish environment. Figure 1.14 shows the market action during the summer of 2008. The market was in a bullish, or upward-trending, pattern from mid-July to mid-August.

FIGURE 1.14:
BULLISH AND BEARISH MARKET CONDITIONS, SUMMER OF 2008

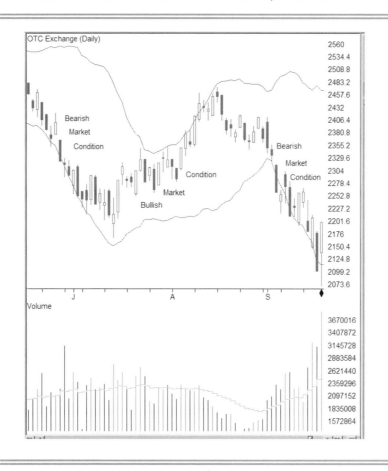

Courtesy of AIQ

A bearish market environment involves seeing consistently lower prices and generally shows a pattern of lower highs and lower lows. In this case, one can generally draw a trend line across the highs of the pattern, and the market is bearish while it trades beneath the trend line. Figure 1.14 illustrates two separate bearish market periods during the summer of 2008. The market was clearly trending down during the last part of June and the first half of July. It was also in a bearish pattern from the middle of August to the middle of September. The market pattern during the four months shown in Figure 1.14 was formed by a bearish period, followed by a bullish period, which was then followed by another bearish period. After studying several charts, these different market periods become easy to recognize.

In a trading range environment, the market moves back and forth between two levels. It runs up to resistance and then backs off, dropping to a support area where it bounces and runs back up toward resistance. Figure 1.15 shows the market action during early 2008. During the six-week period from the middle of January through the end of February, the market moved mostly sideways and did not establish a clear trend either up or down. The market ran up for a few days then reversed and ran down for a few days. It was not setting a pattern of higher highs and higher lows.

If you scan through a daily or weekly chart of the market for the last decade, you can quickly identify a number of bullish, bearish, and trading range periods. The entire chart pattern for the decade is made up of these types of periods in various lengths. Since the market has been, and always will be, made up of bullish, bearish, and trading range periods, it is important to know how a trading system performs during these times. I do not know if next year will be like last year, but I do know that the market action next year will consist of some combination of bullish, bearish, and trading range periods.

Table 1.2 lists seven bullish, six bearish, and five trading range market periods between 2002 and 2009. These periods were picked out by reviewing the daily chart of the market during this period. The interesting part of Table 1.2 is the information showing how the AboveBB system with the below average volume requirement performed in each type of market condition during the indicated test periods.

EARLY 2008 TRADING RANGE MARKET CONDITIONS

Courtesy of AIQ

TABLE 1.2
ABOVEBB WITH BELOW AVERAGE VOLUME TEST RESULTS
BY MARKET CONDITION

TEST PERIOD	MARKET TYPE	WINNING %	ANNUALIZED ROI	# OF TRADES
03/07/03-01/23/04	Bull	41%	-87%	98
08/13/04-12/31/04	Bull	38	-115	44
07/21/06-11/24/06	Bull	44	-90	38
03/14/07-07/20/07	Bull	59	45	49
08/17/07-10/09/07	Bull	50	-0.20	40
03/17/08-06/05/08	Bull	65	200	63
07/16/08-08/18/08	Bull	42	-86	71
01/04/02-10/04/02	Bear	57	108	75
01/23/04-08/13/04	Bear	56	4	46
01/07/05-04/24/05	Bear	69	681	13
05/11/06-07/21/06	Bear	69	180	13
07/20/07-08/17/07	Bear	71	332	7
06/06/08-07/15/08	Bear	71	336	7
11/25/05-05/05/06	Trading Range	48	-87	60
01/05/06-05/11/06	Trading Range	47	-58	40
11/24/06-02/26/07	Trading Range	41	-58	29
10/09/07-11/06/07	Trading Range	53	230	13
01/24/08-02/28/08	Trading Range	51	134	33

In looking at Table 1.2, it is quite striking that the AboveBB system with the below average volume filter showed a positive return in each of the six bear market periods during which it was tested. The market showed significant declines during these periods, and the AboveBB system showed winning trades between 56 and 71 percent of the time. This does not guarantee that it is going to work in every bear market, but it does make the system interesting and worth consideration for this role.

The market decline between January 23, 2004 and August 13, 2004 showed the lowest results, winning only 56 percent of the trades, and yielding an annualized return near breakeven. While this is not a great result, we know that at least in the worst period the system was tested, it faired better than the market. I do not expect any system to work all the time, but the results of this testing indicate that this technique is interesting during periods when the market is clearly declining.

This system is not something I would use during trading range market periods because, as shown in Table 1.2, it showed a negative annualized return during three of the five trading range periods tested, and the percentage of winning trades was not strongly favorable in any of the trading range periods.

I would not use this trading technique during bull market periods since it showed widely varying results with a negative annualized return in five of the bullish periods tested. It had a great run during the first bullish bounce in 2008; however, that one example proves nothing. I am looking for some consistency over similar market conditions and this technique shows reasonable performance during all of the bearish market periods tested, and poor performance during other market periods.

The data in Table 1.2 also provides a hint on what might be expected in trading this system. Good win-loss ratios and annualized returns were shown in most of the bearish market periods. One period, however, showed breakeven returns. Traders have to be willing to experience some periods when a system is not producing strong results. If traders make a few trades that do not work out and then move on to another technique, they may miss the times when a system performs well. Traders need to use money management techniques to ensure that they can ride out slow times when a system does not run strongly.

If I know how a trading system (or trading tool as I call it) performs in each of the three different market conditions, then I can watch the market to determine what the current condition is and then use the tools that have shown good results in that type of market condition. This is the process of Market Adaptive Trading. It takes some practice to quickly recognize the current market conditions, but this is a lot easier than trying to predict where the market is going.

No one has consistently predicted where the market is going over the long run. Remember all those empty suits on the TV news shows telling us everything was fine just before the 2008 crash. They did the same thing before the 2000 crash. Not even (or perhaps especially) the experts can successfully predict market direction consistently; however, you can learn to look at a chart and tell if the market is going up, down, or sideways. And that is actionable information, as opposed to someone's guess of where the market is going to be in three months or a year.

I have found that it is better to look at the performance of trading systems (or money managers) by market condition rather than year. The future market is unlikely to do exactly what it did during the last few years; but, no matter what, it still will be made of bullish, bearish, and trading range periods. Knowing how a trading system performs during these different market conditions is much more useful than knowing how it did during specific years.

TECHNIQUES FOR DETERMINING MARKET CONDITIONS FOR ABOVEBB

There are several interesting techniques for determining market conditions. Drawing trend lines, along with horizontal support and resistance areas on the chart, makes each of the three market conditions clear. This technique is simple, but it works. Markets trading above an ascending trend line are in a bullish environment. Markets trading below a descending trend line are in a bearish environment. Markets trading between horizontal support and resistance areas are in a trading range environment. We can evaluate the effectiveness of different filters for market conditions by testing the performance of the AboveBB system during an extended period of time with and without the market condition filters. The first step is to see how the AboveBB system performs during an extended period without any market condition filters.

Figure 1.16 shows the results of testing the AboveBB with volume filter from January 2, 2002 through December 31, 2008. No market condition filters were used with this test. All signals given by the AboveBB system with the

ABOVEBB WITH VOLUME FILTER TEST RESULTS
2002 THROUGH 2008

AboveBB		Winners	Losers	Neutral
Number of trades in test:	1090	609	473	8
Average periods per trade:	4.06	4	4.13	4.13
Maximum Profit/Loss:		68.64%	(37.33)%	
Average Drawdown:	(2.67)%	(0.78)%	(5.15)%	
Average Profit/Loss:	0.88%	5.22%	(4.69)%	
Average SPX Profit/Loss:	0.34%	0.80%	(0.24)%	
Probability:		55.87%	43.39%	
Average Annual ROI:	79.41%	476.09%	(414.50)%	
Annual SPX (Buy & Hold):	(2.69)%			
Reward/Risk Ratio:	1.43			
Start test date:	01/02/02			
End test date:	12/31/08			

Interval:Daily
Pricing Summary
      Entry price: [Open]
      Exit price: [Open]
Exit Summary
      Hold for 3 periods

FIGURE 1.17:
NASDAQ DURING 2008 WITH FIVE-PERIOD MOVING AVERAGE

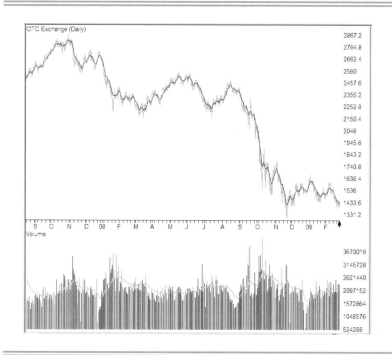

Courtesy of AIQ

volume filter were taken. During this seven-year period, there were about 1,000 trades. Fifty-five percent of the trades were winners, and the annualized ROI clearly beat buy and hold. This is the baseline test of the AboveBB system. If we find that market condition filters improve these results during the same test period, then the market filters are considered helpful. If a market filter does not improve test results during this period, then we should discard the filter.

Moving averages also can be used as filters to help determine the current market conditions. As we have seen, the current market conditions have a clear effect on shorting extensions above the upper Bollinger band. Short-term moving averages tend to follow the price action fairly closely. As moving averages lengthen (or include a longer sample in the calculation of the average), they tend to follow the general trend of the chart rather than hug the day-to-day action. This is best illustrated by looking at a couple of charts.

Figure 1.17 shows about a year and a half of market action from the fall of 2007 to March of 2009. The high-low price bars are shown in gray, and the five-day exponential moving average of the closing price is shown in black. The five-day moving average tends to be close to what you would draw if asked to run a line through the middle of the price action. It tends to smooth out the unusual deviations in price and represent fairly accurately the basic price movements of the market. If we wanted a general idea of what the market was doing, without all the rapid daily fluctuations, we could just look at the five-period moving average. It does not show you every movement of every day, but it gives a clear, and perhaps easier to follow, picture of the general direction of the current price movements.

If we plot the average over the last 20 periods instead of the last five, a different picture emerges. Longer moving averages have a tendency to follow the general trend of the price movement rather than represent the daily action. Figure 1.18 shows a year and a half of market action from the fall of 2007 to March of 2009 with the 20-period exponential moving average shown in black. Notice that when the market is trending, either up or down, the 20-period moving average tends to act almost like a trend line.

During January, February, and early March of 2008, the market was trending down and the 20-period moving average looked similar to a trend line

NASDAQ DURING 2008 WITH 20-PERIOD MOVING AVERAGE

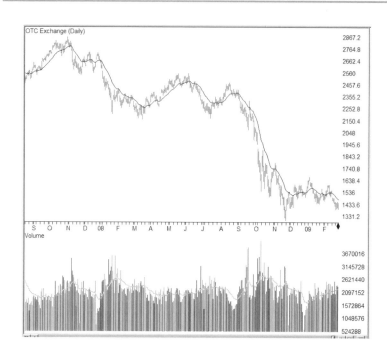

Courtesy of AIQ

that might be drawn across the highs during this period. The market was generally trading just below the moving average. From mid-March to early June, the market was in a brief uptrend and the 20-period average acted like a trend line beneath the lows of the market action. The same behavior was also seen during the market downtrend of September, October, and November of 2008.

The times when the 20-period moving average does not act like a trend line is when the market is basing. When the market is basing, support and resistance should be drawn across the bottom and the top of the basing area. When the market bases in December of 2007, the 20-period moving average basically draws a line right through the middle of the basing area. We see the same behavior when the market bases during December of 2008 and January of 2009.

TESTING ABOVEBB IN BEARISH MARKETS
DEFINED BY MOVING AVERAGES

Observations about how different moving average periods perform can lead to some interesting trading systems and filters. Since the 20-period moving average tends to act like a trend line when the market is bullish or bearish, we should be able to use this moving average to restrict trading to periods of bearish market behavior. We would expect to be whipsawed during trading ranges. If this is the case, then restricting trades in our AboveBB system to periods when the market is below its 20-period exponentially smoothed moving average should improve results during the 2002 to 2009 test period.

Take another look at Table 1.2. The AboveBB system clearly performs better in bearish markets than in bullish or trading range markets. Using the 20-period moving average on the QQQQ as a representation of the market should help us identify bullish and bearish periods in the market. We are not changing the definition of the AboveBB system; we are just using the 20-period moving average on the QQQQ to determine when to trade AboveBB and when to stand aside. We are looking for a practical application of what Table 1.2 tells us. The AboveBB system is unchanged—we are just looking for an aid in determining when to use it, and when to use another one of the techniques in our trading tool box.

For this test, a moving average filter was used to only take trades when the market, as represented by the QQQQ, was below its 20-period simple moving average. During market periods when the NASDAQ 100 was above its 20-period moving average (20MA), the trade signals from the AboveBB system were ignored. When the NASDAQ 100 was below the 20-period simple moving average, the trade signals from the AboveBB system were taken. The results of adding this 20-period moving average filter to the AboveBB with volume filter system are shown in Figure 1.19.

As shown, this filter reduces the number of trades during the 2002 to 2009 period as one would expect, since trades that are available are not being taken when the market is uptrending. Only using the AboveBB system when the market is below the 20-period moving average significantly improves the annualized ROI from 79 to 135. The percentage of winning trades remains about the same as running the test without the moving average filter (results

FIGURE 1.19:
ABOVEBB RESULTS 2002 TO 2009 USING 20-PERIOD MOVING AVERAGE FILTER ON QQQQ

AboveBB		Winners	Losers	Neutral
Number of trades in test:	402	224	175	3
Average periods per trade:	3.99	3.91	4.1	3.00
Maximum Profit/Loss:		68.64%	(37.33)%	
Average Drawdown:	(2.90)%	(0.85)%	(5.58)%	
Average Profit/Loss:	1.48%	6.59%	(5.03)%	
Average SPX Profit/Loss:	0.34%	0.86%	(0.31)%	
Probability:		55.72%	43.53%	
Average Annual ROI:	135.71%	614.99%	(447.33)%	
Annual SPX (Buy & Hold):	(2.69)%			
Reward/Risk Ratio:	1.68			
Start test date:	01/02/02			
End test date:	12/31/08			

Interval:Daily
Pricing Summary
    Entry price: [Open]
    Exit price: [Open]
Exit Summary
    Hold for 3 periods

Courtesy of AIQ

without the moving average filter are shown in Figure 1.16). The significant improvement is the near doubling of the spread between the average winning trade and the average losing trade.

Taking only AboveBB trades when the market is below the 20-period moving average results in trades with a larger average profit and a smaller average loss. If my average winning trade has larger profits and my average losing trade has smaller losses, I am one happy camper.

There are other factors that come into play, but the AboveBB system shows interesting results, and we have found a way to determine when to use it, and when to avoid it, which is a critical part of adapting to the market.

Moving averages can be used alone or in combination to do a variety of different jobs for traders. One combination of moving averages that turns out to be interesting is the five-period exponential moving average of the highs (not the closes, as is usually done) with the 20-period moving average of the closes (the same moving average we used above to determine when to take AboveBB trades, and when to pass on them).

A lot of new traders will focus exclusively on the increase in annualized ROI from 79 to 135. The increase is good, but it is a lot more like a figure of merit than what you will actually see in an account because the numbers are annualized and do not account for commission and slippage, etc. The higher the percentage of winning trades and the wider the spread between the average winning trade and the average losing trade, then the better the system. If I win more often than I lose, and the average winner is bigger than the average loser, then over time there is a great chance of doing well.

When using trend lines to analyze stock charts, we often see trend line breaks (when the price crosses above or below a key trend line) as significant events and a call to action. We have seen that the 20-period exponential moving average can act as a trend line when the market is bullish or bearish. We can combine this substitute trend line with a short-term trend line, which more closely approximates the current action to find "trend line breaks." We can then use these breaks to determine whether to take the trades presented by the AboveBB system or to pass on them.

The five-period average of the highs follows along fairly closely with the highs of the price action. The 20-period average, as we have seen, can look like a trend line when the market is bullish or bearish. When the five-period average of the highs is below the 20-period average of the closes, it is like the highs breaking a trend line, which often indicates a bearish environment. Because the AboveBB system does well in bearish environments (and poorly in bullish and trading range environments), if we take the AboveBB trades when the QQQQ five-period average is below the QQQQ 20-period average, then our results should improve.

When testing a trading system, it is very important to have a visual or a picture of what is going on. Remember, we are looking for ways to determine when to use the AboveBB system and when to ignore the trades. The data of Table 1.2 indicates that we want to focus our trading during bearish market periods. We are looking for ways to determine if the market is bearish. Sometimes the picture can get lost in the math, so I often look at charts to see what is actually happening.

Figure 1.20 shows the same market period, late 2007 to March of 2008, as Figure 1.18. In the case of Figure 1.20, the price chart is colored lighter when the five-period average (5MA) is below the 20-period average (20MA). Prices are shown darker when the five-period average is above the 20-period average. This technique picks up the major downtrends, just like the 20-period; however, it is better at filtering out the periods when the market is in a trading range. Since the AboveBB system is not something we want to use in trading range markets, this should help the test results. It is also very instructive to see how the moving average filters are actually behaving by showing how the interaction of the five- and 20-period moving averages selects specific periods of market behavior (as shown in Figure 1.20).

Figure 1.21 shows the test results for taking AboveBB trades during the 2002 to 2009 period only when the QQQQ five-period average of the highs is below the QQQQ 20-period average of the closes. Figure 1.21 shows a significant improvement in results over both the system without any market condition filter, as shown in Figure 1.16, and the system when the QQQQ is trading below its 20-period average, as shown in Figure 1.19.

In Figure 1.21, the percentage of winning trades increases from below 56 percent to 62 percent, and annualized ROI increases from 135 to over 232. Remember this is when we used two moving averages to determine market conditions rather than just one. The definition of the AboveBB system is the same in both cases; the QQQQ moving averages are used to determine whether to take the trades indicated by the AboveBB system or to ignore them. Since Table 1.2 indicates that AboveBB performs significantly better in declining markets, we use a moving average technique to identify declining markets and then only take AboveBB trades when the moving averages indicate the market is bearish. This process leads us to using the AboveBB

FIGURE 1.20:
MARKET CHART SHOWING PERIODS OF 5MA BELOW 20MA

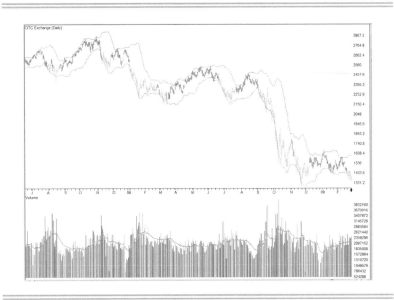

FIGURE 1.21:
TEST RESULTS WITH 5MA AND 20MA

AboveBB				
		Winners	Losers	Neutral
Number of trades in test:	316	196	119	18
Average periods per trade:	3.88	3.38	3.97	4.72
Maximum Profit/Loss:		43.71%	(37.33)%	
Average Drawdown:	92.88)%	(1.01)%	(5.98)%	
Average Profit/Loss:	2.48%	7.11%	(5.13)%	
Average SPX Profit/Loss:	0.61%	1.08%	(0.17)%	
Probability:		62.03%	37.66%	
Average Annual ROI:	232.98%	676.89%	(471.83)%	
Annual SPX (Buy & Hold):	(2.69)%			
Reward/Risk Ratio:	2.28			
Start test date:	01/02/02			
End test date:	12/31/08			

Interval:Daily
Pricing Summary
       Entry price: [Open]
       Exit price: [Open]
Exit Summary
       Hold for 3 periods

Courtesy of AIQ

system in the market environments for which it is best suited. This is the beginning of Market Adaptive Trading, selecting our trading tools based on the current conditions of the market. As traders develop and test a variety of trading tools, they can determine which market environment is best for each tool. The next step is to use techniques like trend line analysis or moving averages to determine the current market conditions and then select the most appropriate trading tools.

Predicting where the market is going to go next is a popular, and largely unsuccessful, activity in the financial press. Traders do not need projections of where the market is going; they just need to adjust their trading techniques based on what the market is actually doing. As we have seen, determining what the market is currently doing is a reasonable thing and there are multiple ways to accomplish the task. This is part of the Market Adaptive Trading process that I use. Remember, the market will not adapt to us—we must adapt to it.

TRADE MANAGEMENT FOR THE ABOVEBB SYSTEM

All of the testing of the AboveBB system so far has used a fixed three-day holding time. This approach is simple and has the advantage that traders do not need to sit and watch a computer all day. Trades are entered based on the rules for AboveBB and then held for three days before exiting. This is just about as simple as it gets. As a practical matter, I will modify the holding period based on the volume pattern of the stock, any changes in market conditions, and how close the stock is to its own support and resistance areas.

Since this system works best in bearish market conditions, I may close the positions early if the market starts moving up on strong, and increasing, volume. I also stay very aware of where the next support and resistance levels are. Stocks tend to bounce at support levels so I look to take profits when a short position nears support, whether or not I have held it for three days. I also watch the volume on the stock's move. If one of my positions is moving on declining volume, I generally exit. Volume measures the interest in a move, and as we will see in later chapters, stocks moving on declining interest are suspect. I will close a stock moving on declining interest and move on to another trade.

VARYING HOLDING TIME FOR ABOVEBB

Table 1.3 shows the effect of varying the holding time when testing the AboveBB with the volume filter and using the five- and 20-period moving averages to determine market conditions. The tests were run for consecutive holding periods of three to six days. The percentage of winning trades varied between 61 and 69 percent. The last column shows the difference between the average percentage gain of winning trades and the absolute value of the average percentage of losing trades. Depending on holding period, the average winning trade was between 1.29 percent and 2.68 percent larger than the average losing trade. The test results in Table 1.3 were for the period of 2002 through 2008, the same test period used in previous tests.

Table 1.3 illustrates several interesting aspects of the AboveBB system. The percentage of winning trades does not vary widely with small increases in holding times. This tells us that it is not critical whether the positions are held three, four, or five days. This gives traders time to look at the positions and determine if there are other factors that indicate whether the positions

TABLE 1.3
EFFECTS OF HOLDING PERIOD ON ABOVEBB WITH BELOW AVERAGE VOLUME AND TWO MOVING AVERAGE FILTER

HOLDING PERIOD	WINNING %	ANNUALIZED ROI	AVERAGE WIN – AVERAGE LOSS
3 days	62	232	1.98%
4 days	64	207	2.68%
5 days	69	182	1.29%
6 days	65	148	2.05%

should be held or closed. If we found a system that only worked if the position was held for exactly three days yet showed losses if held longer, then that would be less interesting. This system, however, has some built-in flexibility with holding times.

I take advantage of this flexibility to look at my position after three days and determine if there is a good reason to hold it. If not, I close the position. Profits are good—take them early and often! If the position has been moving on increasing volume and showing increasing support for the direction it is moving, then I will often give it another day or two. If the position is nearing support (for shorts, or resistance for longs), then I take the profits because, by definition, the stock is reasonably likely to bounce from support. If it bounces, I would be giving back some profits, so I'd rather exit.

When I show this technique to new traders, they frequently ask, "what happens if it breaks through support? Wouldn't you then make more profit by holding the short position?"

Of course, that's true; but, in any given case, we do not know if a stock is going to bounce from support (or retrace from resistance). We believe the bounce is likely, based on the definition of support; so, I want to bank my profits and not risk giving them back if the stock does the normal thing, which is bounce from an area of support. I always want to be in the position to profit (or protect profits) if the market (or an individual stock position) does the normal or expected thing. It is just common sense.

What happens if I took my profits and then the stock continued moving past support? Well, I have my profits and I also have the ability to take another trade. I really have not lost anything at all, except for a round-trip commission. Although, you are using the wrong broker if your commissions are more than a few dollars.

I am a lot more interested in protecting profits and having the opportunity to take another trade than I am in trying to milk the last dime out of every trade. Traders who worry that they missed some potential profit, and are willing to risk real profit to get it, are headed for trouble. Trading is about managing risks and it is a lot harder to go broke taking profits than it is holding on too long. Just ask your "buy and hold" friends about 2008.

REVIEWING TRADE HISTORY FOR ABOVEBB

The statistics for a trading system can provide valuable insight into its performance. Traders should also carefully review the actual trades made during the testing period. Reviewing the actual trades provides an important perspective on what to expect when trading a particular system.

The AboveBB system by itself generated more than 1,000 trades during the 2002 through 2008 test period, as previously shown in Figure 1.16. We added a market condition filter based on the five- and 20-period simple moving averages in order to restrict trading the AboveBB system to bearish periods. Because this was only part of the time, we reduced the number of trades to a little over 300. The system is still generating over 1,000 trades; we are just choosing to ignore some of the trades because the test results indicate that the system performs better during periods of bearish market activity.

Figure 1.22 shows the trades generated by the AboveBB system with the below average volume filter during late 2008. The figure shows that 23 trades were generated during this four-week period. That is an average of one trade a day, but also note that the trades were generated on eight different days, not 23 different days. A four-week period has 20 trading days, and the AboveBB system generated trades on about half of those trading days.

FIGURE 1.22:
ABOVEBB TRADES DURING LATE 2008

	A	B	C	D	E	F	H	I	J
1	Ticker	Entry Date	Entry Price	Exit Date	Exit Price	Profit	Profit%	Con Lose	
2	MIR	12/5/08	19.02	12/10/08	20.05	-1.03	-5.42	1	
3	ITMN	12/4/08	13.22	12/9/08	13.17	0.05	0.38	0	
4	ASTE	12/1/08	29.58	12/4/08	30.8	-1.22	-4.12	1	
5	BVN	12/1/08	15.74	12/4/08	15.56	0.18	1.14	0	
6	EXP	12/1/08	20.6	12/4/08	19.45	1.15	5.58	0	
7	FLR	12/1/08	44.5	12/4/08	43.7	0.8	1.8	0	
8	PCLN	12/1/08	66	12/4/08	58.68	7.32	11.09	0	
9	AYE	11/26/08	32.26	12/2/08	32.79	-0.53	-1.64	1	
10	RGLD	11/26/08	38.44	12/2/08	35.13	3.31	8.61	0	
11	QID	11/24/08	86.47	11/28/08	74.3	12.17	14.07	0	
12	SMN	11/24/08	98.36	11/28/08	76.9	21.46	21.82	0	
13	ALJ	11/11/08	9.61	11/14/08	10.05	-0.44	-4.58	1	
14	FNF	11/11/08	10.03	11/14/08	10.18	-0.15	-1.5	2	
15	OMG	11/11/08	21.85	11/14/08	17.08	4.77	21.83	0	
16	AIR	11/4/08	16.88	11/7/08	14.64	2.24	13.27	0	
17	ASTE	11/4/08	26.43	11/7/08	23.39	3.04	11.5	0	
18	BGG	11/4/08	15.74	11/7/08	15.02	0.72	4.57	0	
19	DLX	11/4/08	13.07	11/7/08	11.65	1.42	10.86	0	
20	ORLY	11/4/08	27.16	11/7/08	24.84	2.32	8.54	0	
21	TOL	11/4/08	23.06	11/7/08	20.75	2.31	10.02	0	
22	BEAV	11/3/08	13.04	11/6/08	12.3	0.74	5.67	0	
23	CLR	11/3/08	31.12	11/6/08	27.06	4.06	13.05	0	
24	LOW	11/3/08	21.66	11/6/08	20.23	1.43	6.6	0	

Courtesy of AIQ

Trading systems generally do not produce multiple trade candidates each and every night. Trades typically come less than every day, and on days that trade candidates occur, there is usually more than one trading opportunity. This is one reason why traders should have more than one trading system for each type of market condition.

The second column from the right in Figure 1.22 shows the percentage profit, or loss, for each trade. Figure 1.19 indicated that for the 2002 through 2008 test period, the AboveBB system showed nearly 56 percent winning trades and an average profit per winning trade of 6.59 percent. These are the averages for the entire test period. New traders often think that they will see 56 percent winners and average profits of 6.59 percent every year, or month, or week. Averages do not work that way—the results can vary from year to year, month to month, or week to week.

Of the 23 trades that AboveBB produced in late 2008, and shown in Figure 1.22, only five were losing trades. There were also eight trades with profits over ten percent, which is not bad for a three-day holding time. Trading during this period showed better-than-average results. Traders who started using the AboveBB system during this period might find it attractive. They may feel since the system did well during this four-week period that they were on the gravy train every month. Remember, you cannot take the results of any particular period and extrapolate them to the next period of equal length. Results vary from period to period, so you need to focus on money management strategies, not just entry patterns.

Figure 1.23 shows another 23 trades taken by the AboveBB system. Note that in this case, it took the system several months to show 23 trades, rather than the four weeks of the previous example. The AboveBB pattern did not stop

Trading is not like driving down the freeway where you have a constant speed and can easily predict when you will make it to the next town. Trading is more like driving through town; where you know it usually takes a half hour to get to the hardware store, but it could be 15 or 45 minutes depending on traffic and weather. When we test a trading system, we know what the long-term averages could be, but they can and will vary for any particular time period.

	A	B	C	D	E	F	H	I	J
190	WLK	2/1/08	20.08	2/6/08	19.35	0.73	3.64	0	
191	IGR	1/31/08	15.16	2/5/08	16.38	-1.22	-8.05	1	
192	TRW	1/31/08	21.6	2/5/08	22.22	-0.62	-2.87	2	
193	TSFG	1/31/08	16.54	2/5/08	16.88	-0.34	-2.06	3	
194	USTR	1/31/08	51.81	2/5/08	55.38	-3.57	-6.89	4	
195	BPOP	1/30/08	13.04	2/4/08	13.94	-0.9	-6.9	5	
196	FHN	1/30/08	19.83	2/4/08	21.01	-1.18	-5.95	6	
197	LPX	1/30/08	15.53	2/4/08	14.93	0.6	3.86	0	
198	CUZ	1/29/08	25.5	2/1/08	26.02	-0.52	-2.04	1	
199	DFS	1/28/08	15.45	1/31/08	16.08	-0.63	-4.08	2	
200	UCBI	1/28/08	17.41	1/31/08	17.63	-0.22	-1.26	3	
201	Snv	1/25/08	11.57	1/30/08	12.46	-0.89	-7.69	4	
202	MPW	1/24/08	11.08	1/29/08	11.87	-0.79	-7.13	5	
203	SATS	1/8/08	31.96	1/11/08	29.77	2.19	6.85	0	
204	DRH	11/29/07	17.35	12/4/07	17.01	0.34	1.96	0	
205	APEI	11/28/07	39.46	12/3/07	42.79	-3.33	-8.44	1	
206	MXB	11/26/07	27.99	11/29/07	26.61	1.38	4.93	0	
207	MXB	11/19/07	24.71	11/23/07	27.3	-2.59	-10.48	1	
208	MTG	11/15/07	23.27	11/20/07	20.6	2.67	11.47	0	
209	BHE	8/23/07	25.32	8/28/07	24.57	0.75	2.96	0	
210	CTB	8/23/07	24.58	8/28/07	24.81	-0.23	-0.94	1	
211	FED	8/23/07	53.06	8/28/07	50.56	2.5	4.71	0	
212	PVTB	8/22/07	35.95	8/27/07	33.88	2.07	5.76	0	

Courtesy of AIQ

occurring, but it took much longer to see 23 trades because of the market conditions filter that we applied. We intentionally decided not to take trades from the AboveBB system when the market was bullish. We did that because the AboveBB system has been shown to perform much better in down markets than up markets.

Figure 1.24 shows the market conditions during the time in which the 23 trades shown in Figure 1.23 were taken. The moving average filter only allows trades to be taken when the five-day exponential moving average of the NASDAQ is below its 20-day exponential moving average. The periods of market activity when this is true are shown in gray in Figure 1.24. Figure 1.24 also shows that there were a half dozen short-term bullish market periods, shown in black, during which no AboveBB trades were taken. The lack of trades from the end of August 2007 to the middle of November shown in Figure 1.23's trade list corresponds directly with a bullish market period shown in black on the market chart of Figure 1.24.

Figure 1.24 shows that we are only using the AboveBB tool during bearish market periods, which are marked by gray. Figure 1.23 illustrates the results of our decision not to use the AboveBB system during those periods. This is the beginning of a Market Adaptive Trading system; in that we have an

MARKET CONDITIONS CHART DURING TRADING PERIOD OF FIGURE 1.23

Courtesy of AIQ

interesting system to use during bearish market periods, and a specific technique for identifying those periods. Later on, we will develop tools for trading during the bullish periods in Figure 1.24, and then we will have a more complete trading system.

ANALYZING CONSECUTIVE LOSING TRADES FOR ABOVEBB

When considering the use of a trading system, it is important to get beyond the statistics and develop an understanding of what it is like to trade it. Just because a system shows winners 60 percent of the time, it does not imply that for every ten trades you will see six winners. In the case of the AboveBB system, we saw that during a fairly long test period (January of 2002 through December of 2008) the system showed winning trades about 62 percent of the time. In order to get a feeling for what it might be like to trade the AboveBB system, it is important to look through the resulting trades and determine how many consecutive losing trades the system produced, because this should affect your decisions on position sizing.

When a coin is flipped, the odds of it coming up tails are 50 percent, or one out of two. If you flip the coin twice, the odds of it coming up tails are one out of four. The chance of it coming up tails five times in a row is "one in two to the fifth power," or one chance in 32. If you do this experiment once (that is just flip the coin five times) the odds of seeing all five flips come up tails is fairly small, about three percent; however, if you run the experiment 30 times, the odds actually favor you seeing at least five tails in a row at least once.

If the coin flip was a trading system, and we show a profit if the coin comes up heads and a loss if it comes up tails, then we might expect to win about half the time. A new trader might feel comfortable taking large positions since he expects to have profitable and losing positions equally. Because of this, he may be willing to take positions representing up to a quarter of his account size. The problem is that if he makes one trade a week, he's quite likely to lose all of his money.

One trade a week is 50 trades a year. When our new trader makes 50 trades, the odds are that at some point during the 50 trades, he will see five tails, or losing trades, in a row. Since he is betting a quarter of his account on each trade, and taking four trades at a time, those highly-probable five losing trades in a row put him out of business.

Our trader thought he was doing something that was relatively harmless because he was expected to win and lose about the same percentage of the time. With large numbers of trades, the problem is that runs of all heads or all tails (the equivalent of winners or losers in a real trading system) are to be expected. Not understanding how many losing trades in a row a system might show and using large position sizes can lead to ruin. Successful trading involves a lot more than just knowing the percentage of winning or losing trades you might expect.

The AboveBB system (with volume and market condition filters) showed losing trades about 38 percent of the time during the 2002 through 2008 test period. The average losing trade was about five percent. If every loss was average, and the trading system showed ten losing trades in a row at some point during the seven-year test period, then the trader's account could be cut in half. I know, 62 percent winning trades sounded great. Remember, traders must understand all aspects of their trading system, and then use appropriate money management strategies to deal with them.

I put all of the trades made using the AboveBB system, during the seven-year test period, into a spreadsheet. Once the trades are in a spreadsheet you can do just about any calculation you please. In this case, I wanted to look at how many running consecutive losing trades occurred. The right-most column in Figure 1.25 shows the number of consecutive losing trades for the AboveBB system. Zero indicates it was a profitable trade; one indicates a single losing trade; two indicates two losing trades in a row; and so on. The largest number of consecutive losing trades in a row during the 2002 through 2008 test period was six.

Figure 1.25 shows that there were six losing trades over a two-day period at the end of January 2008. The average loss for the six trades was 5.45 percent, which is close to the average of -5.13 percent for the 2002 through 2008 test period, as shown in Figure 1.21. The total loss for all six consecutive losing trades was 32.72 percent.

Immediately after the six consecutive losing trades there was a winning trade in LPX, which was followed by five consecutive losing trades over a three-day period. Some traders judge a system based on the maximum number of consecutive losing trades it shows. As we have shown here, this number, like many other statistics, can be misleading.

FIGURE 1.25:
SPREADSHEET CALCULATION OF CONSECUTIVE
LOSING TRADES FOR ABOVEBB

◇	A	B	C	D	E	F	H	I	J
182	MNC	2/4/08	10.68	2/7/08	10.83	-0.15	-1.4	1	
183	PAY	2/4/08	20.93	2/7/08	18.8	2.13	10.18	0	
184	UCBI	2/4/08	19.98	2/7/08	17.52	2.46	12.31	0	
185	WWW	2/4/08	25.96	2/7/08	24.95	1.01	3.89	0	
186	BWS	2/1/08	17.16	2/6/08	15.77	1.39	8.1	0	
187	CAR	2/1/08	13.4	2/6/08	12.06	1.34	10	0	
188	HHS	2/1/08	16.2	2/6/08	15.92	0.28	1.73	0	
189	JLL	2/1/08	77.09	2/6/08	73	4.09	5.31	0	
190	WLK	2/1/08	20.08	2/6/08	19.35	0.73	3.64	0	
191	IGR	1/31/08	15.16	2/5/08	16.38	-1.22	-8.05	1	
192	TRW	1/31/08	21.6	2/5/08	22.22	-0.62	-2.87	2	
193	TSFG	1/31/08	16.54	2/5/08	16.88	-0.34	-2.06	3	
194	USTR	1/31/08	51.81	2/5/08	55.38	-3.57	-6.89	4	
195	BPOP	1/30/08	13.04	2/4/08	13.94	-0.9	-6.9	5	
196	FHN	1/30/08	19.83	2/4/08	21.01	-1.18	-5.95	6	
197	LPX	1/30/08	15.53	2/4/08	14.93	0.6	3.86	0	
198	CUZ	1/29/08	25.5	2/1/08	26.02	-0.52	-2.04	1	
199	DFS	1/28/08	15.45	1/31/08	16.08	-0.63	-4.08	2	
200	UCBI	1/28/08	17.41	1/31/08	17.63	-0.22	-1.26	3	
201	Snv	1/25/08	11.57	1/30/08	12.46	-0.89	-7.69	4	
202	MPW	1/24/08	11.08	1/29/08	11.87	-0.79	-7.13	5	
203	SATS	1/8/08	31.96	1/11/08	29.77	2.19	6.85	0	
204	DRH	11/29/07	17.35	12/4/07	17.01	0.34	1.96	0	

Courtesy of AIQ

If a trader plans a money management strategy for six losing trades in a row and then hits a period where 12 of 13 trades lose money, then he may be surprised and lose more than he is willing to risk. It is important to look through the actual trading history of a system in order to get a feeling for how it performs and what to expect when trading it.

The period in Figure 1.25 showing 12 of 13 losing trades is about the worst case for the AboveBB system over the 2002 through 2008 test period. Imagine getting two groups of new traders together and offering one group the chance to trade a system showing the results shown in Figure 1.21, and the second group the chance to trade a system demonstrating the results shown in Figure 1.25.

Figure 1.21 indicates that the AboveBB system wins 62 percent of the time and has a good spread between the return of the average winner and the loss of the average loser. A lot of traders will express interest in trading this system. Figure 1.25 shows a system that had 12 of 13 consecutive trades showing losses; most new traders will not express interest in trading this system. The interesting thing, of course, is that Figures 1.21 and 1.25 are just different aspects of the same system. This illustrates why analyzing a potential trading system a number of different ways is vitally important.

At this point there is always someone who says, "Why don't we just find a system that always works?" In short, there are no systems that always work.

Are your friends always right; does your car never fail; is your job always fun and interesting? We naturally understand that most things in our life do not

A trading system should be like an old friend. Traders need to understand how it will react in different situations and have a pretty good idea of its strengths and weaknesses. When an old friend makes a few mistakes, we forgive them and move on because the overall relationship is positive and we do not judge it by a few short-term reactions. Trading systems are the same way; sometimes in the short run they can be disappointing, but in the long run the relationship can be beneficial.

always work perfectly. We are willing to deal with the imperfections because there is little alternative, and the overall relationship is beneficial. It is the same for trading systems. Traders do not focus on the short term results because they can be up or down in a given period. Traders have no idea if any specific trade is going to work; they just know that a system has good possibilities over a large number of trades.

In order to get the positive results of Figure 1.21, we will occasionally see rough patches like those shown in Figure 1.25. Figure 1.25 illustrates the worst period in the seven years of trading AboveBB. It is unrealistic to expect that you can trade for seven years and never hit a rough spot. The other interesting thing about the losing period shown in Figure 1.25 is that the next consecutive 13 trades had 12 winners and an average win of 7.44 percent per trade. The average loss during the losing streak was 5.44 percent. The winning streak immediately following the worst losing streak in seven years made up for the losing stretch in about one week.

EFFECT OF EXTENSION ABOVE THE UPPER BOLLINGER BAND

The AboveBB system shorts stocks that are extended at least four percent above the upper band when the move comes on below average volume. Before trading the system I want to know how every part of it works, and one area we have not tested is the effect of the percentage move above the upper band. Figure 1.26 shows the test results of modifying AboveBB to take all trades that move three percent or more above the upper band rather than the four percent requirement in all the previous testing.

Comparing Figure 1.26, with the three percent extension requirement, to Figure 1.21, with the original four percent extension requirement, shows that relaxing the move above the upper band nearly doubles the number of trades while reducing the percentage of winning trades from 62 percent to 58 percent.

Changing the extension above the upper band requirement to be at least five percent instead of at least four percent reduces the number of trades during the 2002 through 2008 period by about a third. It also drops the percentage of winning trades from 62 percent to 60 percent. More is not always better, which is why traders need to test and evaluate every assumption.

A friend told me about an interesting book that had characters called "fair witnesses." These people were totally honest and did not make assumptions. When asked a question, they told the truth and stopped there. As a demonstration, someone asked one of the fair witnesses what color the house on the hill was. He replied, "this side is white." The fair witness reported the truth and made no assumption about the color of the other side of the house. Traders need to seek the truth and not make assumptions about trading systems or the markets. This takes some effort but can pay significant dividends.

FIGURE 1.26:
ABOVEBB USING A THREE PERCENT EXTENSION ABOVE THE BAND, 2002 TO 2008

AboveBB		Winners	Losers	Neutral
Number of trades in test:	602	349	248	5
Average periods per trade:	3.97	3.87	4.1	4.00
Maximum Profit/Loss:		43.71%	(32.57)%	
Average Drawdown:	(2.68)%	(0.83)%	(5.34)%	
Average Profit/Loss:	1.72%	6.17%	(4.51)%	
Average SPX Profit/Loss:	0.63%	1.30%	(0.30)%	
Probability:		57.97%	41.20%	
Average Annual ROI:	158.36%	582.38%	(401.40)%	
Annual SPX (Buy & Hold):	(2.69)%			
Reward/Risk Ratio:	1.93			
Start test date:	01/02/02			
End test date:	12/31/08			

Interval:Daily
Pricing Summary
    Entry price: [Open]
    Exit price: [Open]
Exit Summary
    Hold for 3 periods

Courtesy of AIQ

SELECTING AMONG MULTIPLE
TRADING CANDIDATES

One common question from subscribers to my twice weekly newsletter, The Timely Trades Letter (for a sample of the Letter, email a request to sample@ daisydogger.com), is how to pick the right stock to trade when there are multiple candidates on the nightly screen. I adjust position sizes, the number of positions I trade, and exit strategies based on market conditions. If I have room for one or two trades and four or five candidates show up on the scan, I use backtesting results to determine which factors to consider when prioritizing the available candidates.

Volume relationships play a role in selecting the most appropriate candidates in many different trading systems. In the case of AboveBB, we are only taking trades when the volume on the day that the stock extends at least four percent above the upper band is less than the 21-day moving average of the volume. Figure 1.27 shows the results of trading AboveBB during the 2002 through 2008 period and only taking trades if the volume on the extension is less than 90 percent of the 21-day average. Looking for even lower volume

FIGURE 1.27:
TEST RESULTS WITH VOLUME LESS THAN
90 PERCENT OF AVERAGE

AboveBB		Winners	Losers	Neutral
Number of trades in test:	239	156	82	1
Average periods per trade:	3.82	3.74	3.96	3.00
Maximum Profit/Loss:		43.71%	(37.33)%	
Average Drawdown:	(2.82)%	(0.91)%	(6.49)%	
Average Profit/Loss:	2.61%	7.15%	(5.99)5	
Average SPX Profit/Loss:	0.55%	0.89%	(0.10)%	
Probability:		65.27%	34.31%	
Average Annual ROI:	249.67%	696.76%	(551.42)%	
Annual SPX (Buy & Hold):	(2.69)%			
Reward/Risk Ratio:	2.27			
Start test date:	01/02/02			
End test date:	12/31/08			
Interval:Daily				
Pricing Summary				
Entry price: [Open]				
Exit price: [Open]				
Exit Summary				

Courtesy of AIQ

on the day of the extension above the upper band improves the percentage of winning trades from 62 to more than 65 percent. If I do not want to take all of the trades presented in the AboveBB scan on any particular day, I will take the trade(s) with the lowest volume.

Some trading systems can be affected by the price of the stock, although this is often not as strong of an influence as volume patterns. I ran the 2002 through 2008 test again filtering out all stocks below $20 instead of the $10 price used in the definition of AboveBB. The higher-priced stocks showed an increase in the percentage of winning trades from 62 to 64 percent. When presented with multiple choices on a single day, I can pick the higher-priced stocks as the better candidates.

Horizontal support and resistance levels should always be considered when selecting potential trades. Since stocks often consolidate, or bounce near support and resistance, the distance between the entry point and support (for shorts) or resistance (for longs) is an important consideration when deciding whether or not to take a particular trade. Since AboveBB is looking for short candidates, I want to find trades with "room to run" as the stock pulls back and approaches support.

Trading is based on being positioned to profit if the stock, or the market, does the usual thing in a given situation. Since stocks often bounce from support, candidates with a larger distance to support from the entry are more attractive because they have more "room to run." When an AboveBB pattern occurs near support, it may just drop to support and bounce, thereby limiting potential profits.

The AboveBB scan turned up several candidates on November 3, 2008. One of the candidates, OMG, is shown in Figure 1.28. OMG met all the conditions required by the AboveBB system but was not as attractive as some of the other candidates presented on the same day because the AboveBB pattern occurred just above horizontal support, as illustrated in Figure 1.28. If this was the only candidate, I may have taken the trade; however, since there were multiple candidates presented on the same day, I had the opportunity to choose ones with the most potential. The OMG trade did turn out well—it showed a 2.35 percent profit in three days. A couple of percent every few days can really add up.

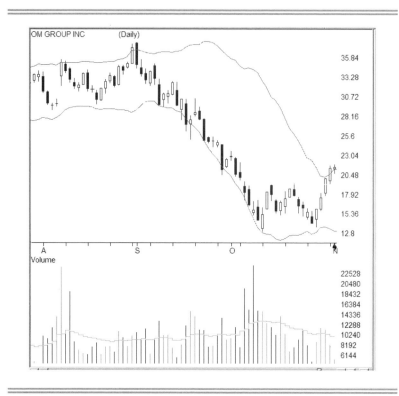

Courtesy of AIQ

VMW was another AboveBB candidate on the same day that OMG came up. As shown in Figure 1.29, VMW had a lot more "room to run," as seen by the distance from the occurrence of the pattern to the next horizontal support level. VMW was a profitable trade; it returned 7.42 percent in three days. The distance to horizontal support is not a guarantee you are going to have a better trade, but it is one of the things I always consider when selecting trades.

There is another volume pattern that I watch because it can strongly affect trading results. When a stock is moving up with a number of well-above-average volume days, or showing accumulation, I will be more interested in it if it is a selection from one of my long trading systems and less interested if it is a candidate from one of my short trading systems.

Courtesy of AIQ

Volume measures the interest in a move. When testing the AboveBB system, we found that moves above the upper band on declining volume, or declining interest, work best. If I see an AboveBB candidate showing a lot of accumulation, I will pass on the trade because there is a lot of interest in the stock when it is moving up.

Figure 1.30 shows an AboveBB candidate from February 15, 2002. EVC demonstrated significant recent accumulation. Notice that it not only showed four very large volume bars while it was moving up, but the average volume had more than doubled in recent weeks. This volume pattern demonstrates very strong interest in the stock and is not the kind of situation in which to take a short trade. Traders taking a short position in EVC would have seen a 7.88 percent loss in just three days.

Courtesy of AIQ

PRACTICAL CONSIDERATIONS

I also apply the same concepts of support, resistance, and accumulation to the market itself to determine if trading is appropriate. If I am trading shorts using AboveBB, or one of my other systems, and the market is approaching support, I become cautious. The reason is that the market often bounces or bases near support and thus shorts would be less attractive. When the market is clearly trending and well away from support, I will use larger position sizes in my trades. I cannot influence what the market does, but I can react to it and reduce my risks by taking smaller position sizes when the market is approaching a support level.

FIGURE 1.31:
MARKET APPROACHING SUPPORT IN MARCH 2008

Courtesy of AIQ

Figure 1.31 shows the NASDAQ during late 2008 and early 2009. As the market was moving down in late February of 2008, the AboveBB system was active because the market's five-period moving average was below its 20-period average. As the market neared the November low, the best approach was to stop taking short trades. This is because the market often will bounce when retesting important lows. Even though the AboveBB system was showing candidates, it was best to ignore them while the market was near support.

Someone usually asks the question: "Yes, but what if the market had broken below support, would it not have been better to hold onto the short positions?" I trade based on what the market usually does, not what I hope may happen, or what sometimes happens. Since the market often bounces when retesting important lows, I will stop taking new shorts and take profits on existing ones when the market approaches support. The market has two choices when it approaches support: it can bounce or it can break below. If the market bounces, I will not incur potential losses from new shorts and will have the profits from the positions I closed. If the market breaks below support, I will have the profits from the positions I closed and can easily take new positions to get back in the game. There is less risk in taking the profits when the market approaches support. It is tough to go broke taking profits while it is easy to go broke by holding on too long.

The AboveBB system is easy to use because it does not require you to watch the market all day. The scan can be run in the evening, and the entry is done at the open the following day. Some traders are able to check on the market from time to time during the day and they often ask about entering a position before the close on the day the pattern occurs, rather than waiting until the next morning. It is easy to check and see if a stock is extended at least four percent above the upper Bollinger band. Verifying that the extension occurred on lower than average volume requires a technique for estimating a stock's volume during trading hours.

The market is open from 9:30 a.m. to 4:00 p.m. EST. I divide these six and one half hours into thirteen half-hour segments and multiply a stock's current volume by an appropriate volume multiplier to estimate the stock's closing volume for the day. If the volume estimate indicates the stock will show below average volume for the day and it is extended at least four percent above the upper Bollinger band, then we have an AboveBB setup.

If volume was evenly distributed during the day, then we would see 1/13 of the day's volume in each half-hour period. We would take the volume at the end of the first half hour of trading and multiply by 13 to estimate the day's volume. At the end of an hour, the stock would have made about 2/13 of the day's volume; so, we would multiply the volume at the end of the first hour by 6.5 to estimate the day's total expected volume.

As a practical matter, stocks trade more heavily during the first half hour than this simple model would predict because of an accumulation of market orders from the previous afternoon and early morning. Because of this, I estimate the stock's volume at the end of the first half hour of trading by multiplying by 10 rather than 13. Table 1.4 shows the multiplication factors I use each half hour to estimate the day's volume. I have this chart posted by my computer and refer to it often.

TABLE 1.4

MARKET TIME AFTER OPEN	MULTIPLICATION FACTOR FOR ESTIMATING ENDING VOLUME
First Half Hour	10
First Hour	6.5
First Hour and a Half	4.3
First Two Hours	3.2
First Two and a Half Hours	2.6
First Three Hours	2.1

Download this chart for your own use from www.traderslibrary.com/TLECorner.

ABOVEBB SUMMARY

The AboveBB system can be an interesting tool in your trading tool box during bearish market periods. The system takes short positions in stocks that have become extended above the upper Bollinger band, as shown in Figure 1.32.

The AboveBB system has only six simple rules and should be used with a moving average technique for determining whether or not the current market conditions are suitable for using AboveBB. The rules defining the AboveBB system are:

- If today's high was more than four percent above the upper band, and
- The volume is less than the 21-day simple moving average, and
- The close is greater than $10, and
- The average volume is at least 300,000 shares, then
- Enter a short position at the opening tomorrow, then
- Hold the position for three days, then
- Close the position on the next open.

The AboveBB system works best in bearish market conditions and should be avoided in bullish or trading range markets. This can be accomplished by only trading AboveBB when the NASDAQ's five-period exponential moving average is below its 20-period exponential moving average.

FIGURE 1.32:
EXAMPLE ABOVEBB PATTERN IN MYGN

Courtesy of AIQ

CHAPTER 1 SELF-TEST

1. Testing a trading system during longer time periods:

    A. Gives a better idea of how it performs in the future.

    B. Guarantees more trades.

    C. Provides more accurate data.

    D. Is not as useful as testing during specific market conditions.

2. Key things to look at in reviewing backtesting results are:

    A. Percentage of winning trades and spread between average winner and average loser.

    B. Annualized ROI.

    C. Holding period.

    D. Maximum profit and number of winners.

3. When a stock moves four percent above the upper Bollinger band:

    A. It is a short candidate in bearish markets.

    B. It is a long candidate in trading range markets.

    C. It is a long candidate in bearish markets.

    D. It should be left alone.

4. Low volume moves above the upper Bollinger band:

    A. Imply the stocks should be left alone.

    B. Improve the odds for taking long positions.

    C. Improve the odds for taking short positions.

    D. Have no effect on trading results.

5. **If backtesting results show winning trades 62 percent of the time:**

   A. You will see six winners for every ten losers.

   B. You will see profits in six weeks out of ten.

   C. You will see a steady stream of profits.

   D. You will have no idea if any particular trade is going to be a winner or loser.

6. **If you short a stock that is extended above the upper band, results may be improved by:**

   A. Picking the stock with low volume on the move above the band.

   B. Picking the stock with high volume on the move above the band.

   C. Trading when the market is in a trading range.

   D. Picking stocks trading under $20.

7. **When shorting stocks extended above the upper band, results are improved by:**

   A. Picking smaller dollar value stocks.

   B. Trading during the first half of the week.

   C. Increasing the holding time from three days to ten days.

   D. Trading when the NASDAQ five-period average is below its 20-period average.

FOR THE ANSWERS,
VISIT WWW.TRADERSLIBRARY.COM/TLECORNER.

CHAPTER 2

BOLLINGER BAND STRATEGY FOR OVERSOLD STOCKS

Stocks are sold at auction based on supply and demand. Sometimes this process results in stocks moving too far too fast, and an inevitable correction results. One way to measure whether or not a stock is oversold is by examining its relationship to the lower Bollinger band. The Bollinger bands measure the volatility of a stock around a simple moving average. Stock prices are contained within the bands about 95 percent of the time. Moves outside the bands are unusual and typically do not last long, as shown in Figure 2.1.

As seen in Figure 2.1, when AMP moves significantly below the lower band, the stock usually bounces back inside the band within two or three days. This same pattern can be observed in a number of different stocks, and the observation forms the basis for a trading system idea. When I see a pattern that happens frequently, I take note and then begin backtesting ideas to find out if the pattern is profitable often enough to be a useful trading tool.

I want to have a variety of different trading tools in my trading tool box so that I can adapt my trading approach to different market conditions. Since strong movements below the band do not happen very often, I do not expect to see a system like this generate trades every day; but, a technique for picking up oversold stocks can be very useful after the market has made an extended decline.

Observations are great, but I do not trade based on my, or anyone else's, observations. I want to test the idea to find out if it really has merit, and if so, what type of market conditions would be most appropriate for using it. In order to test an idea, we need to start with a clear definition of the pattern, and the entry and exit strategies. It is amazing how many people talk about a "trading system" and have no clearly defined exit strategy. Without an exit strategy, you do not have a trading system.

When I talk to traders at trading conferences, I frequently hear them indicating that they just "invert" the definition of a system for longs to get the system for shorts, and visa versa. Once again, this sounds good, but like everything else, it needs to be tested before believing that it works.

FIGURE 2.1:
MOVES BELOW THE LOWER BOLLINGER BAND

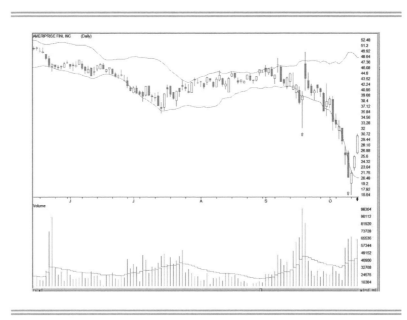

Courtesy of AIQ

One of my daughters is a flight attendant. Her training includes extensive knowledge of evacuation techniques, emergency procedures, and people management along with the more obvious aspects of the job. Most of the time the emergency skills are not called on, but when you need them, it is too late to start training. Trading is also a business where you will not use every technique every day, but when the time comes, you need to have the necessary tools in your trading tool box.

INITIAL BELOWBB SYSTEM BASED ON INVERTING THE ABOVEBB DEFINITION

The seven rules that define the AboveBB system for shorting stocks that become extended above the Bollinger band are outlined in Table 2.1. We investigated this system in Chapter 1 and found it to be interesting. If inverting the rules for an interesting system for shorting stocks leads to an interesting system for taking long positions, then a lot of the work is done. If this is the case, all we need to do is invert the rules of Table 2.1. Inverting these rules leads to the definition shown in Table 2.2 for taking long positions in stocks that are extended below the lower Bollinger band.

TABLE 2.1
WORKING RULES FOR ABOVEBB SYSTEM

- If today's high is more than four percent above the upper band, and
- The volume is less than the 21-day simple moving average, and
- The close is greater than $10, and
- The average volume is at least 300,000 shares, then
- Enter a short position at the opening tomorrow, then
- Hold the position for three days, then
- Close the position on the next open.

TABLE 2.2
INITIAL RULES FOR BELOWBB SYSTEM

- If today's low is more than four percent below the lower band, and
- The volume is less than the 21-day simple moving average, and
- The close is greater than $10, and
- The average volume is at least 300,000 shares, then
- Enter a long position at the opening tomorrow, then
- Hold the position for three days, then
- Close the position on the next open.

Using the rules for BelowBB, which takes long positions in extensions below the lower band as shown in Table 2.2, I tested the system during the seven-year period from the beginning of 2002 through the end of 2008. The results are shown in Figure 2.2 and indicate that the system, as defined in Table 2.2, is not particularly interesting. BelowBB showed winning trades less than half the time, and demonstrated a significant loss in the annualized ROI. The average losing trade showed a greater loss than the average winning trade won.

The AboveBB system, which shorts extensions above the upper band, as defined in Table 2.1, showed a good percentage of winning trades and a positive annualized ROI during the seven-year test period (Figure 2.3). Inverting the rules of a winning system for shorting stocks (AboveBB) did not yield a successful system for taking long positions (BelowBB). Many things that seem logical or reasonable do not turn out that way when fully analyzed. (This seems to be particularly true with politicians.)

BELOWBB TEST RESULTS 2002 THROUGH 2008

BelowBB		Winners	Losers	Neutral
Number of trades in test:	1800	802	937	11
Average periods per trade:	4.07	4.25	3.93	4.09
Maximum Profit/Loss:		43.10%	(50.09)%	
Average Drawdown:	(5.94)%	(1.68)%	(9.46)%	
Average Profit/Loss:	(1.69)%	7.70%	(9.34)%	
Average SPX Profit/Loss	(0.99)%	2.46%	(3.79)%	
Probability:		44.56%	54.83%	
Average Annual ROI:	(151.71)%	661.19%	(867.64)%	
Annual SPX (Buy & Hold):	(2.69)%			
Reward/Risk Ratio:	0.67			
Start test date:	01/02/02			
End test date:	12/31/08			

Interval:Daily
Pricing Summary
      Entry price: [Open]
      Exit price: [Open]
Exit Summary
      Hold for 3 periods

SEVEN-YEAR TEST RESULTS FOR ABOVEBB

AboveBB		Winners	Losers	Neutral
Number of trades in test:	1088	608	473	7
Average periods per trade:	4.06	4.00	4.13	4.00
Maximum Profit/Loss:		68.64%	(37.33)%	
Average Drawdown:	(2.68)%	(0.78)%	(5.15)%	
Average Profit/Loss:	0.88%	5.23%	(4.69)%	
Average SPX Profit/Loss	0.35%	0.81%	(0.24)%	
Probability:		55.88%	43.47%	
Average Annual ROI:	49.47%	476.85%	(414.50)%	
Annual SPX (Buy & Hold):	(2.69)%			
Reward/Risk Ratio:	1.43			
Start test date:	01/02/02			
End test date:	12/31/08			

Interval:Daily
Pricing Summary
      Entry price: [Open]
      Exit price: [Open]
Exit Summary
      Hold for 3 periods

Courtesy of AIQ

Myth: You can invert a profitable system for trading shorts in order to create a profitable system for trading longs.

Fact: Simple inversion may or may not work. In the trading business, assumptions and guesswork can be costly. Each idea or trading technique should be tested on its own before being considered for inclusion in the trader's tool box.

REVISED DEFINITION BASED ON OBSERVATION

Rather than "inverting" the trading rules from an interesting shorting system to get a system for trading longs, it is best to go back to basic observation and determine what the pattern really is. After reviewing a number of charts, I found that stocks were more likely to bounce if the closing price was below the lower band, not just the low of the day.

When the stock closes below the band, it is making a statement. It has not just briefly gone below the band and then bounced up; it has fallen below the band and has stayed there much of the day. An example of this pattern is shown in Figure 2.4.

Based on these observations, I changed the definition of the BelowBB system, as shown in Table 2.3.

A few examples can lead us to interesting ideas to test, but by themselves, a few examples prove nothing. In order to get a better idea of how the revised BelowBB definition affects trading results, I tested the system between January of 2002 and December of 2008. The revised definition produced significantly better results, including a profitable annualized ROI and an improved winning percentage during the test period. The results of this test are shown in Figure 2.5.

RESULTS IMPROVE WHEN THE CLOSE IS BELOW THE BAND

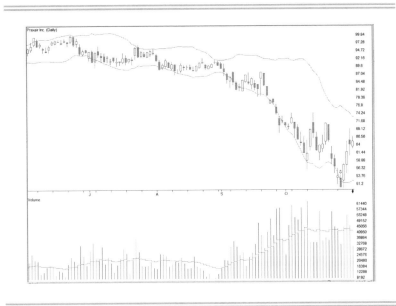

Courtesy of AIQ

TABLE 2.3
IMPROVED BELOWBB DEFINITION

- If today's close is more than four percent below the lower band, and
- The close is greater than $5, and
- The average volume is at least 300,000 shares, then
- Enter a long position at the opening tomorrow, then
- Hold the position for three days, then
- Close the position on the next open.

IMPROVED BELOWBB DEFINITION TEST RESULTS

BelowBB		Winners	Losers	Neutral
Number of trades in test:	7187	3826	3321	40
Average periods per trade:	4.43	4.50	4.34	4.42
Maximum Profit/Loss:		160.24%	(69.22)%	
Average Drawdown:	(4.39)%	(1.25)%	(8.06)%	
Average Profit/Loss:	0.83%	7.89%	(7.30)%	
Average SPX Profit/Loss	0.36%	2.32%	(1.89)%	
Probability:		53.24%	46.21%	
Average Annual ROI:	68.30%	639.61%	(613.36)%	
Annual SPX (Buy & Hold):	(2.69)%			
Reward/Risk Ratio:	1.25			
Start test date:	01/02/02			
End test date:	12/31/08			
Interval:Daily				
Pricing Summary				
Entry price: [Open]				
Exit price: [Open]				
Exit Summary				
Hold for 3 periods				

Courtesy of AIQ

TEST RESULTS FOR BOTTOM OF THE RANGE CLOSE

Since test results were improved by selecting setups that closed below the lower Bollinger band, I next looked at whether where the close occurred within the day's trading range affected results.

Adding a requirement to take trades only when the closing price for the stock occurred within the bottom 20 percent of the day's trading range improved results. The annualized ROI increased from 68 to 133 percent and the percentage of winning trades increased from 53 to 56 percent. These test results are shown in Figure 2.6.

It appears that when stock prices move below the lower band, it is like stretching a rubber band; it causes prices to snap back inside. Closing below the band instead of just briefly moving below it stretches the "rubber

TEST RESULTS FOR BOTTOM 20 PERCENT CLOSE

BelowBB		Winners	Losers	Neutral
Number of trades in test:	5107	2889	2195	23
Average periods per trade:	4.47	4.52	4.41	4.26
Maximum Profit/Loss:		120.13%	(69.22)%	
Average Drawdown:	(4.43)%	(1.38)%	(8.49)%	
Average Profit/Loss:	1.64%	8.49%	(7.36)%	
Average SPX Profit/Loss	0.73	2.72%	(1.88)%	
Probability:		56.57%	42.98%	
Average Annual ROI:	133.85%	685.68%	(609.41)%	
Annual SPX (Buy & Hold):	(2.69)%			
Reward/Risk Ratio:	1.52			
Start test date:	01/02/02			
End test date:	12/31/08			

Interval:Daily
Pricing Summary
      Entry price: [Open]
      Exit price: [Open]
Exit Summary
      Hold for 3 periods

Courtesy of AIQ

band" more. Closing in the bottom 20 percent of the day's trading range and being below the band stretches the "rubber band" even farther, resulting in better moves.

This knowledge is not only useful for the BelowBB system, but can be used in trade management when using other systems. If excursions below the lower band do not last long and are the basis for a trading system taking longs, then it would not make much sense to hold short positions in declining stocks when they move below the lower band. I use this information to help manage my short trades and frequently take profits when short positions approach the lower band.

The DVretrace system (to be discussed in Chapter 4) is one of my "bread and butter" shorting systems. It generates a consistent and frequent supply of shorting candidates. The analysis of the BelowBB system indicates that I should take profits on short positions that extend below the lower band. One of the great things about testing trading systems is that we gain knowledge about the behavior of stocks and the market, which can be applied to a number of different trading tools. Knowing that oversold stocks are likely to bounce around the lower band is useful knowledge for managing trades from any of the other systems in my tool box.

EFFECT OF ELIMINATING GAP DOWNS AND EXTENSION BELOW THE BAND

Figure 2.7 illustrates an interesting observation; stocks that gap down often continue down in the short run. In Figure 2.7, BIDU shows a gap down in late September and the stock continues down for two more weeks. It showed a gap down in late October, which only lasted two bars before bouncing, but the gap down in mid-November resulted in another strong continuation move down.

FIGURE 2.7:
STOCKS THAT GAP DOWN OFTEN CONTINUE DOWN IN THE SHORT RUN

Courtesy of AIQ

BelowBB		Winners	Losers	Neutral
Number of trades in test:	1998	1177	812	9
Average periods per trade:	4.48	4.54	4.38	4.11
Maximum Profit/Loss:		120.86%	(69.22)%	
Average Drawdown:	(4.72)%	(1.53)%	(9.40)%	
Average Profit/Loss:	2.85%	9.76%	(7.14)%	
Average SPX Profit/Loss	0.22	2.42%	(2.97)%	
Probability:		58.91%	40.64%	
Average Annual ROI:	232.10%	783.78%	(595.11)%	
Annual SPX (Buy & Hold):	(2.69)%			
Reward/Risk Ratio:	1.98			
Start test date:	01/02/02			
End test date:	12/31/08			
Interval:Daily				
Pricing Summary				
Entry price: [Open]				
Exit price: [Open]				
Exit Summary				
Hold for 3 periods				

Courtesy of AIQ

Remember, nothing in trading works all the time. Traders are looking for general rules that provide an edge and work more often than not. They are not hung up on looking for things that always work. In the example of Figure 2.7, gaps down generally lead to a short-term decline. If this pattern occurs more often than not, then filtering out stocks that have gapped down should improve the results of the BelowBB system. The important thing is to make observations about stock behaviors and then test them. I do not want to trade based on something that happens in a few examples. I want to test those ideas and then find things that provide a trading edge.

Figure 2.8 shows the results of testing BelowBB during the seven-year test period between 2002 and 2008 with two filters added to the definition shown in Table 2.3. The first filter is the one tested above that only takes trades when the close is in the bottom 20 percent of the day's range. The second filter requires that today's open be equal to or greater than yesterday's close, which selects stocks that have not gapped down on the day they make their excursion and close below the lower Bollinger band.

By focusing BelowBB on stocks that did not gap down on the day the pattern forms, the annualized ROI increased from 133 to 232 and the percentage of winning trades increased from 56 percent to nearly 59 percent. The spread between the average winning trade and the average losing trade also improved. Stocks that did not open with a gap on the day they made the move below the lower band tended to bounce back more in the short term than stocks that had a gap down.

We found that declining stocks that close at least four percent below the lower Bollinger band tend to bounce, and that taking long positions in these oversold stocks has the potential to stand as a trading system. The next step is to determine how sensitive the system is to the distance the stock closes beneath the lower band. Table 2.4 shows the results of running the test five times and varying the extension of the close below the lower band from three percent to seven percent.

TABLE 2.4
EFFECT OF EXTENSION OF CLOSE BELOW THE LOWER BAND

LOWER BAND EXTENSION	WINNING %	ANNUALIZED ROI	# OF TRADES	AVG. WIN-AVG. LOSS
3%	56.8	162	3195	1.92%
4%	58.9	232	1998	2.62%
5%	60.5	292	1288	3.21%
6%	62.2	370	860	4.06%
7%	62.6	407	603	4.41%

The first column in Table 2.4 shows the percentage that the closing price of the stock was below the lower band. The next three columns show the percentage of winning trades, the annualized ROI, and the number of trades during the seven-year test period of 2002 through 2008. The last column shows the difference between the average winning trade and the average losing trade (absolute value of). Larger winning percentages are good for obvious reasons. Larger numbers in the last column indicate that the average winning percentage is greater than the average losing percentage. Remember, the bigger this number, the better.

Table 2.4 shows a direct correlation between the percentage the close is below the lower band and the percentage of winning trades. The farther below the band the stock closes, the higher the percentage of winning trades we see. The difference between the average winner and the average loser also increases as distance grows between the close and the lower band. We see a higher percentage of winning trades, and we gain more on the average trade. This result is something I use frequently when looking at potential trades for this system.

Based on these results, I changed the BelowBB definition to look for stocks that were at least five percent below the lower band, rather than the four percent used in the initial definition. I did not move all the way to seven percent because it cuts the number of trades in half. I would rather see more trades available. Then, if there are more trades on the scan than I am interested in, I can prioritize them based on the amount of extension below the lower band.

I do not want to keep adding filters in order to drive up all the numbers in a backtest. I want to use the backtesting as a guide to formulate general rules that I can use not only for finding potential trades, but to also prioritize those potential trades. Using the seven percent move below the lower band creates better test results, but test results are just one indication of what might happen going forward. In the real world, I want to see a number of trades from several different tested systems and then pick the best of the trades that are available based on a variety of risk and reward factors.

Using the five percent extension below the band yields more potential trading candidates that can then be analyzed based on various risk/reward measurements, such as the distance to the next resistance level. I do not want to blindly trade any system, I want trading candidates from systems that have shown promising results. Then, I will use the analysis of current market conditions to determine whether to take any trades at all, and, if I take any of the trades, I will focus on selecting the best of what is available in terms of potential risk and reward.

If a long setup forms a point under strong resistance, I am not nearly as interested in it as a setup that forms three points under weak resistance. The most likely thing for a stock to do at resistance is stall or bounce, so I want to pick trades with more "room to run."

Using the five percent number instead of the seven percent number showed about twice as many trades. This gives us more opportunity to consider other factors, such as support and resistance areas, before making any trades. Trading systems are not magic boxes that lead to wealth—they are just one of the tools that you use along with market conditions and risk management techniques to increase your odds of success.

The revised definition of BelowBB is shown in Table 2.5.

TABLE 2.5
REVISED BELOWBB DEFINITION

- If today's close is more than five percent below the lower band, and
- The close is greater than $5, and
- The average volume is at least 300,000 shares, and
- The close is in the bottom 20 percent of the day's range, and
- The open is greater than or equal to yesterday's close, then
- Enter a long position at the opening tomorrow, then
- Hold the position for three days, then
- Close the position on the next open.

ANALYZING TRADE HISTORY

When analyzing a potential trading system, it is important to look beyond the basic statistics and try to get a feel for how the system might work in actual practice. Knowing how often a trading system wins is important, but I also want some idea of how those wins are distributed in terms of profit-sizing and time. If a system wins frequently, but most of the profit comes from just a few trades, then it may look good on paper but not be useful in actual practice. One way to check on how the profits are distributed is to look at all of the trades sorted by profit size.

Figure 2.9 shows the results of all trades during the 2002 through 2008 period sorted in descending order of profitability. There were two trades with profits of over $20, and ten trades with profits between $9 and $10. The profitable trades are distributed in a typical bell curve with fewer large profit trades and an increasing number of trades as the profit level declines. This is normal, and a result of the natural statistics of the trading system. Traders are not doing a great job because they hit a couple of $15 profit trades, or doing a poor job if they see a series of trades making just $1. This is the natural distribution of trades. It is not what you are doing; it is how the system works.

FIGURE 2.9:
BELOWBB TRADES SORTED BY PROFIT IN DESCENDING ORDER

Ticker	Held	Entry Date	Entry Price	Exit Date	Exit Price	Profit
CME	3	10/28/2008	244.49	10/31/2008	268	23.51
RKH	5	10/10/2008	71.95	10/15/2008	95.28	23.33
POT	3	10/6/2008	87.25	10/9/2008	103.05	15.8
ISRG	5	10/8/2008	179	10/13/2008	194	15
DVN	5	10/10/2008	58.17	10/15/2008	72.75	14.58
IYG	5	10/10/2008	47.69	10/15/2008	62	14.31
TNH	3	11/13/2007	89.76	11/16/2007	103	13.24
DECK	3	1/8/2008	132.02	1/11/2008	145.04	13.02
MTB	5	10/10/2008	64	10/15/2008	76.5	12.5
ENER	5	10/10/2008	31.65	10/15/2008	42.82	11.17
MS	5	10/10/2008	9.19	10/15/2008	20.23	11.04
BXP	5	10/10/2008	65	10/15/2008	76	11
IYF	5	10/10/2008	46.35	10/15/2008	56.95	10.6
MAA	5	11/21/2008	24.56	11/26/2008	35	10.44
SPG	5	10/8/2008	70.66	10/13/2008	80.66	10
AMP	5	10/10/2008	19.25	10/15/2008	29	9.75
RMBS	6	2/13/2004	25.11	2/19/2004	34.73	9.62
ACE	5	10/10/2008	36.99	10/15/2008	46.47	9.48
DIA	5	10/10/2008	82.39	10/15/2008	91.84	9.45
ICE	6	1/18/2008	134.82	1/24/2008	144.27	9.45
STT	5	11/20/2008	29.59	11/25/2008	38.66	9.07
PFG	5	10/10/2008	14.99	10/15/2008	24.04	9.05
RNR	5	10/10/2008	32.05	10/15/2008	41.08	9.03
URS	3	11/13/2007	53.23	11/16/2007	62.25	9.02
XL	3	1/22/2008	37	1/25/2008	46	9
CF	3	10/6/2008	51.3	10/9/2008	60.29	8.99
JNJ	5	10/10/2008	55.4	10/15/2008	64.31	8.91
SPW	5	10/8/2008	42.53	10/13/2008	51.36	8.83
INT	5	10/10/2008	14.65	10/15/2008	23.11	8.46
PKX	5	10/8/2008	63.77	10/13/2008	72.1	8.33
ABT	5	10/10/2008	47.97	10/15/2008	56.1	8.13
DVY	5	10/10/2008	38.4	10/15/2008	46.53	8.13
TMK	5	10/10/2008	37.5	10/15/2008	45.5	8
IVE	5	10/10/2008	42.75	10/15/2008	50.52	7.77
BK	5	10/8/2008	21.87	10/13/2008	29.45	7.58
AB	5	9/18/2008	33.01	9/23/2008	40.53	7.52
VTR	5	10/10/2008	32	10/15/2008	39.48	7.48
UBSI	5	10/10/2008	22	10/15/2008	29.33	7.33
IWN	5	10/10/2008	46.2	10/15/2008	53.45	7.25
GENZ	5	10/10/2008	62.63	10/15/2008	69.85	7.22

Courtesy of AIQ

Knowing this makes it a lot easier when you see your trades picking up a series of small profits after a few big wins. It is not that you are missing something—it is just how trading works.

Figure 2.10 shows the losing trades from the BelowBB test during the 2002 through 2008 test period sorted from largest losing trade to smallest losing trade. There were only two losing trades above $10, and the distribution of losing trades looks like a relatively normal distribution indicating that the profits, or losses, are more likely due to the pattern itself rather than some event.

FIGURE 2.10:
BELOWBB LOSSES SORTED IN DESCENDING ORDER

Ticker	Held	Entry Date	Entry Price	Exit Date	Exit Price	Profit
PRU	5	10/3/2008	62	10/8/2008	45.94	-16.06
THC	5	10/30/2002	39.55	11/4/2002	29.21	-10.34
0	5	10/8/2008	103.01	10/13/2008	93.41	-9.6
IRF	5	6/21/2002	34.5	6/26/2002	25.1	-9.4
ALL	5	10/8/2008	37.6	10/13/2008	28.84	-8.76
DIG	5	10/8/2008	40.55	10/13/2008	31.9	-8.65
WCG	3	10/29/2007	31.55	11/1/2007	22.93	-8.62
JEC	5	10/3/2008	45.14	10/8/2008	36.55	-8.59
GDI	5	10/3/2008	30.66	10/8/2008	23.5	-7.16
PWR	5	6/28/2002	10.07	7/3/2002	3.1	-6.97
RATE	6	7/3/2008	33.83	7/9/2008	26.93	-6.9
FST	5	10/8/2008	31.85	10/13/2008	25.34	-6.51
ESV	5	10/8/2008	41.75	10/13/2008	35.27	-6.48
JOYG	5	9/5/2008	50.33	9/10/2008	44.01	-6.32
AKS	5	9/5/2008	40.41	9/10/2008	34.18	-6.23
SII	5	10/8/2008	42.2	10/13/2008	36.04	-6.16
GGP	5	10/3/2008	10.87	10/8/2008	4.95	-5.92
CSIQ	5	10/3/2008	16.9	10/8/2008	11	-5.9
PXD	5	10/8/2008	37.74	10/13/2008	31.95	-5.79
BUCY	5	9/5/2008	49.8	9/10/2008	44.22	-5.58
BHI	3	10/6/2008	48.04	10/9/2008	42.48	-5.56
WGOV	5	10/3/2008	31.15	10/8/2008	25.61	-5.54
BIDU	3	1/24/2006	57.5	1/27/2006	52	-5.5
XL	5	10/8/2008	11.95	10/13/2008	6.78	-5.17
OIS	5	10/8/2008	23.5	10/13/2008	18.58	-4.92
GB	5	5/14/2004	29.65	5/19/2004	24.81	-4.84
BRY	5	10/8/2008	23.49	10/13/2008	18.69	-4.8
APC	5	10/8/2008	34.05	10/13/2008	29.33	-4.72
VLO	5	10/3/2008	26.2188	10/8/2008	21.5	-4.7188
CVTX	5	8/6/2003	26.24	8/11/2003	21.73	-4.51
TNB	3	10/6/2008	31.15	10/9/2008	26.65	-4.5
FCX	6	1/18/2008	83.71	1/24/2008	79.27	-4.44
RYAAY	5	10/3/2008	20.75	10/8/2008	16.33	-4.42
CNA	5	10/8/2008	19	10/13/2008	14.63	-4.37
DDM	5	10/8/2008	39.66	10/13/2008	35.38	-4.28
NOV	5	10/8/2008	30.42	10/13/2008	26.19	-4.23
MLM	3	10/6/2008	84.6	10/9/2008	80.44	-4.16
CCO	5	10/8/2008	10.35	10/13/2008	6.2	-4.15
RDN	3	8/6/2007	23.27	8/9/2007	19.13	-4.14

Courtesy of AIQ

Another important aspect of analyzing trading system results is to review the trades sorted by calendar date. I am looking for trades to be relatively consistent over time and not all clumped around a couple of dates. I want to be sure that the trades are due to the pattern regularly occurring and not due to some event that may or may not recur in the future.

Figure 2.11 shows the BelowBB trades that happened between the middle of July and the beginning of October in 2008. Trades are generally evenly distributed through time. Some days may not have any setups and other days may have several, but the trades are not all clumped around one or two dates. Scrolling through all the calendar periods indicates that the pattern shown in Figure 2.11 is typical, with one exception.

FIGURE 2.11:
BELOWBB TRADES SORTED BY DATE

Ticker	Held	Entry Date	Entry Price	Exit Date	Exit Price	Profit
RYAAY	5	10/3/2008	20.75	10/8/2008	16.33	-4.42
MTRX	5	10/3/2008	14.29	10/8/2008	11.06	-3.23
IT	5	10/3/2008	19.77	10/8/2008	17.39	-2.38
HIG	5	10/3/2008	29.97	10/8/2008	28.14	-1.83
GNTX	5	10/3/2008	12.18	10/8/2008	11.19	-0.99
RRI	3	9/30/2008	9.51	10/3/2008	5.97	-3.54
AN	3	9/30/2008	11.08	10/3/2008	11	-0.08
AINV	3	9/30/2008	14.69	10/3/2008	15.5	0.81
DDR	3	9/30/2008	29.23	10/3/2008	30.09	0.86
TRV	3	9/30/2008	39.4	10/3/2008	42.68	3.28
DISCA	5	9/19/2008	16.27	9/24/2008	17.07	0.8
AYR	5	9/18/2008	9.99	9/23/2008	12.62	2.63
MXB	5	9/18/2008	20.01	9/23/2008	25.25	5.24
AB	5	9/18/2008	33.01	9/23/2008	40.53	7.52
PBY	5	9/11/2008	6.23	9/16/2008	6.32	0.09
KBR	5	9/10/2008	18	9/15/2008	18	0
IO	5	9/10/2008	13.1	9/15/2008	13.82	0.72
AG	5	9/10/2008	48.67	9/15/2008	49.82	1.15
FLR	5	9/10/2008	57	9/15/2008	60.91	3.91
HL	3	9/9/2008	5	9/12/2008	4.6	-0.4
NG	3	9/9/2008	4.87	9/12/2008	4.73	-0.14
FTK	3	9/8/2008	13.35	9/11/2008	11.39	-1.96
JOYG	5	9/5/2008	50.33	9/10/2008	44.01	-6.32
AKS	5	9/5/2008	40.41	9/10/2008	34.18	-6.23
BUCY	5	9/5/2008	49.8	9/10/2008	44.22	-5.58
DELL	5	9/3/2008	20.8	9/8/2008	20.61	-0.19
HAR	3	8/19/2008	33.88	8/22/2008	34.66	0.78
MENT	3	8/18/2008	10.69	8/21/2008	11.4	0.71
NCTY	5	8/14/2008	19	8/19/2008	18.58	-0.42
SBGI	5	8/8/2008	5.95	8/13/2008	6.01	0.06
ENS	5	8/8/2008	27.31	8/13/2008	29	1.69
RRI	5	8/6/2008	14.98	8/11/2008	17.23	2.25
EXM	3	8/5/2008	29.6	8/8/2008	30.23	0.63
OSG	3	8/5/2008	66.94	8/8/2008	67.64	0.7
SWC	3	8/4/2008	8.16	8/7/2008	7.47	-0.69
MLI	5	7/25/2008	26.51	7/30/2008	25.89	-0.62
AGU	5	7/25/2008	83.71	7/30/2008	86.34	2.63
GAP	3	7/21/2008	18.49	7/24/2008	17.83	-0.66
ACE	5	7/16/2008	45.9	7/21/2008	49.1	3.2
DAKT	3	7/15/2008	17.12	7/18/2008	18.1	0.98

Courtesy of AIQ

There were two days in 2008 that generated more than 50 BelowBB trades each day. These unusual days occurred in early October when the news media was talking about a potential total collapse of the financial system. Fifty trades a day is about ten times the normal activity. In trading, when something unusual happens, it is almost always a sign to be cautious. With the exception of this period in October 2008, the distribution of trades is relatively normal for this type of system.

The market dropped 21 percent in a few days in early October 2008. This is unusual activity for the market and strong moves like this will affect most trading systems. In the case of BelowBB, it resulted in an unusually large number of trading opportunities as the strong market move caused a number of stocks to become oversold. Barring this unusual period of a few days, BelowBB shows nine losing trades in a row in January 2003, and seven losing trades in a row in December 2007. In general, the winning and losing trades were relatively evenly distributed.

Based on this review of losing trades, I want to use a position-sizing strategy that allows me to see at least ten losing trades in a row without an unacceptable loss. I remember attending a conference and hearing a trader say that if the worst case during a seven-year period was nine losers in a row, than he felt comfortable being more aggressive because large numbers of consecutive losers do not happen often. My approach, on the contrary, is to make sure I am always trading for the long run.

The Bollinger band systems are looking for overbought and oversold stocks. These conditions generally occur when the market has been running for a

Think about it. If a trader risks a large portion of his account on each trade and they all go against him at some point, he could suffer a crippling loss. He might make good money using large position sizes when things are going well. But when the natural statistics take over, and the inevitable string of consecutive losses comes, he will be hurt and possibly even broke. Ten years from now, I expect that I will still be in the game and he will be doing something else. There is a correlation between risk and reward; I would rather focus on managing risks and making sure I can trade for the long term rather than swing for the fences and risk the large loss. Different traders will make different choices—just make sure you fully understand the implications of the choices you make.

while and occur less often when the market is indecisive or basing in a tight range. I do not expect to see a number of setups for overbought and oversold stocks every day, which matches the data shown in Figure 2.11.

BelowBB generates a few trades, then takes a week or so off and then generates another few trades. Pullback and retracement systems (discussed in other chapters of this book) tend to generate trading candidates more frequently than either of the Bollinger band systems because the natural rhythm of stock movement is frequently showing runs and pullbacks. The Bollinger band systems are more specialized tools that look for stocks that have run too far in one direction. This happens less often than either pullbacks or retracements in trending stocks.

EFFECT OF HOLDING TIME ON RESULTS

Up to this point, all of the testing has used a fixed three-day holding time. Positions are entered, held for three days, and then closed. Table 2.6 shows the results of testing this choice. In general, the testing indicates that holding more than three or four days diminishes results. I use this information by looking at my position after three days and determining if there is a clear reason to continue holding. If not, then I close the position. If after three days, I see that the market is moving up strongly or the position is moving up on increasing volume, I will consider holding longer. I also look to see what my other trading opportunities are at that time. I am not fixated on any one trade; I always want to be in the best of what is available.

TABLE 2.6
EFFECT OF HOLDING TIME ON BELOWBB

HOLDING TIME	WINNING %	ANNUALIZED ROI	AVERAGE WIN-AVERAGE LOSS
3 Days	60.5	292	3.21%
4 Days	61.5	243	3.00%
5 Days	56.5	118	2.14%
6 Days	54.1	73	1.76%

EFFECT OF MARKET CONDITIONS
ON TEST RESULTS

One of the best ways to determine market conditions is through direct observation. It is usually clear whether or not the market is moving up, down, or sideways. Traders can also use a dual moving average technique to get a visual representation of market conditions. As we discussed previously, the five-period moving average (5MA) generally follows the price action relatively closely and the 20-period moving average (20MA) usually moves in the direction of the intermediate-term trend. Let's illustrate this with a few examples and demonstrate what it means for our BelowBB system.

Figure 2.12 shows a chart of the NASDAQ with periods when the five-period simple moving average of the highs is below the 20-period moving average of the lows. During these periods, the market is generally bearish. The technique does not pick up the exact beginning and ending of bearish periods since there is always some lag with moving average systems. As a general

FIGURE 2.12:
GENERALLY BEARISH WHEN THE 5MA IS BELOW THE 20MA

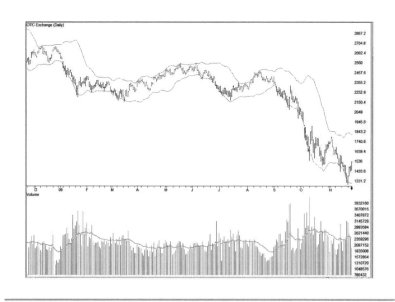

Courtesy of AIQ

purpose indicator, it helps provide a visual representation to assist in determining market conditions.

Figure 2.13 shows another NASDAQ period with areas of the chart when the five-period exponential moving average of the highs is greater than the 20-period exponential moving average of the lows. As seen, this technique provides a reasonable approximation of periods when the market is generally bullish.

We can use this technique as a filter in backtesting. We would only take BelowBB trades when the market is either generally bullish or generally bearish. Running the tests during the 2002 through 2008 period using these market condition filters can give us a basic idea of how the market environment affects the BelowBB results.

Figure 2.14 shows the results of running the BelowBB test during the 2002 through 2008 period and limiting trades to periods when the five-period moving average of the highs is above the 20-period moving average of the close. This results in fewer trades, as one would expect since trades are only taken when the market is bullish.

FIGURE 2.13:
GENERALLY BULLISH WHEN THE 5MA IS ABOVE THE 20MA

Courtesy of AIQ

BELOWBB RESULTS 2002-2008, USING 5MA ABOVE 20MA FILTER

BelowBB		Winners	Losers	Neutral
Number of trades in test:	365	205	157	3
Average periods per trade:	4.30	4.30	4.31	3.67
Maximum Profit/Loss:		42.84%	(27.32)%	
Average Drawdown:	(3.15)%	(1.12)%	(5.88)%	
Average Profit/Loss:	1.56%	6.53%	(4.90)%	
Average SPX Profit/Loss	(0.07)%	0.36%	(0.63)%	
Probability:		56.16%	43.01%	
Average Annual ROI:	132.47%	554.26%	(414.89)%	
Annual SPX (Buy & Hold):	(2.69)%			
Reward/Risk Ratio:	1.74			
Start test date:	01/02/02			
End test date:	12/31/08			

Interval:Daily
Pricing Summary
      Entry price: [Open]
      Exit price: [Open]
Exit Summary
      Hold for 3 periods

FIGURE 2.15:
BELOWBB RESULTS 2002-2008, USING 5MA BELOW 20MA FILTER

BelowBB		Winners	Losers	Neutral
Number of trades in test:	925	577	342	6
Average periods per trade:	4.58	4.68	4.43	4.33
Maximum Profit/Loss:		120.86%	(59.22)%	
Average Drawdown:	(5.77)%	(1.84)%	(12.49)%	
Average Profit/Loss:	4.42%	12.37%	(8.93)%	
Average SPX Profit/Loss	0.53%	3.29%	(4.12)%	
Probability:		62.38%	36.97%	
Average Annual ROI:	351.92%	965.89%	(736.16)%	
Annual SPX (Buy & Hold):	(2.66)%			
Reward/Risk Ratio:	2.34			
Start test date:	01/02/02			
End test date:	12/31/08			

Interval:Daily
Pricing Summary
      Entry price: [Open]
      Exit price: [Open]
Exit Summary
      Hold for 3 periods

Courtesy of AIQ

It also results in a lower annualized ROI and a slightly lower percentage of winning trades. Based on this test, it appears that the 5 x 20 moving average filter results in slightly lower performance, but not dramatically so. Bullish market conditions influence the BelowBB trading results, but not strongly so.

Taking BelowBB trades only when the five-period moving average is below the 20-period moving average restricts trading to periods when the market is often bearish and yields the results shown in Figure 2.15. During these market periods, the BelowBB system shows about three times as many trades as we saw when looking at instances when the five-period average was above the 20-period average. It also shows generally improved results. Using this moving average filter improves the annualized ROI and the percentage of winning trades.

The interesting thing about using the moving average filter for market conditions is that the results indicate that the percentage of winning trades only varies a small percent depending on whether or not the filter is used. For this reason, I generally do not use a market condition's filter on the BelowBB system and will look at all the trades it produces. I will use other factors such as distance to resistance in both the stock and the market along with what other trading system candidates are available in order to decide whether or not to take trades shown by the BelowBB scan.

Myth: Trading the BelowBB system in bullish environments will be more profitable because it is a system that trades longs.

Fact: The only way to truly understand how a system performs in different market conditions is to do the work and run the tests. Assumptions based on logical ideas may not always pan out. Like Ronald Reagan used to say, "Trust but verify."

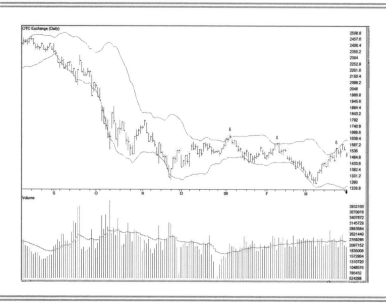

Courtesy of AIQ

The upper Bollinger band will often act as resistance to market moves, particularly in trading range markets. This tendency to retrace from the upper band during trading range conditions is illustrated in Figure 2.16. In strongly trending markets, the market may "ride the bands." It is quite common, however, for the market to base or retrace when hitting the upper band during a trading range environment. Since I always want to be positioned to profit when the market does the normal or usual thing, I take profits on positions when they approach the upper band during a trading range environment. I also will avoid taking BelowBB trades when the market is close to the upper band. I use my knowledge of how the market and the individual trading systems perform to help prioritize my trades.

The market also tends to base or retrace near horizontal resistance points as shown in Figure 2.17. During the first part of 2009, the market confirmed a double bottom pattern, as shown in Figure 2.18. The left and right bottoms are marked with a "B" on the chart, and the confirmation high, which also acts as horizontal resistance, is marked by a "C." When the market ran up off the right bottom, it stalled, or based, for a few days as it approached the hori-

MARKET MOVING INTO HORIZONTAL RESISTANCE

Courtesy of AIQ

zontal resistance from point "C," which is also marked by a horizontal line in Figure 2.18. The next horizontal resistance area is the middle line, which comes from the peak in early November. The market touched the second horizontal resistance area in early May and then retraced slightly.

Retracing or basing near horizontal resistance is normal market behavior. During these times, the market is resting. It is more difficult for trading set-ups to trigger and move, so I cut back on the number of trading positions I take and also reduce position sizes. When a BelowBB pattern shows up and the market is not near resistance, I am interested. If the market is close to resistance, I pass on the opportunity and look at other techniques.

I also use the time stop (sell after three days) as a guideline, rather than a hard and fast rule. When one of my positions approaches resistance, I take the profits and move on, especially if the market is in a trading range environment. Figure 2.19 shows a BelowBB setup that moved up strongly and reached horizontal resistance in just two days. When the stock moves into resistance, I close it and take my profits to another trade whether it has been

TENDENCY TO BASE OR RETRACE NEAR HORIZONTAL RESISTANCE

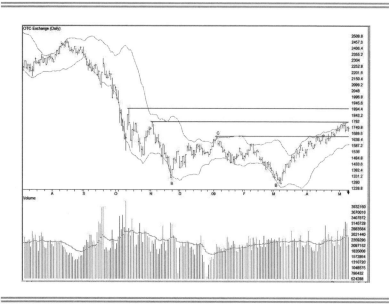

Courtesy of AIQ

one, two, three, or four days. The most likely thing for a stock to do at resistance is retrace, by definition. If the stock is likely to retrace, then I want to have my profits and move on and not just hold on for three days. Trading systems are not magic formulas to be blindly followed; traders must use all the knowledge and skills about how stocks and the market perform to manage trades.

Volume patterns are another important trade management tool. When I have a long position (from any of my trading systems) that starts going up on declining volume, I generally take profits and close the position, whether or not I have held it for the amount of time used in the testing. Stocks moving up on declining volume are generally weak because fewer people are willing to pay higher prices for the stock. This means that I want to take my money and put it to work in another trade.

Figure 2.19 shows a BelowBB setup that was moving up on declining volume (noted by the arrows on the chart) and closing this position on the second

Courtesy of AIQ

day preserved a profit, whereas waiting until three days would have resulted in a loss.

BELOWBB SUMMARY

Stocks are sold at auction based on supply and demand. Sometimes this process results in stocks moving too far too fast, and an inevitable correction results. One way to measure whether or not a stock is oversold is by examining its relationship to the lower Bollinger band. When a stock closes below the band, it is making a statement. It has not just briefly gone below the band and then bounced up; it has fallen below the band and has stayed there much of the day. Since the Bollinger bands contain the large majority of a stock's price action, extensions below the lower band tend to pop back inside the band quickly, which creates opportunities for long trades.

BelowBB looks for oversold stocks that meet the conditions outlined below.

- If today's close was more than five percent below the lower band, and
- The close is greater than $5, and
- The average volume is at least 300,000 shares, and
- The close is in the bottom 20 percent of the day's range, and
- The open is greater than or equal to yesterday's close, then
- Enter a long position at the opening tomorrow, then
- Hold the position for three days, then
- Close the position on the next open.

Adding a requirement to only take trades when the closing price for the stock occurs within the bottom 20 percent of the day's trading range improves results. It appears that when stock prices move below the lower band it is like stretching a rubber band which causes them to snap back inside. Closing below the band instead of just briefly moving below it stretches the rubber band more. Closing in the bottom 20 percent of the day's trading range and being below the band stretches the rubber band even farther, resulting in better moves. This knowledge is not only useful for the BelowBB system, but can be used in trade management when using other systems. If excursions below the lower band do not last long, and are the basis for a trading system taking longs, then it would not make much sense to hold short positions in declining stocks when they move below the lower band. I use this information to help manage my short trades and frequently take profits when short positions approach the lower band.

Our testing showed a direct correlation between the percentage the close is below the lower band and the percentage of winning trades. The farther below the band the stock closes, the higher percentage of winning trades we see. The difference between the average winning and the average losing trade also increases as the close is farther below the lower band. As the distance between the close and the lower band increases, we see a higher percentage of winning trades and we gain more on the average trade. This result is something I use frequently when looking at potential trades from this system.

If a long setup forms a point under strong resistance, I am not nearly as interested in it as a setup that forms three points under weak resistance. The most likely thing for stocks to do at resistance is stall or bounce, so I want to pick the trades with more room to run. Trading systems are not magic boxes that lead to wealth, they are just one of the tools that the trader uses along with market conditions and risk management techniques.

The Bollinger band systems are looking for overbought and oversold stocks. These conditions generally occur when the market has been running for a while and occur less often when the market is indecisive or basing in a tight range. I do not expect to see a number of setups for overbought and oversold stocks every day. BelowBB generates a few trades, then takes a week or so off, and then generates another few trades. Pullback and retracement systems (discussed in other chapters in this book) tend to generate trading candidates more frequently than either of the Bollinger band systems because the natural rhythm of stock movement is frequently showing runs and pullbacks. The Bollinger band systems are more specialized tools that look for stocks that have run too far in one direction. This happens less often than either pullbacks or retracements in trending stocks.

CHAPTER 2 SELF-TEST

1. Trading effectively requires:

    A. Knowledge of economic forecasts and expert opinion.

    B. Watching CNBC to stay on top of the news.

    C. A clearly defined entry and exit strategy.

    D. An opinion on market direction.

2. Inverting the rules for trading shorts yields a good system for trading longs.

    A. True

    B. False

    C. Only in a trading range market.

    D. Only if you trade high volume stocks.

3. When taking long positions on extensions below the lower Bollinger band:

    A. Results improve if trading in a bearish market.

    B. Results improve if the stock closes below the band.

    C. Results improve if the stock closes above the band.

    D. Results improve if it is February.

4. When taking long positions on extensions below the lower Bollinger band:

    A. Results improve if the stock did not gap down on the move below the band.

    B. Results improve if the stock did gap down on the move below the band.

    C. Gaps have little effect on the results.

    D. Results improve if the stock gaps below the band during bearish markets.

5. **When taking long positions on extensions below the lower Bollinger band:**

   A. The relationship of the close to the lower band is not important.

   B. There is a direct correlation between the distance the close is below the band to results.

   C. Results improve if the stock moves below the band, then closes above it.

   D. The close should be near the top of the day's range.

6. **Examining the actual positions during a test period:**

   A. Proves the system's effectiveness.

   B. Shows the trades are evenly spaced.

   C. Helps to determine a position sizing strategy.

   D. Is not as important as the annualized ROI.

7. **When taking long trades on extensions below the lower band:**

   A. The results are best in trading range market conditions.

   B. The results improve when holding times are lengthened from three to six days.

   C. The results decline when holding times are lengthened from three to six days.

   D. Positions can be held indefinitely.

FOR THE ANSWERS, VISIT WWW.TRADERSLIBRARY.COM/TLECORNER.

CHAPTER 3

PULLBACKS IN UPTRENDING STOCKS

Good trading systems often begin with a repeated observation. Seeing something happen ten times does not prove that it is a good trading system, but it makes it worth investigating. One of the basic observations about stocks' behavior is that stocks usually do not go straight up or straight down—instead they tend to move in waves. A stock may run up a bit, then retrace (pull back) for a few sessions and then continue the original upward movement.

A variety of interesting pullback systems exist for traders. Pullbacks are one of the bread and butter techniques of trading because they occur frequently and can be found in most market conditions. Most traders should have more than one pullback system in their trading tool box. There are many interesting pullback systems; some are based on the percentage of retracement, some on pullbacks to key moving averages, some on pullbacks for a specific number of days, and some on pullbacks with specific volume patterns.

The pullback technique researched here involves stocks that retrace a move, or pull back, on declining volume.

DVPULLBACK DEFINITION

Volume analysis is an important part of trading. Volume measures the interest in a move. It isn't necessarily the absolute level of the volume that is key—it is often the volume pattern or the recent changes in volume that tell the story.

My youngest daughter played soccer throughout high school and college. If I was talking to someone at the game and all of a sudden the crowd noise increased significantly, we both knew to quickly look on the field because something important was happening. For stocks, volume is like the crowd noise. The level of noise, or volume, changes depending on the importance of what is going on in the game.

Strong stocks tend to move up to lots of cheering, or volume; and they tend to retrace, or pullback, on light volume. The light volume pullback is not necessarily a significant change in behavior, which is noted by the quiet crowd or low volume. As a stock goes through a rhythmic cycle of upward movement followed by a brief retracement and then continuation of the upward movement, we can use volume clues to determine if the retracements are a normal part of the stock's rhythm, or the beginning of a change in trend.

Figure 3.1 illustrates how stocks tend to move in waves. They run up for a bit, and then pull back, and then continue the original movement. The stock in Figure 3.1 hit a bottom in late November. Then it ran up for a week, pulled back for a few days, then continued the run up after the first week in December. The process repeated, with the stock running up until mid-December when it pulled back again for a few days and then resumed the upward movement for the rest of the month.

If volume measures the interest in a move, then light volume pullbacks may indicate that there are few sellers during normal pullbacks along its generally upward movement. If there is little interest in selling on the pullbacks

Courtesy of AIQ

and strong interest on buying during the upward movements, then traders may be interested in taking positions as the light volume pullbacks end.

Figure 3.2 shows an example of a stock that moved up on relatively strong volume and then pulled back on light volume, which declined every day. The pullback period is marked between the arrows on the price chart. Note how during this period, the volume declined every day. There was not only low interest in selling during the pullback, but the interest declined every day. After a few days, the stock resumed its upward movement and the volume increased.

Trading a system based on seeing a few examples of when it worked is just asking for trouble. It is amazing how many people do this. A few examples prove nothing! Before risking money on any trading strategy, you need to

DECLINING VOLUME PULLBACK PATTERN

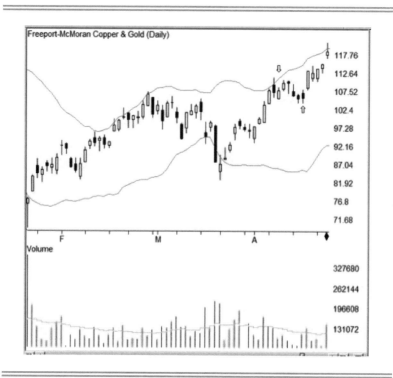

Courtesy of AIQ

know how often the system produced winning trades over a large number of trades, during different time periods, and during different market conditions. You should thoroughly examine a trading system until you fully understand how it behaves under a variety of conditions. Only then, after the system is well-known, should you consider using it.

In order to test a trading system, it needs to be clearly defined using nouns and numbers, not adjectives. Words like big, strong, fast, et cetera, do not convey specific information. Trading systems using adjectives will be interpreted by different traders in different ways, which can lead to unexpected results. If you can't explain a trading system to a 12-year-old child in a few minutes, there is likely something wrong with it.

Pullback systems have four key parts to them. First, we examine the definition of a pullback, which comes from observing the price action. Second, we look at the trigger condition, which is used as an indication that the pull-back may be ending. Third, we review the entry or the taking of a position. Fourth, we have our exit strategy.

Trading strategies need to have:

1. A setup condition, or the price and volume pattern on the pullback;

2. A trigger condition, which indicates it is time to enter a position; and,

3. An exit strategy.

When I am trading, I know exactly how I am going to exit the position before I ever enter it. Entering a position without a clear exit strategy usually ends up tangled in emotions or hunches. Trading on emotions or hunches leads to losses. Marry your spouse for life, but just date stocks. Always have an exit strategy. Always.

In order to test this declining volume pullback idea, I named the system DVpullback and started with the following definitions:

A DVpullback occurs if:

• The stock shows three consecutive lower highs, and
• The stock shows three consecutive days of lower volume than the previous day.

A price trigger occurs if:

• Today's high is greater than yesterday's high, and
• The close is greater than $5, and
• The 21-day simple moving average of the volume is greater than 200,000.

The entry strategy is:

• If a DVpullback occurred yesterday, and

- A trigger occurs today, then
- Buy at the open tomorrow.

The exit strategy is:

- Hold for three days; meaning the entry day, the next day, and the following day, then
- Sell at the following day's open.

INITIAL TESTING OF DVPULLBACK SYSTEM

In order to get a basic idea of whether or not a new trading idea is worth investigating, I first do a quick test in a recent calendar year. I pick an up year for testing bullish systems and a down year for testing bearish systems. If the candidate trading system does not work in a bullish (or bearish for shorting systems) calendar year, then it may not be worth investing further effort.

When testing a trading system idea, I will typically end up running the backtesting program several hundred times. Testing is a lot of work, but so are most helpful things. Trading is not an instant path to riches—it requires effort and hard work. Much of the effort needs to go into research and analysis long before the first trade is ever made.

> In the volume example above, I talked about my youngest daughter playing soccer through high school and college. She did not just show up for college the first day and get a soccer scholarship. She put years of effort into practice, conditioning, and competitive tournaments. Successful traders also need to put in time analyzing systems, understanding how the market behaves, and honing their skills. It will take time, it will require effort, and it will cost you something to become an effective trader.

Figure 3.3 shows the market conditions during 2007, which was the period used for the initial test of the DVpullback system. Calendar 2007 had a

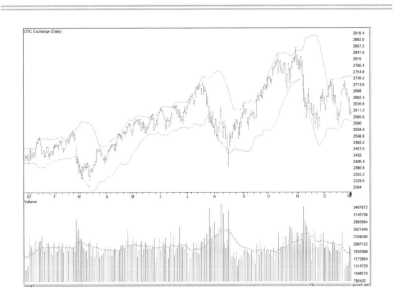

Courtesy of AIQ

mixture of different market conditions. There was a drop early in the year, followed by a bullish run until July. Then, we saw another steep drop followed by another run during the fall, and ended the year with a wide trading range during November and December. The year was not all bullish, but if a bullish scan has promise, it should show some indications of that during 2007.

I coded the system definition for DVpullback in AIQ Systems Trading Expert Pro and ran a backtest during calendar 2007. My database of stocks used for the test consisted of about 2,500 stocks. Obviously, there are more than 2,500 stocks, but I am not interested in trading low volume stocks because of the potential for wide bid/ask spreads. Low volume stocks may also be difficult to get in or out of when things are moving rapidly. I have found from experience that 2,500 stocks provide plenty of trading opportunities, and there is no need to take the additional risks noted above.

FIGURE 3.4:
INITIAL TEST RESULTS FOR DVPULLBACK

TriggeredDVPullback

		Winners	Losers	Neutral
Number of trades in test:	2345	1298	1033	14
Average periods per trade:	4.56	4.57	4.55	4.43
Maximum Profit/Loss:		26.57%	(21.95)%	
Average Drawdown:	(1.69)%	(0.55)%	(3.13)%	
Average Profit/Loss:	0.53%	3.20%	(2.81)%	
Average SPX Profit/Loss	0.26%	0.81%	(0.42)%	
Probability:		55.35%	44.05%	
Average Annual ROI:	42.68%	255.46%	(225.01)%	
Annual SPX (Buy & Hold):	2.05%			
Reward/Risk Ratio:	1.43			
Start test date:	01/02/07			
End test date:	12/31/07			

Interval:Daily
Pricing Summary
     Entry price: [Open]
     Exit price: [Open]
Exit Summary
     Hold for 3 periods

Courtesy of AIQ

The results of the initial DVpullback backtest are shown in Figure 3.4. During calendar year 2007, the software found 2,345 DVpullback trades, of which more than 55 percent were profitable trades. The annualized ROI of 42.68 percent was better than that for the market itself, and the average winning trade showed a 3.2 percent profit while the average losing trade showed a 2.8 percent loss. If we translate the statistics to English: the system has profitable trades more often than losing trades, the annualized return is better than buying the market, and on average, winning trades pay more than losing trades cost. These numbers indicate that the system is worth further investigation.

Many traders new to backtesting tend to zero in on the annualized ROI number and avoid looking at the rest of the information. The annualized ROI is generally the last thing I review.

It is not the number you will see in your account for a variety of obvious reasons. The number is annualized; it assumes you took all 2,345 trades available, and it does not include commission and slippage. I use the annualized ROI more like a figure of merit, where more is usually better. I focus on systems that have a good percentage of winning trades, and ones where the average winner gains more than the average loser loses. If those conditions are met, then over the long haul, trading should be profitable.

Most traders will not take as many trades as are available during the test period, and most may not use the system all year because of changing market conditions. Remember, I do not want to just blindly trade a system; I want to adapt to the current market conditions by using the tool from my trading tool box most suited to the current market based on extensive testing information.

Fifty-five percent winning trades is a good start; however, this percentage is the average across a large number of trades. This does not imply that for every ten trades you will have winners five or six times. There will be strings of winning and losing trades. The test data give an idea of how a system performs, and it is important to look beyond the statistics to see how the trades are distributed and how long the winning and losing streaks are, as we illustrated in the first chapter.

EFFECT OF UPTREND FILTER ON DVPULLBACK RESULTS

The initial rules for the DVpullback did not take into consideration whether or not the stock was trending up, trending down, or basing. The next step is to add a filter that selects stocks in an uptrend and looks for the DVpullback pattern in those uptrending stocks. As shown in Figure 3.5, an uptrend exists when a stock is making a series of higher highs and higher lows.

As a stock moves through the normal runs and retracements, it tends to make a series of peaks, or highs, if it is an uptrend. The lowest value during a given period also tends to be rising. Figure 3.5 marks the series of higher highs with an "H" and the series of higher lows with a "L." When the series of highs are clustered around the same level, the stock is generally in a trading range. When the series of highs and lows have increasing values, the stock is generally in an uptrend.

FIGURE 3.5:
UPTRENDING STOCK

Courtesy of AIQ

Figure 3.6 shows an example of a DVpullback occurring in an uptrending stock. In Figure 3.6, the stock ticker symbol RIG was in an uptrending period because it was making a series of higher highs, as marked "H." It was also showing a series of higher lows, as marked by "L."

In late December, RIG made a series of three lower highs, as marked by the down arrows on the price plot in Figure 3.6. While RIG was making a lower high for three days in a row, it was also showing lower volume each day

FIGURE 3.6:
DVPULLBACK IN AN UPTRENDING STOCK

Courtesy of AIQ

that a lower high occurred. This pattern of three consecutive lower highs and three consecutive lower volume days meets the basic requirements of a DVpullback.

After the three consecutive lower highs, the RIG setup triggered by showing a high above the previous day's high, as marked in Figure 3.6 by the "T." The entry strategy for DVpullback is to enter at the open the day following a trigger. The entry is marked by an "E." The exit strategy for DVpullback is to hold for three days, including the entry day, and then exit.

In the case of RIG, a position would have been entered on December 12, 2007 at $135.47. The position would have been held for three trading days and then exited at the open the following day, which resulted in an exit on December 26, 2007 at $145.56 for a profit of $10.09.

Figure 3.6 illustrates how to identify and trade the DVpullback pattern; but, while one example is interesting, it proves nothing. Traders need to see how the addition of the uptrending stock requirement affects results over a large number of trades.

In the case of the DVpullback, the entry and exit strategies are based solely on the daily charts. The scan can be run in the evening and if a DVpullback is triggered, traders can double check the market conditions and enter a trade the next day. There is nothing in the DVpullback definition that requires a trader to be glued to the screen all day.

Adding a rule to the DVpullback definition that requires the stock to be in an uptrend before a DVpullback trade is taken improves the overall results during the initial 2007 test period, as shown in Figure 3.7. The number of

FIGURE 3.7:
DVPULLBACK WITH UPTREND RULE, 2007 TEST RESULTS

TriggeredDVPullback		Winners	Losers	Neutral
Number of trades in test:	962	554	404	4
Average periods per trade:	4.53	4.53	4.54	4.25
Maximum Profit/Loss:		26.57%	(20.01)%	
Average Drawdown:	(1.51)%	(0.48)%	(2.95)%	
Average Profit/Loss:	0.61%	3.00%	(2.68)%	
Average SPX Profit/Loss	0.28%	0.77%	(0.39)%	
Probability:		57.59%	42.00%	
Average Annual ROI:	48.77%	241.99%	(215.35)%	
Annual SPX (Buy & Hold):	2.05%			
Reward/Risk Ratio:	1.54			
Start test date:	01/02/07			
End test date:	12/31/07			
Interval:Daily				
Pricing Summary				
Entry price: [Open]				
Exit price: [Open]				
Exit Summary				
Hold for 3 periods				

Courtesy of AIQ

trades decreased from 2,345 to 962 because the system was only looking at uptrending stocks during the 2007 test period. The percentage of winning trades increased from 55 percent to over 57 percent, and the annualized ROI increased from 42 percent to over 48 percent. Restricting DVpullback trades to stocks that are uptrending improves results. This rule will be included in the standard definition of DVpullback and used in all subsequent tests.

A lot of people think that traders are glued to a screen, watching the market all day. The work in trading is done long before any trades are placed and involves carefully testing and analyzing a potential trading system. Actually placing the trades is a small part of the job and does not require one to be glued to the screen all day.

USING BOLLINGER BAND SYSTEM TEST DATA TO IMPROVE DVPULLBACK RESULTS

One of the great things about testing a variety of potential trading systems is that insights developed from analyzing one system can be used when examining another. In previous chapters, we learned that moves outside the Bollinger bands usually do not last long. Based on this observation, we developed an interesting shorting system based on excursions above the upper band. The Bollinger bands tend to contain the large majority of the price action and significant excursions outside the bands tend to move quickly back inside by either retracement or basing. The upper band tends to act as resistance and the normal thing for a stock to do at resistance, especially in a trading range market, is to pull back.

Figure 3.8 shows a DVpullback pattern in CME that occurred in late October and is marked by the down arrows on the chart. CME was in an uptrend. It showed three consecutive lower highs and three consecutive lower volume days. These conditions meet the DVpullback setup conditions, and CME triggered the following day by making a higher high on increasing volume. After the trigger day, CME ran up to approach the upper Bollinger band

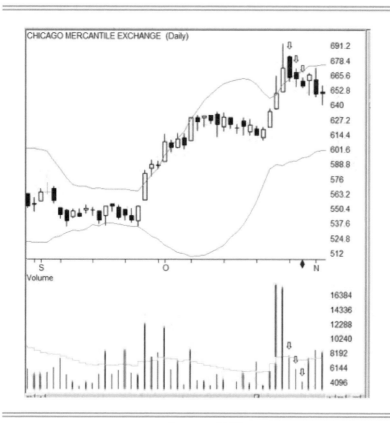

Courtesy of AIQ

and then dropped to end up with a $5.48 loss in three days. The upper band acted as resistance and stopped the run.

Figure 3.9 shows a DVpullback that occurred in CEL during late May. CEL made three lower highs on declining volume each day and then triggered by making a higher high. The DVpullback setup is marked by the down arrows in Figure 3.9 and the trigger is marked by the letter "T."

After triggering, the stock was held for three days and then sold for a nine percent profit. In this case, the DVpullback pattern occurred well below the upper Bollinger band. After the trigger, CEL ran up to the area of the upper band and then stalled, but because the setup occurred well below the band, there was plenty of "room to run" and the trade resulted in a nice profit. In

FIGURE 3.9:
DVPULLBACK PATTERN OCCURRING WITH ROOM TO RUN

Courtesy of AIQ

general, the farther from resistance a pattern occurs, the more "room to run" it has before stalling at resistance.

When offered several trading opportunities, one of the things I use to prioritize them is to look at how much room there is between the entry point for the trade and the next resistance area. Since the most likely thing for a stock to do is run up to resistance and then stall, I often take profits as a stock approaches resistance. If the upper Bollinger band tends to act as resistance, then I would expect that eliminating DVpullback trades that occur above or near the upper band may improve results. It is an interesting theory, although I do not trade theories or hunches. I trade systems that have demonstrated results. We need to test this idea to see if it has merit.

THE ROOM-TO-RUN FILTER

Figure 3.10 shows the results of testing DVpullback during 2007 with the uptrending stock filter, which is now a standard part of the system, and an additional "room-to-run" filter. The room-to-run filter only takes DV-pullback trades if they occur at least two daily ranges below the upper Bollinger band.

As shown in Figure 3.10, adding the room-to-run filter increased the percentage of winning trades from 57 percent to 60 percent, and increased the annualized ROI from 48 percent to 67 percent. The test results are significantly improved when the DVpullback pattern forms at least twice the daily range of the trigger day below the upper Bollinger band.

If we reduce the room-to-run requirement from twice the trigger day range below the upper Bollinger band to just one times the trigger day range below the upper band, we get the results shown in Figure 3.11. As compared to the original room-to-run definition, the performance during the test period decreased. Annualized ROI dropped from 67 percent to 59 percent, and the percentage of winning trades dropped about a point. The results are still better than those without the room-to-run filter (see Figure 3.7). This indicates that the filter is helpful and that the farther the DVpullback forms below the upper Bollinger band, the better.

The improved results of the room-to-run filter indicate that this rule should be added to the system definition. Subsequent tests will include both the room-to-run rule and the uptrending stock rule. The testing process so far has given us a much better feel for what to look for with the DVpullback pattern. We have found that stocks should be in an uptrend and that the pullback pattern should occur below the upper Bollinger band.

As a practical matter, when I run the DVpullback scan every evening, I do not calculate whether or not the pullback has occurred more than two daily ranges below the upper band. There is no need to calculate the daily range to three decimal points and then see if the pattern formed that much below the band. I am looking for general rules that can be easily determined by a visual scan. The system shows improvement if the pattern forms at least one daily range below the band, and even more improvement if it forms at least two

FIGURE 3.10:
DVPULLBACK 2007 TEST WITH ROOM-TO-RUN RULE

TriggeredDVPullback

		Winners	Losers	Neutral
Number of trades in test:	362	220	138	4
Average periods per trade:	4.52	4.50	4.54	4.25
Maximum Profit/Loss:		17.39%	(20.01)%	
Average Drawdown:	(1.33)%	(0.38)%	(2.89)%	
Average Profit/Loss:	0.83%	3.01%	(2.63)%	
Average SPX Profit/Loss:	0.38%	0.82%	(0.31)%	
Probability:		60.77%	38.12%	
Average Annual ROI:	67.03%	244.11%	(211.04)%	
Annual SPX (Buy & Hold):	2.05%			
Reward/Risk Ratio:	1.83			
Start test date:	01/02/07			
End test date:	12/31/07			

Interval:Daily
Pricing Summary
      Entry price: [Open]
      Exit price: [Open]
Exit Summary
      Hold for 3 periods

FIGURE 3.11:
DVPULLBACK WITH "ONE TIMES RANGE ROOM-TO-RUN"

TriggeredDVPullback

		Winners	Losers	Neutral
Number of trades in test:	713	424	285	4
Average periods per trade:	4.51	4.53	4.49	4.25
Maximum Profit/Loss:		26.57%	(20.01)%	
Average Drawdown:	(1.46)%	(0.48)%	(2.94)%	
Average Profit/Loss:	0.74%	3.05%	(2.70)%	
Average SPX Profit/Loss:	0.32%	0.83%	(0.43)%	
Probability:		59.47%	39.97%	
Average Annual ROI:	59.47%	246.16%	(219.55)%	
Annual SPX (Buy & Hold):	2.05%			
Reward/Risk Ratio:	1.68			
Start test date:	01/02/07			
End test date:	12/31/07			

Interval:Daily
Pricing Summary
      Entry price: [Open]
      Exit price: [Open]
Exit Summary
      Hold for 3 periods

Courtesy of AIQ

daily ranges below the band. I use this information by scanning through the candidates presented by the DVpullback each evening and discard the ones that form obviously close to the band. I then use the results from some of the other filters to prioritize the candidates. I am looking for the best of what is available, and use all the tools we are developing here to prioritize the setups.

EFFECT OF HOLDING TIME ON DVPULLBACK TEST RESULTS

Up to this point, the exit strategy has been to hold for three days and then sell. Before using a system, I want to be sure I have tested and analyzed every variable and am not trading on assumptions. I started using the three-day holding time because that number comes up over and over again in different swing trading systems as one of the more effective exit strategies. A lot of traders new to backtesting focus on complicated percentage of capital protection strategies, or moving average systems for exits. I have found that using a three-day time stop is generally effective and easy to use.

I ran the backtest five more times during the 2007 test period and varied the holding time between two and six days. The results are shown in Table 3.1. The three-day holding period shows the best winning percentage, but the

TABLE 3.1
EFFECTS OF HOLDING TIME ON DVPULLBACK 2007 TEST RESULTS

HOLDING TIME	WINNING %	ANNUALIZED ROI
2 Days	57.18	73%
3 Days	60.77	67
4 Days	56.23	31
5 Days	56.79	40
6 Days	56.21	33

other holding periods still show strong annualized ROI numbers and winning percentages above 56 percent. These test results indicate that traders do not need to be in a rush to exit at exactly three days, but can use other information to determine whether or not to exit early or hold longer.

As a practical matter, I look at the position on the third day and determine whether or not there is a clear reason to be holding longer. If not, I close the position. In determining whether or not there is a reason to hold longer, I look at the market price and volume pattern, the distance to resistance, and the other opportunities available to trade. If one or more of these factors indicates the position is worth holding, I will continue the trade. If none of these factors provide a reason to continue, I will close the position after three days and move on to the next trade.

EFFECT OF MARKET CONDITIONS ON DVPULLBACK HOLDING TIME

The current market conditions play a key role in determining exit strategies. Stocks behave differently in trading range markets than they do in trending markets. Since a key part of trading is adapting to the market, traders' exit strategies should change with the market conditions.

The market is the summation of a large number of individual stocks. In trading range markets, as illustrated in Figure 3.12, most stocks tend to "pop and drop" rather than show strong trends. When the market is in a trading range then, almost by definition, most stocks cannot be trending.

When the market is in a trading range, it tells you that the typical stock is not going to run far before it retraces. Realize that in trading range markets, you should focus on shorter holding times and quick profits. In trading ranges, you are trying to piece together a trend in your account from the brief pops in several different stocks rather than the rare single stock that is trending. Traders pick up the initial move on a stock that triggers. Then, they close it and then pick up another pop to keep repeating the process.

Looking for stocks that run far in a trading range is likely to be frustrating, so you must adapt to what the market is giving you. If you use the same ap-

FIGURE 3.12:
TRADING RANGE MARKET CONDITIONS

Courtesy of AIQ

proach in all market conditions, you are likely to get a lot of practice exercising stops.

During December of 2007, the market was in a trading range. In late December HTLD formed a DVpullback setup and triggered, as shown in Figure 3.13. After the trigger, HTLD moved up briefly and then dropped. This is the type of "pop and drop" that is typical in a trading range. I do not try to predict where the market is going because history has shown that is a very hard game to win consistently. I simply look at the current market conditions and then adjust my trading strategy, which is something most people can do well. In a trading range market, I usually do not hold past three days and will often exit early if the trade is approaching support or resistance.

TRADING RANGE POP AND DROP

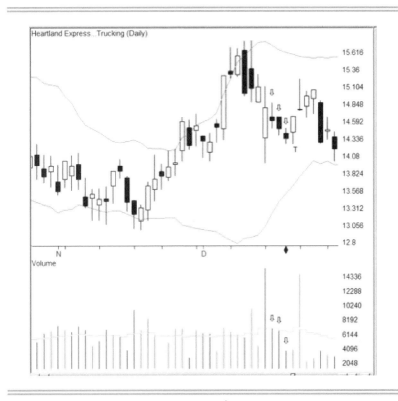

Courtesy of AIQ

When the market is trending, stocks tend to run longer because they have the wind in their sails. The market is the sum of a large number of stocks. To make a trend out of a large number of stocks, many of them need to be running for more than just a few days. Once again, it is the observation of the market conditions that tell traders how to trade. Traders do not trade a new shiny system just because they have it. They trade a system because testing indicates it is appropriate for the current market conditions and then they use the market conditions to determine the most appropriate exit strategy.

DVPULLBACK IN SCHN DURING A TRENDING MARKET

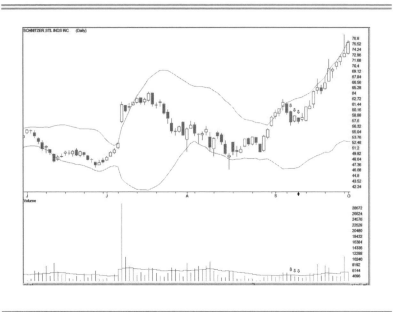

Courtesy of AIQ

In trending markets, I often hold well past three days. During September of 2007, the market was in an uptrend. In the second week of September, SCHN formed a DVpullback setup and then triggered, as shown in Figure 3.14. The entry for the SCHN trade was September 14, 2007 and SCHN moved up during 11 of the following 12 days.

When the market is trending, we see fewer pop and drops and longer movements after a stock has triggered, so I increase my holding times.

Table 3.2 is the same holding time test that was used to produce the information in Table 3.1 except that the tests were run during the market uptrend of September 2007. The data in Table 3.1 is based on running the holding time tests during the full year.

Table 3.2 shows that the percentage of winning trades is generally better across the different holding times tested. This is something we will explore further when we examine how the DVpullback system performs in different

TABLE 3.2
HOLDING TIME TESTS DURING SEPTEMBER 2007 MARKET UPTREND

HOLDING TIME	WINNING %	ANNUALIZED ROI
2 Days	60.47	143%
3 Days	71.79	182
4 Days	54.05	104
5 Days	56.76	107
6 Days	71.43	115

market conditions. It also shows that the longer, six-day holding time provides a significant improvement in the percentage of winning trades.

When the test was run for the full year (see Table 3.1), the longer six-day holding time provided okay results but did not show a significant improvement as compared to the four- or five-day holding periods. In comparison, we can see that testing indicates that during a trending period, the longer holding time is a viable option.

This is one reason why I adapt my trading style, including exit strategy, to the market conditions. Different market conditions favor different trading systems and exit strategies. Reading the market conditions and adapting the trading style based on market conditions is a process I call Market Adaptive Trading.

Table 3.3 continues the holding time testing process by looking at the results of trading DVpullback using different holding times during the market trading range period of November 14, 2007 to October 9, 2008. During this period, when the market was in a trading range, the percentage of winning trades and the annualized ROI were significantly less than the same test run when the market was in a bullish period. In fact, during the trading range market conditions, two of the three holding periods longer than three days showed annualized losses.

TABLE 3.3
HOLDING TIME TESTS BETWEEN NOVEMBER 14, 2007 AND OCTOBER 9, 2008, TRADING RANGE MARKET

HOLDING TIME	WINNING %	ANNUALIZED ROI
2 Days	49.12	20%
3 Days	54.39	14
4 Days	56.14	-11
5 Days	56.14	2
6 Days	52.63	-6

As noted above, stocks tend to pop and drop when the market is in a trading range. This behavior implies that stocks run briefly after the trigger and the best strategy is to exit quickly. This approach is born out by the results of Table 3.3. Stocks behave differently in trending markets than they do in trading range markets. I adapt my trading style to the market conditions by usually not holding pullbacks more than two or three days during periods when the market is in a trading range and by holding for longer time periods when the market is trending.

In the case of DVpullback, the trader who liked to hold about a week would likely see interesting results during bullish markets and struggle with trading during trading range periods. He may even think that the system "just does not work well in trading ranges," when in fact it may be his lack of knowledge that is the issue. Never trade something you have not tested and do not fully understand. Details like adjusting exit strategies based on market conditions can make a big difference in results.

To learn more, visit www.daisydogger.com, or send an email to sample@daisydogger.com to see my current market analysis and the setups I am watching in the current market.

At a recent trading conference, several traders were talking about exit strategies at lunch and one noted that he "liked to hold positions for about a week." When asked, he had no reason for the decision, it just "felt right" to him. Trading on tips, emotions, or what "just feels right" is unlikely to produce good long-term results. Trading should be based on the careful analysis and testing of each trading system. Testing does not eliminate risk or guarantee results, but it can help to give a good idea of how a system has actually performed.

In trading ranges, I generally do not hold longer than three days. I will exit sooner if the stock approaches the upper Bollinger band or a horizontal resistance point. I do not want to hold out for the last dime; I want to be taking profits as the stock approaches resistance. In a trading range market, it is generally better to get out too early than too late. Once again, it is tough to go broke taking profits.

When I say this at trading conferences, there is usually someone who says, "Yes, but if the stock broke through resistance, wouldn't you have been better off holding longer?" The answer is obvious, and irrelevant. Trading is about managing risk, not trying to squeeze every last dime out of a trade.

Eventually, almost all resistance areas are broken. I, however, want to go with the odds and be positioned to profit if the stock does the normal thing and retraces.

If it does retrace, I have my profits and can use them in a new trade. If the stock breaks above resistance, I still have my profits and can take another trade. From a risk management standpoint, I am better off taking the profits. I don't worry about what a stock does after I'm out. I'm off to the next trade. One of the keys to trading is learning what usually happens in a given situation and then being positioned to profit if it does.

In a trending market, I will allow the position more room to run and will actively manage the exit. This approach comes from testing a number of trading systems in different market conditions and seeing how holding times affect the results. When the market is trending, I will still look to close positions when either the market or my position approaches resistance.

If the position is not close to resistance, then I watch the volume pattern. If it is going up on generally large volume and down on generally small volume, I will give it some room. I use trend lines to manage the exit and I look for signs of distribution in the position to indicate that it may be best to exit and move on to another position. The basic rule is that if there is not a clear reason to hold the exit, then move into another position that does have a clear position to hold.

Many people go through life acting on their feelings and don't learn from experience. They often end up someplace they did not want to be, and too often they feel it is someone else's fault. When traders act on feelings, they often lose money in the long run. Trading without testing a system and carefully analyzing how it behaves is asking for trouble. The market does not care what you think or how you feel; it does what it wants. Traders need to understand this to be successful.

EFFECT OF TRIGGER DAY VOLUME ON DVPULLBACK TEST RESULTS

Volume patterns have an important effect on many trading systems. Volume measures the interest in a move. It shows how many people are interested in the current price pattern and how they are voting with real money. Rather than listen to the talking heads on the business channels, it is better to look at the volume patterns and see what people are actually doing with their money.

Figure 3.15 shows the results of running the DVpullback test during the 2007 initial test period with an additional requirement: that trades are only taken if the volume on the trigger day is greater than the previous day's volume. The "increased trigger day volume" requirement increases

TriggeredDVPullback		Winners	Losers	Neutral
Number of trades in test:	231	143	85	3
Average periods per trade:	4.45	4.41	4.54	4.00
Maximum Profit/Loss:		12.09%	(8.31)%	
Average Drawdown:	(1.13)%	(0.35)%	(2.47)%	
Average Profit/Loss:	0.97%	2.84%	(2.14)%	
Average SPX Profit/Loss	0.52%	0.93%	(0.14)%	
Probability:		61.90%	36.80%	
Average Annual ROI:	79.88%	235.56%	(171.74)%	
Annual SPX (Buy & Hold):	2.05%			
Reward/Risk Ratio:	2.24			
Start test date:	01/02/07			
End test date:	12/31/07			

Interval:Daily
Pricing Summary
        Entry price: [Open]
        Exit price: [Open]
Exit Summary
        Hold for 3 periods

Courtesy of AIQ

the annualized ROI from 67 percent to over 79 percent. It also increases the percentage of winning trades from 60 percent to nearly 62 percent. If the volume increases on the day of the trigger, it indicates that as the price goes up, there are more people interested in owning the stock. This interest leads to better results (as shown).

The research outlined above indicates that when the DVpullback pattern forms below the upper Bollinger band, it has room to run and the test results are improved. There are other aspects of the volume price pattern and where it forms that can affect the test results. Some pullbacks in trending stocks are very shallow. They just make a minor correction in the uptrend. Other pullbacks are deeper and show up on the charts as obvious rest periods in a trending stock.

I once asked a group of traders which would perform better, shallow or deep pullbacks. A lively discussion ensued. One group "knew" that shallow pullbacks would perform better because the basic uptrend was hardly affected and that was a sign of strength. Another group thought that shallow pullbacks might just be part of the daily "noise" in a stock's movement and thus deeper pullbacks would perform better because the stock had a chance to rest.

The interesting thing is that no one in either group had tested the premise. They had strong feelings about which was better and were acting on those feelings, but they did not have any data to indicate which type of pullback performed better.

EFFECT OF PULLBACK DEPTH ON DVPULLBACK TEST RESULTS

Successful traders are curious and always wanting to learn how things work and what the normal course of action is in a given market condition or trading setup. When asked whether shallow or deep pullbacks worked best, successful traders are likely to have one of two responses. They will either say, "I don't know, and we should investigate it." Or they will say, "we tested it and the results were...." Guessing what will happen in a given situation involves taking an unknown risk. Traders are focused on managing risk, and learn to position themselves to profit if the usual thing happens and to take small losses when the unusual happens.

Myth: Eliminating shallow pullbacks from the DV-pullback system will degrade results because shallow pullbacks are a sign of strength.

Fact: Initial testing shows that when shallow pullbacks (defined as those setups that occur above the five-period moving average) are eliminated, results improve.

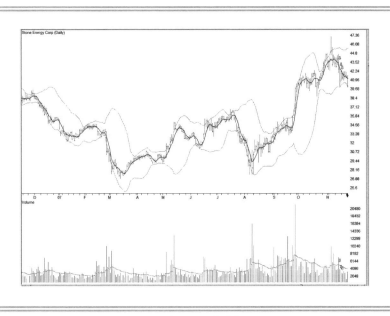

Courtesy of AIQ

Figure 3.16 shows a stock with a DVpullback that formed in mid-November, marked by the arrows on the chart. The thick gray line on the chart is the five-period moving average (5MA) of the closing price. Note how the five-period moving average follows the price pattern and tends to filter out much of the daily noise. The five-period moving average provides a good representation of the general price action. We can use the five-period moving average to filter out shallow pullbacks in a trending stock by requiring that the DVpullback trigger occur below it. Triggers that occur above the 5MA are shallow pullbacks and may simply be part of the daily noise or fluctuation in prices.

In order to test whether or not eliminating shallow pullbacks has an effect on DVpullback results, I ran the test again during the 2007 initial test period and eliminated all DVpullback setups that occurred above the five-period moving average. The results are shown in Figure 3.17. Using this technique increased the annualized ROI from 67 percent to 80 percent, and increased the percentage of winning trades from 60 percent to nearly 64 percent. This

TriggeredDVPullback

		Winners	Losers	Neutral
Number of trades in test:	243	155	87	1
Average periods per trade:	4.43	4.45	4.41	3.00
Maximum Profit/Loss:		17.39%	(20.01)%	
Average Drawdown:	(1.39)%	(0.40)%	(3.18)%	
Average Profit/Loss:	0.98%	3.15%	(2.89)%	
Average SPX Profit/Loss	0.46%	0.88%	(0.27)%	
Probability:		63.79%	35.80%	
Average Annual ROI:	80.49%	258.97%	(239.12)%	
Annual SPX (Buy & Hold):	2.05%			
Reward/Risk Ratio:	1.94			
Start test date:	01/02/07			
End test date:	12/31/07			

Interval:Daily
Pricing Summary
      Entry price: [Open]
      Exit price: [Open]
Exit Summary
      Hold for 3 periods

Courtesy of AIQ

indicates that for this test, shallow pullbacks (those where the trigger occurs above the 5MA) do not perform as well. And, the percentage of winning trades may be significantly improved by taking only DVpullback trades when the trigger occurs below the five-period moving average.

Figure 3.18 shows a DVpullback pattern occurring in mid-December, as marked by the arrows on the chart. The middle line is the 20-period moving average (20MA), which provides a good indication of the general trend of the stock. Pullbacks that occur below the 20-period moving average would generally be ones that triggered below the general trend of the stock, and hence could be considered deep pullbacks.

Running the DVpullback test again during the 2007 initial test period with a filter that only takes DVpullback trades that have triggers occurring below the 20MA should provide an indication of how the system performs when only trading deep pullbacks. The results of this test are shown in Figure 3.19. During the test period, we found that our filter decreased the annualized

FIGURE 3.18:
20MA TENDS TO FOLLOW GENERAL TREND

FIGURE 3.19:
EFFECT OF ONLY TRADING DEEP PULLBACKS

TriggeredDVPullback

		Winners	Losers	Neutral
Number of trades in test:	145	87	57	1
Average periods per trade:	4.63	4.62	4.68	3.00
Maximum Profit/Loss:		17.38%	(8.31)%	
Average Drawdown:	(1.59)%	(0.46)%	(3.34)%	
Average Profit/Loss:	0.69%	2.98%	(2.80)%	
Average SPX Profit/Loss	0.42%	0.89%	(0.30)%	
Probability:		60.00	39.31%	
Average Annual ROI:	54.01%	235.13%	(218.09)%	
Annual SPX (Buy & Hold):	2.05%			
Reward/Risk Ratio:	1.62			
Start test date:	01/02/07			
End test date:	12/31/07			

Interval:Daily
Pricing Summary
      Entry price: [Open]
      Exit price: [Open]
Exit Summary
      Hold for 3 periods

Courtesy of AIQ

ROI from 67 percent to 54 percent and decreased the percentage of winning trades slightly.

Trading only deep pullbacks (ones with the trigger occurring below the 20MA) during the test period reduces results, but it still interests me. The testing above indicates a fairly strong positive effect from eliminating trades that trigger above the 5MA and a small negative effect from taking only deep pullback trades. As a practical matter, I usually do not take DVpullback trades that occur above the 5MA. The results for deep pullback trades are not as strong, so I will use that as a second order of prioritization for available trades. When presented with more trades than I am interested in taking, given the current market conditions, I will pick the ones occurring above the 20MA first.

When trading, I am not holding out for the perfect trade because there is no such thing. Trading is about managing risks, and I use the current market conditions to determine how many trades to take and the appropriate position size to use. I use the DVpullbacktesting information to help prioritize the available trades. Setups with more room to run are prioritized above

Sometimes I will see traders trading weaker patterns because they have had a good winning streak and are "using the house's money." This is nonsense; profits are yours! There is no house! Each trade must stand on its own. Do not be tempted to trade weaker patterns after a winning streak. Stick to what works. Dance with the one that brought you.

Sometimes traders will start trading more aggressively when they are down in an attempt to get back to even. Drawdowns are a fact of life in trading. Trading is not like drawing a paycheck. You do not get paid because it is Friday. I research the systems and then use that information when trading. If I have a losing streak, I know that is to be expected and just stay focused on using the knowledge and skills that come from fully testing and analyzing trading systems.

ones with little room to run. Setups triggering on stronger volume compared to the previous day's volume are prioritized above ones with lower trigger day volume. Setups with shallower pullbacks are prioritized above ones with deeper pullbacks. I then look at the setups that are triggering and start from the top of the prioritized list and work down until I run out of setups or fill the number of positions I want.

Serious traders will go through a learning curve as they study market behavior and how their trading systems function. They will have times when they run into situations that have not been experienced or researched, and they may be unsure of what to do. This is normal. It is the price of admission to the trading business.

My general rule is that when I am unsure, I close the position. It is hard to go broke taking profits, so my focus is having a clear reason to stay in a position, not wondering whether or not I should get out. If there is no clear reason to hold, I take profits and move on to another trade.

DVPULLBACK TEST RESULTS DURING THE THREE MAJOR MARKET CONDITIONS

Up to this point, the testing for DVpullback has been done during the 2007 calendar year period. This initial test period was picked because it had a mix of market conditions and was an environment where we would expect the DVpullback pattern to work. If it does not work where it should, then there is little point in expending a lot of energy testing a variety of time periods.

The 2007 calendar year testing was a quick check to see how the system would behave. Since the DVpullback showed promise, we now need to understand how it will perform in different market conditions.

It is very difficult to successfully predict future market direction, but it is reasonably straightforward to look at what the market is currently doing and then select trading tools and techniques that have performed well in that type of environment in the past. Testing a trading system in each of the three types of market environments provides a useful tool that can then be applied, as appropriate, in similar conditions in the future. We do not need to predict; we can observe our test information and then select the most appropriate trading tools.

Table 3.4 shows the results of running the DVpullback test during six different bull market conditions. These bullish market conditions span different years and are of different lengths. The only commonality is that they are all periods when the market is trending up.

TABLE 3.4
DVPULLBACK TEST RESULTS DURING DIFFERENT
BULLISH MARKET PERIODS

TEST PERIOD	MARKET TYPE	WINNING %	ANNUALIZED ROI	# OF TRADES
08/13/04-12/31/04	Bull	62.9	123	124
07/21/06-11/24/06	Bull	68.6	88	138
03/14/07-07/20/07	Bull	64	85	117
08/17/07-10/09/07	Bull	69.7	158	43
03/17/08-06/05/08	Bull	64.2	71	98
07/16/08-08/18/08	Bull	56.2	5	16

The DVpullback system shows profitable trading during all six bullish market periods. The percentage of winning trades is above 56 percent in all of the bullish test periods, and above 62 percent in five of the six bullish test periods. The lowest annualized ROI and winning percentage came during 2008 when the market was down significantly for the year. Even though the market was down for the year in 2008, DVpullback performed well during one of the bounces.

The results shown in Table 3.4 are interesting and indicate that in a variety of test periods (spanning different amounts of time and occurring in different years), the DVpullback system shows interesting results when the market is trending up. Of course the market is not always trending up, so we need to understand how DVpullback performs when the market is bearish or trending down.

Table 3.5 shows the test results for DVpullback during six different bearish market periods. These bearish periods also occur in different years and last for various lengths of time. The only thing they have in common is that the market is generally trending down during these periods.

TABLE 3.5
DVPULLBACK TEST RESULTS DURING DIFFERENT
BEARISH MARKET PERIODS

TEST PERIOD	MARKET TYPE	WINNING %	ANNUALIZED ROI	# OF TRADES
01/04/02-10/04/02	Bear	41	-53	104
01/23/04-08/13/04	Bear	44	-52	151
01/07/05-04/22/05	Bear	53	38	82
05/11/06-07/21/06	Bear	41	-9	41
07/20/07-8/17/07	Bear	12	-287	8
06/06/08-07/15/08	Bear	55	12	18

The performance results for DVpullback are very different during bearish market periods. The system lost money in four of the six bearish periods. DVpullback was profitable in all six bullish market test periods, and it showed losses in most of the bearish market periods.

This is more proof for how the market environment plays a strong role in the results of many trading systems. Trading the same system in all market environments can lead to large swings in the account.

Successful traders adapt to the market by using trading systems, position sizing, and exit strategies that are suitable for the current market conditions. One way to adapt to changing market conditions is to have a number of different trading systems in your trading tool box and a clear understanding of how these tools work in bull, bear, or trading range markets. As the market moves through these three different environments, you can select the most appropriate tools from your tool box.

Table 3.6 shows the results of testing DVpullback during five different trading range markets. The system showed profits during each of the trading ranges, but the annualized ROI and the percentage of winning trades was lower than the results for testing DVpullback in bullish market conditions. The average winning percentage for the five trading range markets tested was 55 percent. The average winning percentage for the six bullish markets tested was 64 percent.

TABLE 3.6
DVPULLBACK TEST RESULTS DURING DIFFERENT
TRADING RANGE MARKET PERIODS

TEST PERIOD	MARKET TYPE	WINNING %	ANNUALIZED ROI	# OF TRADES
11/25/05-05/05/06	Trading Range	55	42	169
01/05/06-05/11/06	Trading Range	59	46	138
11/24/06-02/26/07	Trading Range	49	22	106
10/09/07-11/06/07	Trading Range	62	154	32
01/24/08-02/28/08	Trading Range	50	29	46

How do I use the information from the test results in actual practice? In trending markets, I trade bigger positions and more of them because the DVpullback test results show a larger percentage of winning trades and a larger annualized ROI in that market environment. In a trading range market, the winning percentage and the annualized ROI drop off, so I reduce position sizes and the number of positions I trade to compensate for the increased risk. I avoid using DVpullback when the market is trending down, and instead use one of the other tools in my trading tool box. Once again, I focus on adapting all aspects of trading to the current market conditions.

Some trading systems only show interesting results in one of the three market conditions. These systems are still useable, but traders need to be careful when market conditions are changing quickly. DVpullback shows interesting results in two of the three types of market conditions and thus it is more "forgiving" when market conditions are changing.

MOVING AVERAGE FILTER FOR DETERMINING MARKET CONDITIONS

Most traders can observe recent market action to determine if the current conditions are bullish, bearish, or in a trading range. We can also develop a market filter to help with this process. Figure 3.20 shows the market environment over a nine-year period from 2000 through 2008. The market ended up slightly below where it started out during this period, so a buy and hold strategy would likely have been flat to down. The market, however, was not flat during this period; it had several bullish, bearish, and trading range environments. There were plenty of opportunities for traders.

The labeled periods in Figure 3.20 are when the market's five-period exponential moving average of the highs is above the 20-period simple moving average of the closes. Note that when the 5MA is above the 20MA, the market is generally in a bullish or trading range environment. When the 5MA is not above the 20MA, the price chart is generally bearish.

The bullish periods (labeled in Figure 3.20) correspond to the market conditions during which we have found that the DVpullback shows interesting results. The bearish periods on the price chart correspond to periods when the DVpullback is not profitable. Based on what we see from Figure 3.20, it looks like the "5MA above the 20MA" might be a good filter for deciding whether or not to take DVpullback trades. This idea seems logical, but as

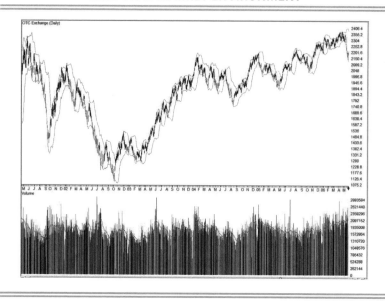

Courtesy of AIQ

traders, we want to test and verify any idea or potential trading system before actually considering using it.

Figure 3.21 shows the test results for DVpullback during the nine-year period of 2000 to 2008. During this time period, the market was down slightly and DVpullback showed an annualized ROI of 75 percent, with 57 percent of the trades profitable. The percentage of profitable trades is lower than what we saw for the average of the six bullish market environments because this multi-year period is a combination of bullish periods (where we saw strong results), trading range periods (where DVpullback showed interesting results), and bearish market periods (where DVpullback generally lost money). Since we have shown that DVpullback performs better during bullish periods than bearish market environments, we would expect the overall results to be lower for a long time period.

Figure 3.22 shows the results of running the DVpullback test again during the 2000 to 2008 time period with the addition of a filter that only takes the trades when the five-period exponential moving average of the highs is above the 20-period simple moving average of the closes. This is the moving

FIGURE 3.21:
DVPULLBACK TEST RESULTS DURING 2000 TO 2008,
WITH NO MARKET FILTERS

TriggeredDVPullback		Winners	Losers	Neutral
Number of trades in test:	2465	1411	1034	20
Average periods per trade:	4.36	4.34	4.40	4.05
Maximum Profit/Loss:		126.25%	(28.71)%	
Average Drawdown:	(1.76)%	(0.66)%	(3.30)%	
Average Profit/Loss:	0.91%	3.66%	(2.84)%	
Average SPX Profit/Loss	0.43%	1.05%	(0.41)%	
Probability:		57.24%	41.95%	
Average Annual ROI:	75.95%	308.34%	(235.22)%	
Annual SPX (Buy & Hold):	(3.76)%			
Reward/Risk Ratio:	1.76			
Start test date:	12/29/00			
End test date:	12/31/08			

Interval:Daily
Pricing Summary
      Entry price: [Open]
      Exit price: [Open]
Exit Summary
      Hold for 3 periods

FIGURE 3.22:
DVPULLBACK TEST RESULTS DURING 2000 TO 2008,
USING 5MA OVER 20MA FILTER

TriggeredDVPullback		Winners	Losers	Neutral
Number of trades in test:	1988	1173	799	16
Average periods per trade:	4.29	4.28	4.32	3.94
Maximum Profit/Loss:		33.39%	(28.71)%	
Average Drawdown:	(1.64)%	(0.66)%	(3.12)%	
Average Profit/Loss:	1.07%	3.66%	(2.71)%	
Average SPX Profit/Loss	0.61%	1.18%	(0.22)%	
Probability:		59.00%	40.19%	
Average Annual ROI:	91.15%	312.33%	(228.98)%	
Annual SPX (Buy & Hold):	(3.76)%			
Reward/Risk Ratio:	1.98			
Start test date:	12/29/00			
End test date:	12/31/08			

Interval:Daily
Pricing Summary
      Entry price: [Open]
      Exit price: [Open]
Exit Summary
      Hold for 3 periods

Courtesy of AIQ

average filter that selects periods of bullish and trading range market activity and rules out bearish market periods.

Using this filter increased the percentage of winning trades from 57 percent to 59 percent and increased the annualized ROI from 75 percent to 91 percent. The results are better than running DVpullback during the same test period without the filter because trades were not taken during bearish market periods when DVpullback was proven to not perform as well.

In addition to determining if the market action is trending up, trending down, or moving in a trading range, traders can use this moving average filter to help determine market conditions and then determine whether to use DVpullback or another tool in the trader's toolbox.

If you want to see the trend lines I am watching in the current market, send a request to sample@daisydogger.com. When learning how to use new tools, it is often best to work with someone who has experience in the area.

USING TREND LINES TO DETERMINE MARKET CONDITIONS

Another technique for determining the current market conditions is to use trend lines. When the market is trending up, it by definition forms a series of higher highs and higher lows. Drawing an ascending trend line under the lows of the recent market movement provides a tool for monitoring the market environment. As long as the market is trading above the ascending trend line, the market is in a bullish environment. Trend lines generally get you in a little after a bullish move has started and out a little before the change to the next market environment. Trend lines do not catch the entire bullish move; but almost by definition, any move worth trading does not require you to be in during the first few days. In the long run, it may be better to miss the beginning portion of a few moves than to get in too early and be whipsawed on false breakouts.

FIGURE 3.23:
ASCENDING TREND LINE DURING A BULLISH
MARKET ENVIRONMENT

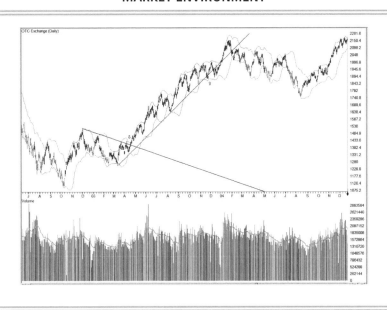

Courtesy of AIQ

Figure 3.23 shows an ascending trend line marking a bullish market move along with the period when the five-period exponential moving average of the highs is above the 20-period simple moving average of the closes, which is marked on the price chart. The labeled region is the period that would be traded using the moving average filter. It starts with a trading range period before the ascending trend line forms, and ends with another trading range period after the ascending trend line has been broken. Trading the DVpullback system using the moving average filter resulted in 54 percent winning trades. Trading DVpullback while the market was above the ascending trend line resulted in 64 percent winning trades. Each technique improves the DV-pullback results as compared to just taking all the trades in the period.

The mechanical moving average filter is helpful. Trend lines can be used to better focus in on specific market conditions and improve results. Using these techniques takes some practice.

Figure 3.24 shows five trend lines that were used to follow the market movement during a three-year period. The first ascending trend line was broken

TREND LINES DURING MARKET MOVEMENTS

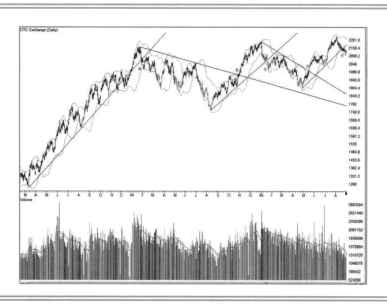

Courtesy of AIQ

at point A. When an ascending trend line is broken, the market is likely to base or retrace. I respond to the break of an ascending trend line by reducing position sizes and the number of positions traded until the next market move becomes clear. Trend line breaks imply that something is changing and until the next market condition is clear, I want to reduce risk and protect previous profits.

At point B in Figure 3.24, the market broke above a descending trend line indicating I should look to use a bullish system. This run did not last long and the new trend line was broken at point C. When there is a break below an ascending trend line, it indicates caution and reduced position sizes until the new market conditions become clear.

At point D, the market breaks above the new descending trend line and the process repeats. The market decides how long it will run during a move. You cannot influence it, but you need to react to it. Some traders get frustrated when market moves do not last for months at a time. Successful traders just trade the current conditions using tools they have fully analyzed. It does not matter how long a move lasts, they are always ready for the next move with another one of the tools in their tool box.

When I go to a trading conference, I often ask how many traders are bullish, and a number of hands go up. I then ask how many traders are bearish and more hands go up. I then ask how many traders do not care if the market is bullish or bearish. This usually generates some chuckles and a couple of hands. The serious traders do not care whether the market is going up or down; they know it is out of their control and they have tools to deal with both conditions… so it does not matter. The traders laughing at this question usually have interesting stories of significant drawdowns from guessing incorrectly. Try not to be bullish or bearish, just focus on where the market's key trend lines and support and resistance levels are and adapt to what the market is actually doing.

DVPULLBACK SUMMARY

The DVpullback system is an interesting trading system in bullish market conditions and may be used with reduced position sizes in trading range markets. The definition of the DVpullback system is outlined below.

A DVpullback occurs if:

- The stock shows three consecutive lower highs, and
- The stock has three consecutive days of lower volume than the previous day, and
- The stock is in an uptrend, which is defined as the highest high of the last two weeks is higher than the highest high of the previous two weeks, and the lowest low of the last two weeks is higher than the lowest low of the previous two weeks.

A price trigger occurs if:

- Today's high is greater than yesterday's high, and
- The close is greater than $5, and
- The 21-day simple average of the volume is greater than 200,000, and
- The stock has "room to run," which is defined as when the stock is at least two daily ranges below the upper Bollinger band on the price trigger.

The entry strategy is:

- If a DVpullback occurred yesterday, and
- A trigger occurs today, then
- Buy at the open tomorrow.

The exit strategy is:

- Hold for three days: the entry day, the next day, and the following day, then
- Sell at the following day's open.

Traders should be more aggressive and exit more quickly when the market is in a trading range. Market conditions should also affect the exit strategy. When the market approaches resistance, the upper Bollinger band, or a trend line, consider taking profits on most positions.

Results are improved by only taking trades that have volume on the trigger day above the volume of the previous day. As a general rule, I pay close attention to this rule when using DVpullback in trading range markets and have a little more flexibility in strongly trending markets.

Traders can use their own observations of the market to determine if conditions are suitable for DVpullback. They can also use the moving average filter developed in this chapter to identify bullish and trading range markets for using DVpullback. Finally, traders can use market trend lines to determine if bullish conditions exist, and then use DVpullback when the market is trading above an ascending trend line.

Testing a trading system does not guarantee future results, and trading always involves risk. Traders should do their own analysis and then only trade with funds they can afford to lose. No one should trade with the rent money; there will be times when a string of consecutive losses occurs, and that is just a part of trading.

CHAPTER 3 SELF-TEST

1. Seeing ten successful trading examples in a book or magazine:

    A. Demonstrates the effectiveness of the system.

    B. Illustrates how the system should be used.

    C. Proves nothing.

    D. Implies the system should be tried.

2. Trading strategies need to have:

    A. Shown that they work through a number of successful trade examples.

    B. A clear entry and exit definition consisting of nouns and numbers, not adjectives.

    C. Been tested over a long calendar period.

    D. Worked well for someone else.

3. When trading pullbacks in trending stocks, one should look for:

    A. Stocks pulling back on increasing volume.

    B. Stocks in a trading range.

    C. Stocks in a bearish mode.

    D. Stocks pulling back on declining volume.

4. Results for trading pullbacks in trending stocks can be improved by:

    A. Watching charts most of the day.

    B. Trading stocks above the upper Bollinger band.

    C. Trading stocks below the upper Bollinger band.

    D. Trading stocks that are declining.

5. Results for trading pullbacks in trending stocks can be improved by:

    A. Trading during bullish market conditions.

    B. Trading during bearish market conditions.

    C. Trading during trading range market conditions.

    D. Trading without considering market conditions.

6. Results for trading pullbacks in trending stocks can be improved by:

    A. Focusing on trades with declining volume on the day the setup triggers.

    B. Focusing on trades with increasing volume on the day the setup triggers.

    C. Focusing on trades with very small volume on the day the setup triggers.

    D. Volume on the trigger day does not matter.

7. Results for trading pullbacks in trending stocks can be improved by:

    A. Taking trades when the stock is above the five-period moving average.

    B. Taking trades when the stock is below the five-period moving average.

    C. Focusing on trades that pull back below the 20-period moving average.

    D. Ignoring the depth of the pullback.

8. Results for trading pullbacks in trending stocks can be improved by:

    A. Trading during bullish market conditions.

    B. Trading during bearish market conditions.

    C. Trading during trading range market conditions.

    D. Trading without reference to market conditions.

9. Results for trading pullbacks in trending stocks can be improved by:

    A. Trading when the NASDAQ 5MA is above the NASDAQ 20MA.

    B. Trading when the NASDAQ 5MA is below the NASDAQ 20MA.

    C. Trading when the NASDAQ is below an ascending trend line.

    D. Trading without reference to the NASDAQ.

FOR THE ANSWERS,
VISIT WWW.TRADERSLIBRARY.COM/TLECORNER.

CHAPTER 4

RETRACEMENTS IN DOWNTRENDING STOCKS

Traders need tools in their trading tool box that allow them to have a tradable edge in each of the three types of market conditions. When the market is in a bearish, or downtrending, environment, I trade retracements in declining stocks. There are a number of different retracement patterns that are interesting. Retracements are one of the "bread and butter" patterns for downtrending market environments because they provide frequent trade setups and interesting results.

DVRETRACE DEFINITION

The system researched in this chapter is based on the observation that declining stocks or markets usually do not go straight down. Declining stocks tend to move in waves; they often run for a bit, retrace for a bit, and then continue the decline, as shown in Figure 4.1. The question on any bounce, or retrace, in a declining stock is whether or not the bounce (retrace) is a bottom and the beginning of a new uptrend or just a normal correction in a downtrending movement.

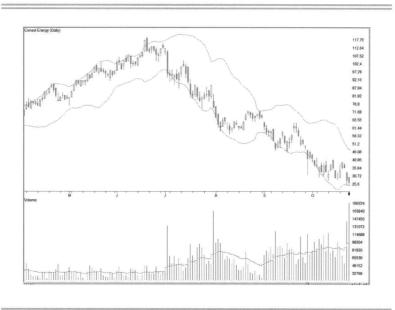

Courtesy of AIQ

Volume patterns play a key role in determining how serious a move is. The volume bars indicate the amount of interest in a move. Big bars indicate lots of interest and small bars indicate little interest. If a stock is generally declining and it bounces on light volume, it should indicate that there is less interest in the stock as it retraces (bounces). Put another way, there are fewer people willing to buy at higher prices.

This is an interesting observation and theory, but you know by now that we need to test observations before trading them. The world is full of things that sound good but may not represent the truth. "The check is in the mail." "Officer, I was not speeding." Successful traders do not take things at face value; they test them to see what really happens.

In order to test a system, we first need a clear definition. Clear definitions use nouns and numbers, not adjectives. The path and course of action are clear and not left up to the interpretation of the user.

Some politicians have mastered the ability to speak in such a way that different people hear what they want to hear. They rarely commit to a specific definition of something so that more groups can feel their views are supported. Traders are not trying to find something that feels good. They are trying to clearly understand how a trading tool has performed. Trading system definitions need to be as specific and unambiguous as possible so that they can be tested and used effectively.

The initial retracement system definition, called DVretrace, consists of three parts. The retrace is an upward movement in the stock that is measured by a series of three consecutive higher lows. The trigger condition is used to indicate that the retracement pattern of consecutive higher lows has ended. The entry is made at the open the day after a trigger occurs, and the stock is held three days and then exited at the following open. There is also a basic price and volume filter included in the retracement definition, which is intended to filter out stocks that may have large bid/ask spreads or may be difficult to exit at a given price when conditions are rapidly changing.

The definition for the DVretrace system is:

A DVretrace occurs if:

- The stock is in a downtrend, defined as when the highest close in the last two weeks is lower than the lowest close of the previous month, and
- There are three consecutive higher lows, and
- There are three consecutive days of lower volume, and
- The close is greater than $5, and
- The 21-day simple average of the volume is greater than 200,000.

A trigger occurs if:

- Today's low is less than yesterday's low.

If a DVretrace occurred yesterday, and a trigger occurs today, then

- Short at the open tomorrow.
- Hold for three days. Day one is the entry day; then hold two more days, and
- Buy to cover at the next open.

Figure 4.2 shows an example of a DVretrace pattern. Genco Shipping is in a clear downtrend, and from August through October, it had been setting a series of lower highs and lower lows on the chart. In mid-October, the stock made a series of three consecutive higher daily lows as marked by the down arrows on the chart. At the same time the stock made the three higher lows, the volume declined every day, as marked by the down arrows on the volume chart in Figure 4.2.

INITIAL TESTING OF DVRETRACE PATTERN

Before using a system, I want to know how it performed over hundreds of trades in different time periods and market conditions. Only then will I have some idea of what to expect when using the tool. In order to get a quick idea of whether or not the DVretrace system is worth investigating, I looked at all of the trades it generated during 2008. When first looking at a system, I want to do a quick test during a period when it ought to work. If it shows some promise, I will continue investigating it in different time periods and market conditions. Since DVpullback is a shorting system, if it did not work in 2008, it may not be worth investigating further.

Figure 4.3 shows the results of backtesting the DVretrace system during calendar year 2008. During the 2008 test period, DVretrace saw 863 trading opportunities. The annualized result for all trades was 161 percent, which represents a clear improvement over the market's 36 percent decline during the same period. Sixty-one percent of the trades were profitable, and the average winning trade yielded 6.74 percent while the average losing trade lost 5.91 percent. This initial test indicates that DVretrace performed well during the 2008 market decline and may be worth further investigation.

FIGURE 4.2:
DVRETRACE PATTERN

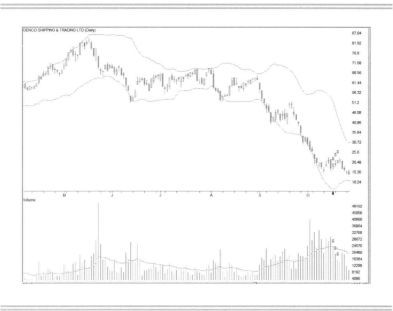

Courtesy of AIQ

Backtesting is a tool to help traders understand how a system has performed, but it is not a guarantee of future results, nor is it a guarantee of the results you would see in your account. Backtesting data gives traders an idea of how a system has performed and provides insights into how the system behaves. Remember, the annualized ROI calculation assumes that all trades were taken and the results were annualized. I use the ROI number as a figure of merit. More is better, and it is just one indication of whether or not a system is worth trading. I am more interested in the percentage of winning trades and the difference between the average winning trade and the average losing trade.

If a system wins more often than it loses, and the average winning trade is larger than the average losing trade, then over the long run, the system has profit potential. If a system shows 60 percent winning trades, it does not imply that six of every ten trades will be winners. All systems have winning and losing streaks. Traders need to understand this and use position sizing to manage risks and allow them to ride out the normal losing streaks in trading. The benefit of backtesting is that traders can get an idea of how a system

TriggeredDVretrace				
		Winners	Losers	Neutral
Number of trades in test:	863	534	325	4
Average periods per trade:	4.40	4.64	4.01	4.50
Maximum Profit/Loss:		47.68%	(68.99)%	
Average Drawdown:	(3.55)%	(1.16)%	(7.53)%	
Average Profit/Loss:	1.94%	6.74%	(5.91)%	
Average SPX Profit/Loss	1.76%	3.18%	(0.56)%	
Probability:		61.88%	37.66%	
Average Annual ROI:	161.05%	530.22%	(538.77)%	
Annual SPX (Buy & Hold):	(36.32)%			
Reward/Risk Ratio:	1.87			
Start test date:	01/02/08			
End test date:	12/31/08			

Interval:Daily
Pricing Summary
      Entry price: [Open]
      Exit price: [Open]
Exit Summary
      Hold for 3 periods

Courtesy of AIQ

has performed over many trades, although it will not provide any indication of whether or not any particular trade will be profitable.

EFFECT OF TRIGGER DAY VOLUME ON DVRETRACE TEST RESULTS

In Chapter 3, we researched the DVpullback system and found that taking trades with increasing volume on the trigger day improved results. Figure 4.4 shows the results of adding a filter to DVretrace that only takes trades if the volume on the trigger day is greater than the previous day's volume. Increasing volume on the trigger day results in an increase in the percentage of winning trades from 61 percent to 63 percent and leaves the annualized ROI about the same.

If instead we require the volume on the trigger day to be at least 110 percent of the previous day's volume, we find that the test results are not signifi-

TriggeredDVretrace

		Winners	Losers	Neutral
Number of trades in test:	648	410	236	2
Average periods per trade:	4.42	4.67	3.99	5.00
Maximum Profit/Loss:		47.68%	(68.99)%	
Average Drawdown:	(3.84)%	(1.26)%	(8.37)%	
Average Profit/Loss:	1.93%	6.71%	(6.35)%	
Average SPX Profit/Loss	1.98%	3.44%	(0.53)%	
Probability:		63.27%	36.42%	
Average Annual ROI:	159.21%	524.30%	(580.92)%	
Annual SPX (Buy & Hold):	(36.32)%			
Reward/Risk Ratio:	1.83			
Start test date:	01/02/08			
End test date:	12/31/08			

Interval:Daily
Pricing Summary
      Entry price: [Open]
        Exit price: [Open]
Exit Summary
      Hold for 3 periods

Courtesy of AIQ

cantly improved, as shown in Figure 4.5. More is not always better. Rather than assume, traders need to test all ideas. Just because a filter improved results for one trading system does not mean that the same filter will improve results for a different system.

If instead of looking at the relationship of the volume on the trigger day to the previous day's volume, we look at the relationship of the trigger day's volume to the average volume, we get the results shown in Figure 4.6. In this case, DVretrace trades were only taken if the volume on the day of the trigger was above average. Average volume is defined as the simple moving average of the volume over the last 21 days. This is essentially the average volume over the last month. As shown in Figure 4.6, requiring above average volume on the day of the trigger diminishes results. The percentage of winning trades and the annualized ROI both drop. The annualized ROI is nearly cut in half.

FIGURE 4.5:
EFFECT OF "110 PERCENT TRIGGER DAY VOLUME" ON DVRETRACE TEST RESULTS

TriggeredDVretrace

		Winners	Losers	Neutral
Number of trades in test:	580	367	212	1
Average periods per trade:	4.42	4.66	3.99	5.00
Maximum Profit/Loss:		47.68%	(68.99)%	
Average Drawdown:	(4.01)%	(1.30)%	(8.73)%	
Average Profit/Loss:	1.78%	6.62%	(6.57)%	
Average SPX Profit/Loss	1.92%	3.39%	(0.61)%	
Probability:		63.28%	36.55%	
Average Annual ROI:	147.44%	517.77%	(602.01)%	
Annual SPX (Buy & Hold):	(36.32)%			
Reward/Risk Ratio:	1.74			
Start test date:	01/02/08			
End test date:	12/31/08			

Interval:Daily
Pricing Summary
        Entry price: [Open]
        Exit price: [Open]
Exit Summary
        Hold for 3 periods

FIGURE 4.6:
EFFECT OF "ABOVE AVERAGE VOLUME" ON TRIGGER DAY

TriggeredDVretrace

		Winners	Losers	Neutral
Number of trades in test:	212	123	87	2
Average periods per trade:	4.40	4.66	4.02	5.00
Maximum Profit/Loss:		41.08%	(68.99)%	
Average Drawdown:	(4.27)%	(0.98)%	(9.02)%	
Average Profit/Loss:	0.92	6.63%	(7.13)%	
Average SPX Profit/Loss	1.78%	3.21%	(0.21)%	
Probability:		58.02%	41.04%	
Average Annual ROI:	76.29%	519.59%	(647.29)%	
Annual SPX (Buy & Hold):	(36.32)%			
Reward/Risk Ratio:	1.31			
Start test date:	01/02/08			
End test date:	12/31/08			

Interval:Daily
Pricing Summary
        Entry price: [Open]
        Exit price: [Open]
Exit Summary
        Hold for 3 periods

Courtesy of AIQ

Myth: Taking trades with increasing volume on the trigger day will always improve results because volume shows increased interest in the stock.

Fact: You must test each system's filters separately. In the case of DVretrace, above average volume on the trigger day did not improve results.

From this series of tests related to the volume pattern on the trigger day, it appears that for DVretrace, it is not necessarily the magnitude of the volume on the day of the trigger that is important. It is the relationship of the volume to the previous day's volume that matters. Increasing volume on the trigger day indicates that as the price was moving below the previous day's low, there was more interest in the move than there was the previous day when another consecutive higher low was formed.

Volume patterns are important in analyzing market moves, and play a large role in many trading systems. Volume indicates how much interest there is in a move. When there is a lot of interest in a move, then it may be more likely to continue.

In police work there is a saying, "follow the money." In trading it is often good to "follow the volume." In this case, when a downtrending stock is retracing (or bouncing up) on low volume and then it continues the downward movement on increasing volume, there is less interest in rising prices and more interest in declining prices. With some systems, the effect of volume patterns can be dramatic. With other systems, such as DVretrace, the effect is less dramatic but still interesting. We will include the requirement that the trigger day volume be larger than the previous day's volume in the DVpullback definition and use it in subsequent testing.

EFFECT OF AVERAGE VOLUME AND STOCK PRICE ON DVRETRACE RESULTS

The DVretrace definition includes an average volume filter that ignores all stocks with a 21-day simple moving average of the daily volume less than 200,000. This is a standard filter that I use on most systems to make sure the stocks have reasonable bid/ask spreads and that there is enough volume to get easily in and out of a trade. If you try to sell a 2,000 share position in a stock which only trades around 20,000 shares a day, you will find that it can be difficult, especially if things are moving quickly. Trading stocks with average volume above 200,000 shares reduces this problem.

One of my newsletter (The Timely Trades Letter) subscribers asked me what I thought the effect would be if the minimum average volume requirement was increased from 200,000 to 500,000. He felt that larger volume stocks had more activity, and hence, the trading results should be better. During my active trading career, I have learned that trading based on hunches, guesses, feelings, and tips is often a bad idea. Rather than guess, I tested the idea.

To test whether larger volume stocks improve results, let's look at Figure 4.7. This figure shows the results of trading DVretrace during calendar year 2008 with an additional requirement that trades are taken only in stocks that have a 21-day simple moving average volume above 500,000. The results shown in Figure 4.7 are not significantly different than those shown in Figure 4.4, which is the test that includes the now standard "increasing volume on the day of the trigger" filter. The results are about the same whether the trades include stocks with average volumes above 200,000 or above 500,000. The average volume of the stock is not nearly as significant to results as the increasing volume on the day of the trigger.

When I told my subscriber that the average volume of the stocks traded with DVretrace did not matter much, he then asked if the price of the stock would have an effect on results. I ran a quick test using a filter that only took DVretrace trades if the price of the stock was at least $25. (The DVretrace definition includes the standard filter that requires the price of the stock to be at least $5.)

FIGURE 4.7:
EFFECT OF INCREASING THE AVERAGE VOLUME
REQUIREMENT TO 500,000

TriggeredDVretrace

		Winners	Losers	Neutral
Number of trades in test:	553	351	201	
Average periods per trade:	4.47	4.69	4.07	5.0(
Maximum Profit/Loss:		47.68%	(68.99)%	
Average Drawdown:	(3.80)%	(1.25)%	(8.27)%	
Average Profit/Loss:	2.03%	6.80%	(6.28)%	
Average SPX Profit/Loss	2.13%	3.58%	(0.39)%	
Probability:		63.47%	36.35%	
Average Annual ROI:	165.97%	528.84%	(562.75)%	
Annual SPX (Buy & Hold):	(36.32)%			
Reward/Risk Ratio:	1.89			
Start test date:	01/02/08			
End test date:	12/31/08			

Interval:Daily
Pricing Summary
       Entry price: [Open]
       Exit price: [Open]
Exit Summary
       Hold for 3 periods

FIGURE 4.8:
EFFECT OF INCREASING MINIMUM STOCK PRICE TO $25

TriggeredDVretrace

		Winners	Losers	Neutral
Number of trades in test:	278	184	93	1
Average periods per trade:	4.56	4.77	4.15	5.00
Maximum Profit/Loss:		24.99%	(20.63)%	
Average Drawdown:	(2.70)%	(1.04)%	(6.02)%	
Average Profit/Loss:	2.17%	5.83%	(5.06)%	
Average SPX Profit/Loss	2.66%	4.00%	0.03%	
Probability:		66.19%	33.45%	
Average Annual ROI:	173.28%	446.54%	(445.34)%	
Annual SPX (Buy & Hold):	(36.32)%			
Reward/Risk Ratio:	2.28			
Start test date:	01/02/08			
End test date:	12/31/08			

Interval:Daily
Pricing Summary
       Entry price: [Open]
       Exit price: [Open]
Exit Summary
       Hold for 3 periods

Courtesy of AIQ

The results of running the DVretrace scan during calendar 2008 using a minimum $25 stock price are shown in Figure 4.8. Trading only the higher dollar value stocks improved results. The annualized ROI increased about 10 points, and more important, the percentage of winning trades increased from 63 percent to 66 percent. This is an interesting improvement, but rather than incorporate it into the standard definition of DVretrace, I use it as one of the tools for prioritizing trade opportunities when the scan shows more DVretrace setups than I need.

ADAPTING TRADING STYLE TO CURRENT MARKET CONDITIONS

As the market changes between bullish, bearish, and trading range conditions, I adapt my trading style to match the current market. I change trading systems based on the test results for each of my trading tools in the three different market conditions. I also adjust position sizes and the number of trading positions based on the current market conditions.

In a bullish market, stocks tend to trigger and run for a bit. In trading range market conditions, stocks tend to "pop and drop." I respond to trading range market conditions by using shorter holding times and reduced position sizes than in a trending market. Traders who focus on understanding and managing risk reduce their exposure when the market conditions present increased risk. Strongly trending markets are the most favorable conditions; they do not eliminate risk but the rewards are generally better than during trading range markets. Because trading ranges present increased risk, I reduce position sizes to respond appropriately.

Traders can also adjust their risk profile by changing the number of trading positions they use. The number of trading positions is the number of stocks that you are willing to hold at one time. When a position hits its target or a stop loss point, then I have an open trading position and can take another trade. I will hold more trading positions in a strongly trending market than I will in a trading range market because the risks are lower. My total risk is the summation of the amount at risk in each trade. I am willing to take on more risk in trending markets so I can trade a greater number of positions.

I look for differing numbers of trades to take depending on the market conditions, and how many "open slots" I have. The market conditions determine how many trades, or trading positions, I will hold at any one time. The number of open slots depends on how many of my trading positions have just hit their targets or stops. When a trading position has hit its target, or stop, I have an open slot that can be filled by another setup that triggers. Since there will be times when my trading tools generate more interesting setups than I have open slots, it is important to have a way to prioritize setups.

System test results can be helpful in developing techniques for prioritizing the setups that are generated by the tools in my trading tool box. The test results shown in Figure 4.8 indicated that higher-dollar stocks tend to have a higher winning percentage. When I see more DVretrace setups than I have room to take (based on the number of open slots), I can select the ones that are above $25 and pass on the setups that occur at prices below $25. If there are still more setups than open slots, I will prioritize them based on the risk/reward ratio of each setup.

The risk assumed in a trade is the distance between the entry point and the initial stop loss. I generally place an initial stop loss order just above the high of the retracement pattern in DVretrace setups because if the pattern triggers and then moves against me to set a higher high, it is an indication that the pattern is not working well. The potential reward for a trade depends on the market conditions. In a trading range, stocks tend to pause or bounce at the Bollinger bands, a nearby support or resistance area, or a recent high or low. I usually set a limit order just before these areas to close the trade before the run stalls.

When presented with too many setups, I pick the ones with the best risk/reward ratio. I look for small risks and large rewards. In a trading range market, the risk/reward ratio will not be as favorable as it will be in trending markets. I am looking for the best of what is available rather than a specific number.

DVRETRACE TEST RESULTS IN DIFFERENT MARKET CONDITIONS

Now that we have a working definition of DVretrace and an idea of how to prioritize multiple trades, we need to evaluate the system in more than just one calendar period. Since the market conditions of one calendar period generally do not repeat in the next calendar period, we need to test different market conditions rather than different calendar periods. We want to see how DVretrace performs in multiple bullish, multiple bearish, and multiple trading range environments. When we have that information, we will have a better idea of how to use the system.

Table 4.1 shows the test results for DVretrace during six different bullish market environments, which span different years and different lengths of time. The only common element is that the market was trending up during each of these periods. During the bullish market periods, DVretrace lost money in three of the six periods and the percentage of winning trades was below 50 percent in half of the test periods. Based on these results, DVretrace should not be used during bullish market conditions.

Table 4.2 shows the results of testing DVretrace during six different bearish market periods. The results paint a different picture than those of Table 4.1. DVretrace shows profits in all bearish markets tested, with an average winning percentage of 59 percent across the six different bear market periods. The percentage of winning trades was above 50 percent in all bear markets and ranges from a low of 51.8 percent to a high of 75 percent.

This type of testing allows us to get away from trying to predict targets for the market, which is a tough game to win consistently. Instead of trying to predict market targets, I just need to be able to look at the current market conditions and determine if they are bullish, bearish, or trading range. This is much easier to do consistently than trying to predict where the market is going, and traders can use one or more of the three techniques for determining current market conditions that were outlined in previous chapters.

TABLE 4.1
DVRETRACE TEST RESULTS DURING SIX DIFFERENT
BULLISH MARKET PERIODS

TEST PERIOD	MARKET TYPE	WINNING %	ANNUALIZED ROI	# OF TRADES
08/13/04-12/31/04	Bull	30.5%	-149%	72
07/21/06-11/24/06	Bull	42.6	-58	75
03/14/07-07/20/07	Bull	60.2	34	73
08/17/07-10/09/07	Bull	52.2	27	69
03/17/08-06/05/08	Bull	28.9	-100	45
07/16/08-08/18/08	Bull	57.1	49.7	84

TABLE 4.2
DVRETRACE TEST RESULTS DURING SIX DIFFERENT
BEARISH MARKET PERIODS

TEST PERIOD	MARKET TYPE	WINNING %	ANNUALIZED ROI	# OF TRADES
01/04/02-10/04/02	Bear	51.8%	1%	110
01/23/04-08/13/04	Bear	53.3	65	120
01/07/05-04/22/05	Bear	56.7	50	67
05/11/06-07/21/06	Bear	54.6	11.7	75
07/20/07-08/17/07	Bear	66.7	176	15
06/06/08-07/15/08	Bear	75.0	203	24

TABLE 4.3
DVRETRACE TEST RESULTS DURING SIX DIFFERENT
TRADING RANGE MARKET PERIODS

TEST PERIOD	MARKET TYPE	WINNING %	ANNUALIZED ROI	# OF TRADES
11/25/05-05/05/06	Trading Range	53.9%	110%	63
01/05/06-05/11/06	Trading Range	52.0	57	52
01/07/05-04/22/05	Trading Range	42.1	-30	19
11/24/06-02/26/07	Trading Range	73.7	483	19
10/09/07-11/06/07	Trading Range	49.0	-95	43

Table 4.3 shows the results of testing DVretrace in five different trading range markets. Two of the five trading range periods show losses and winning percentages below 50 percent. The average percentage of winning trades for the five trading range market periods shown in Table 4.2 is slightly over 54 percent. DVretrace can produce a small profit when the market is in a trading range environment, but the results are not as consistent as we saw for using DVretrace during bear market environments.

The market condition testing information shown in Tables 4.1, 4.2, and 4.3 indicate that the most consistent results for using DVretrace occur in bearish market conditions. Based on this information, I would be interested in having DVretrace as one of the tools in my trading toolbox for use during bear markets.

To review, the process I use for trading starts with an analysis of the current market conditions. First, I determine if the market is currently bullish, bearish, or in a trading range environment. I then open the drawer in my trading tool box that contains tools suitable for the current market conditions and run the scans to find trading setups. I then prioritize the trading setups based on risk/reward ratio, trigger volume pattern, etc., and select the best of what is available for trades to add to my portfolio.

REAL WORLD TRADING TIPS

Immediately after entering a trade, I enter a stop loss just under the low of the pattern for long trades and just above the high of the pattern for short trades. I also enter a limit order just under resistance for longs or just above support for shorts, and the two orders are linked in an "order cancels order" format. The stop and limit orders provide basic trade management; if the stock moves quickly in either direction, the orders will take me out.

Sometimes a trade will take off the next day and quickly move outside the Bollinger bands or test a recent high. In this case, the limit order captures the move without me having to be there watching all day. I use the three-day holding period that testing found to be effective as a starting point for the exit strategy.

My testing has shown that a three-day holding period can be an effective exit strategy during trading range markets and that longer holding times can be used during trending markets. In practice, I use this as a guideline and not as a hard and fast rule. If a position approaches support or resistance, I will generally take the profit whether or not it has been three days. The most likely thing for a stock to do at a key support or resistance level is to bounce or retrace. If the stock is going to bounce or retrace from support or resistance most of the time, then in the short-term, the run is over and I am better off taking profits.

When a stock approaches support or resistance, it is either going to break through or retreat from it. If, based on the definition of support and resistance, the stock retreats most of the time, then by taking profits in the support or resistance area I will maximize my return and not "give back" profits as the stock retreats. In the cases where the stock does not retreat, and moves through support or resistance, I will still have my profits and can roll them into another position. I do not need to continue making money on a specific stock. I can roll my profits into whatever is working.

Traders need to focus on managing risk and being positioned to profit based on the most probable outcome. If the normal thing for declining stocks to do is bounce at support, then I want to take advantage of this knowledge and use it to prioritize trades based on the risk/reward ratio, and also to take profits when a short position approaches support. If I have a long position and the stock is moving up toward resistance, then I want to take profits before the resistance area in case the stock follows the normal pattern and retraces from resistance. In both cases, I want to maximize my profits by following the statistically sound strategy.

Some traders are reluctant to take profits when a short position approaches support because they do not want to be wrong. They worry that they will "miss out" if the stock keeps going down instead of bouncing. This is trading on emotion and ego, not logic.

If the stock is most likely to bounce at support, then most of the time you are better off closing the short position before it gets to support. There is no way to know what will happen on any particular trade. There are no magic indicators or super systems that will tell you the outcome on a specific trade. You are not smart if the trade worked and you are not dumb if the trade failed. The smart way to trade is to be positioned to profit if the market and the stock you are trading do the normal or expected thing. I do not want to bet on the unusual, I want to bet on the normal thing happening.

Earlier, we developed an indicator for market conditions based on the five- and 20-period moving averages. One would expect this technique to improve the results of DVretrace over long calendar periods based on the results of the market condition period testing done above. And, while expectations are interesting, testing is better; so we need to establish that the moving average market conditions indicator helps when using DVretrace.

Figure 4.9 shows the results of testing DVretrace during the seven-year period from the beginning of 2002 through 2008. This seven-year period included a number of bullish, bearish, and trading range market periods; so, we would expect the average results to be below what we saw for bearish

TriggeredDVretrace		Winners	Losers	Neutral
Number of trades in test:	1833	1000	821	12
Average periods per trade:	4.44	4.54	4.32	4.00
Maximum Profit/Loss:		47.68%	(68.99)%	
Average Drawdown:	(2.60)%	(0.77)%	(4.86)%	
Average Profit/Loss:	0.77%	4.80%	(4.14)%	
Average SPX Profit/Loss	0.59%	1.75%	(0.81)%	
Probability:		54.56%	44.79%	
Average Annual ROI:	62.91%	385.84%	(350.06)%	
Annual SPX (Buy & Hold):	(2.69)%			
Reward/Risk Ratio:	1.41			
Start test date:	01/02/02			
End test date:	12/31/08			

Interval:Daily
Pricing Summary
      Entry price: [Open]
      Exit price: [Open]
Exit Summary
      Hold for 3 periods

Courtesy of AIQ

conditions in Table 4.2 and above what we saw for bullish conditions in Table 4.1. Figure 4.9 shows that the annualized ROI for the seven-year period was 62 percent and that 54 percent of the trades were profitable.

ANALYZING ACTUAL TRADE INFORMATION AND DISTRIBUTION OF TRADES

Testing shows the average annualized ROI and the percentage of winning trades over the entire test period. These results are usually not evenly distributed. There is some normal random fluctuation and a strong influence by the current market conditions. Figure 4.10 shows the actual trade information for the DVretrace trades that were taken during March of 2008.

Of the 23 trades taken during March, 19 of them were losing trades. The full test period had winning trades 54 percent of the time. This sounds interesting because if you win more often than you lose and the average winning trade is a larger than the average loss, then over time there is a good chance you will be profitable. The averages, however, do not tell you anything about each individual trade or small groups of trades. In this case, 19 losing trades out of 23 is not a good result, but it is part of the overall 54 percent winning trades. Clearly, there must be some good winning streaks in there to end up with a 54 percent winning average.

If a trader without any knowledge of how DVretrace performed over long time periods and in different market conditions started using the system in March of 2008, he would likely stop after a long string of losses. He would conclude that the system did not work and then continue his search for a "good" trading system. A trader that had fully tested and analyzed DVretrace would know that when the market is in a trading range and moving to a bullish period, as it was during this time, that he should be using another tool in his trading toolbox.

An uninformed trader tends to think that trading is some magic formula that should produce good results all the time. An informed trader realizes that no trading system works all the time—he must observe the market conditions in order to select the most appropriate tools to use.

During September and the first week of October 2008, DVretrace showed very intriguing results. As shown in Figure 4.11, DVretrace showed profits in 22 of the 24 trades during this period. An uninformed trader who started using DVretrace in September may feel he had found the "super trading system," or perhaps that he was really "catching on" to this trading thing. I have heard both of those reactions several times at trading conferences. The informed trader, who has fully tested all of his trading systems and learned to read the market, would know that the market conditions were favorable for DVretrace and would have selected it as one of the tools to be used during this period.

Just because a trading system shows favorable results in one type of market condition does not imply that it will also show favorable results when condi-

DVRETRACE RESULTS DURING MARCH 2008

Ticker	Held	Entry Date	Entry Price	Exit Date	Exit Price	Profit
SEPR	5	4/4/2008	19.57	4/9/2008	21.74	-2.17
VOD	3	4/1/2008	30.19	4/4/2008	31.79	-1.6
CBM	3	3/31/2008	6.96	4/3/2008	7.14	-0.18
CHY	3	3/31/2008	12.4	4/3/2008	13.07	-0.67
ATHR	5	3/28/2008	21.56	4/2/2008	22.74	-1.18
BGP	5	3/28/2008	5.86	4/2/2008	5.84	0.02
BMS	5	3/28/2008	25.4	4/2/2008	26.62	-1.22
EWA	5	3/28/2008	25.91	4/2/2008	26.64	-0.73
GOOG	5	3/28/2008	447.46	4/2/2008	469.9	-22.44
ITT	5	3/28/2008	52.49	4/2/2008	54.28	-1.79
LMT	5	3/28/2008	100.38	4/2/2008	101.9	-1.52
NTGR	5	3/28/2008	19.97	4/2/2008	20.3	-0.33
QSFT	5	3/28/2008	13.2188	4/2/2008	13.375	-0.1563
SINA	5	3/28/2008	34.45	4/2/2008	37	-2.55
TBL	5	3/28/2008	13.85	4/2/2008	14.37	-0.52
TNB	5	3/28/2008	36.05	4/2/2008	38.06	-2.01
RYAAY	5	3/27/2008	28	4/1/2008	28.46	-0.46
UNH	5	3/26/2008	35.25	3/31/2008	34.4	0.85
BLKB	3	3/24/2008	24.95	3/27/2008	25.39	-0.44
WBMD	3	3/24/2008	26.44	3/27/2008	25.49	0.95
STP	6	3/18/2008	31.3	3/24/2008	31.79	-0.49
EEFT	5	3/14/2008	20.37	3/19/2008	20.22	0.15
EW	5	3/14/2008	44.3	3/19/2008	46.25	-1.95
GVA	5	3/14/2008	31.92	3/19/2008	32.46	-0.54
STMP	5	3/14/2008	9.84	3/19/2008	9.92	-0.08
MSFT	5	2/29/2008	27.69	3/5/2008	27.75	-0.06
SBNY	5	2/29/2008	27.03	3/5/2008	25.8	1.23

Courtesy of AIQ

tions change. Testing a system does not guarantee future results, but it can help to develop a better understanding of a trading system. The test data above indicated that DVretrace shows promise in declining markets but is a poor choice in bullish markets.

Note from Figure 4.11 that DVretrace does not produce the same number of trades every day. Sometimes there will be a week with no trades at all, and sometimes there will be a day with six or more trades. This is not unusual for a trading system. If the system shows 300 trades when tested over a calendar year, it does not imply that there is one trade a day. It is normal to see periods with no trades, and periods with several trades a day. And, as we've discussed, there will be times when the system generates more trades than the trader can take in one day.

The testing averages are based on the computer taking each and every trade, no matter how many arrive in one day. In real life, traders will not take all the trades generated by a single system for a variety of reasons. This is one

DVRETRACE RESULTS DURING DECEMBER 2007

Ticker	Held	Entry Date	Entry Price	Exit Date	Exit Price	Profit
GNW	3	10/7/2008	6.9	10/10/2008	3.61	3.29
LQD	3	10/7/2008	88	10/10/2008	80	8
WYE	3	10/7/2008	37.1	10/10/2008	30.65	6.45
CAH	3	10/6/2008	49.73	10/9/2008	43.2	6.53
IBN	3	10/6/2008	21.08	10/9/2008	18.3	2.78
IFX	3	10/6/2008	5.21	10/9/2008	4.65	0.56
KCE	3	10/6/2008	36.39	10/9/2008	33.09	3.3
MS	3	10/6/2008	22.49	10/9/2008	17.98	4.51
TSN	3	10/6/2008	11.5	10/9/2008	11.4375	0.0625
IBM	3	9/30/2008	115.83	10/3/2008	105.16	10.67
SLG	3	9/30/2008	68.04	10/3/2008	55.98	12.06
EWM	5	9/24/2008	8.67	9/29/2008	8.5	0.17
HERO	5	9/24/2008	17.9	9/29/2008	15.71	2.19
NBR	5	9/24/2008	26.21	9/29/2008	25.33	0.88
NFX	5	9/24/2008	39.41	9/29/2008	32.94	6.47
SLT	5	9/24/2008	10.35	9/29/2008	9.18	1.17
XME	5	9/24/2008	56.16	9/29/2008	50.49	5.67
EMR	3	9/16/2008	42.15	9/19/2008	44.86	-2.71
NAT	3	9/16/2008	30.05	9/19/2008	33.01	-2.96
EWS	5	9/3/2008	11.08	9/8/2008	11.04	0.04
STLD	5	9/3/2008	22.78	9/8/2008	22.41	0.37
TOT	5	9/3/2008	67.49	9/8/2008	65.02	2.47
VTIV	6	8/28/2008	22.17	9/3/2008	21.89	0.28
CIEN	6	8/27/2008	17.55	9/2/2008	17.42	0.13

Courtesy of AIQ

of the reasons that traders will not see the backtested results in actual practice. Backtesting can provide an understanding of how a trading system works, but it does not guarantee future results. I use backtesting to develop some general principles about how a trading system performs, but do not expect to see the same annualized ROI or winning percentage in my account going forward.

You must look through the trades and see how they are grouped in terms of time and profit levels to get a better understanding of whether or not the trading technique is suitable for use. Once again, there are no guarantees. Gathering information on a trading system is like presenting information to a jury that then makes a decision based on the preponderance of the evidence. To have a good case, you need a lot of evidence from multiple sources looked at in different ways.

Figure 4.12 shows trades from an eight-day trading period in July of 2008. There were two DVretrace trades on July 14, one on July 15, three on July 16, and no trades on July 17, 18, or 21. The three-day period with no DVretrace trades was followed by 13 trades on July 22. The summary statistics for a trading system give you an idea of how it has performed over a number of trades during the test period. The summary information is very interesting, but traders need to look at the actual trade information to get a better feel for how the system works and what to expect.

Since it is unlikely, and perhaps unwise, to take 13 trades from a single system in a single day, traders need a way to prioritize potential trades and select the few most appropriate ones to trade. This is why I test the volume and price filters, so I can use that information along with risk/reward ratios to prioritize among multiple trades. I would not trade any system just based on the summary statistics.

FIGURE 4.12:
DVRETRACE TRADES IN JULY OF 2008

Ticker	Held	Entry Date	Entry Price	Exit Date	Exit Price	Profit
TRN	5	7/23/2008	36.25	7/28/2008	34.32	1.93
TSM	5	7/23/2008	9.98	7/28/2008	9.94	0.04
USB	5	7/23/2008	29.9	7/28/2008	28.89	1.01
VMED	5	7/23/2008	11.85	7/28/2008	11.09	0.76
ACG	3	7/22/2008	8.09	7/25/2008	8.08	0.01
ACH	3	7/22/2008	27.01	7/25/2008	25.9	1.11
BDC	3	7/22/2008	33.17	7/25/2008	35.12	-1.95
CR	3	7/22/2008	36.87	7/25/2008	37.14	-0.27
EWW	3	7/22/2008	54.65	7/25/2008	53.3	1.35
HMIN	3	7/22/2008	15.8	7/25/2008	15.51	0.29
JOSB	3	7/22/2008	23.07	7/25/2008	24.63	-1.56
LM	3	7/22/2008	31.51	7/25/2008	37.96	-6.45
MGA	3	7/22/2008	59.9	7/25/2008	59.71	0.19
MYE	3	7/22/2008	8.25	7/25/2008	9.52	-1.27
PHK	3	7/22/2008	11.07	7/25/2008	11.26	-0.19
RTH	3	7/22/2008	86.88	7/25/2008	88.27	-1.39
VECO	3	7/22/2008	15.63	7/25/2008	16.39	-0.76
EWY	5	7/16/2008	47.58	7/21/2008	49.57	-1.99
PKX	5	7/16/2008	125.19	7/21/2008	122.05	3.14
VWO	5	7/16/2008	43.55	7/21/2008	45.06	-1.51
HCN	3	7/15/2008	43.65	7/18/2008	47.24	-3.59
CHDX	3	7/14/2008	15.91	7/17/2008	17.93	-2.02
CSGS	3	7/14/2008	11.78	7/17/2008	14.84	-3.06

Courtesy of AIQ

USING THE MOVING AVERAGE MARKET CONDITIONS INDICATOR WITH DVRETRACE

Figure 4.13 shows the market over an 18-month period in the last half of 2007 and 2008. The gray sections of the price chart are periods when the five-period exponential moving average of the highs is below the 20-period exponential moving average of the close. This dual moving average system provides a reasonable way to identify periods when the market is bearish or in a trading range. Since our testing has indicated that the DVretrace results are dependent on the current market conditions, this tool can be useful in helping to decide whether or not using DVretrace is appropriate.

The five-period moving average is a good representation of the highs without all the daily noise. The 20-period moving average generally follows the intermediate-term trend. When the five-period moving average of the highs (representing the short-term trend of the highs) is below the 20-period moving average of the closes, (the intermediate-term trend) then prices are generally trading below the intermediate-term trend and hence the market is most likely in a downtrending period.

Adding the 5 x 20 MA filter to DVretrace and running the test from 2002 through 2008 yields the results shown in Figure 4.14. As compared to DVretrace during the same period without the filter (as shown in Figure 4.9), we see that the percentage of winning trades increases from 54 percent to 59 percent and the annualized ROI doubles. These results are consistent with what we obtained from testing the DVretrace system in different market conditions, as shown in Tables 4.1 and 4.2.

No trading system makes money all the time. Trading systems have up and down periods as a normal part of the process. Testing can help provide insights into how to minimize the swings and manage risks. In the case of DVretrace, the testing data makes a good case that results may be improved by only using the system during bearish market conditions and using other techniques when the market is bullish or in a trading range.

Trading tools are not magic formulas that lead to guaranteed riches. They are patterns that repeat and provide an edge in trading. Your job is to fully analyze and understand each trading system and then focus on the most appropriate trading system for the current market conditions.

FIGURE 4.13:
5 X 20 MOVING AVERAGE MARKET CONDITIONS FILTER

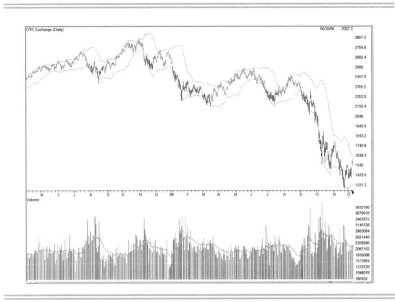

FIGURE 4.14:
DVRETRACE RESULTS USING 5 X 20 MARKET CONDITIONS
FILTER DURING 2002-2008

TriggeredDVretrace

		Winners	Losers	Neutral
Number of trades in test:	913	543	367	3
Average periods per trade:	4.42	4.63	4.11	5.00
Maximum Profit/Loss:		47.68%	(68.99)%	
Average Drawdown:	(3.22)%	(1.04)%	(6.49)%	
Average Profit/Loss:	1.49%	5.95%	(5.00)%	
Average SPX Profit/Loss	1.34%	2.74%	(0.73)%	
Probability:		59.47%	40.20%	
Average Annual ROI:	122.88%	469.05%	(452.22)%	
Annual SPX (Buy & Hold):	(2.69)%			
Reward/Risk Ratio:	1.73			
Start test date:	01/02/02			
End test date:	12/31/08			

Interval:Daily
Pricing Summary
       Entry price: [Open]
       Exit price: [Open]
Exit Summary
       Hold for 3 periods

Courtesy of AIQ

Retracements in Downtrending Stocks • 165

DVRETRACE SUMMARY

The DVretrace system is an interesting trading system in bearish market conditions and should not be used in bullish or trading range markets. The definition of the DVretrace system is outlined below, and an example DVretrace trade is shown in Figure 4.15.

A DVretrace occurs if:

- The stock is in a downtrend, defined as when the highest close in the last two weeks is lower than the lowest close of the previous month, and
- There are three consecutive days of higher lows, and
- There are three consecutive days of lower volume, and
- The close is greater than $5, and
- The 21-day simple average of the volume is greater than 200,000.

A trigger occurs if:

- Today's low is less than yesterday's low.

If a DVretrace occurred yesterday and a trigger occurs today, then

- Short at the open tomorrow.
- Hold for three days. Day one is the entry day; then hold two more days, and
- Buy to cover at the next open.

I use the three-day holding period as a guideline. Market conditions should also affect the exit strategy. When the market approaches support, the lower Bollinger band, or a trend line, consider taking profits on most positions.

Results are improved by only taking trades that have a stock price above $25 on the trigger day. I use this information to help prioritize potential trades when the scan presents multiple opportunities on the same day. Other factors that should be considered in prioritizing trades include the distance between the entry point and the initial stop loss, the distance to the lower Bollinger band, the distance to the recent low, and the distance the market has to its next support area.

Courtesy of AIQ

Traders can use their own observation of the market to determine if conditions are suitable for DVretrace. They can also use the 5 x 20 moving average filter to identify bearish markets for using DVretrace. Finally, traders can use market trend lines to determine if bearish conditions exist and then use DVretrace when the market is trading below a descending trend line.

CHAPTER 4 SELF-TEST

1. **Results for trading retracements in downtrending stocks can be improved by:**

    A. Trading stocks with increasing volume on the trigger day.

    B. Trading stocks with decreased volume on the trigger day.

    C. Trigger day volume does not strongly affect results of this system.

    D. Trading stocks with above average volume on the trigger day.

2. **Results for trading retracements in downtrending stocks can be improved by:**

    A. Trading higher volume stocks.

    B. Trading lower volume stocks.

    C. Trading higher priced stocks.

    D. Trading lower priced stocks.

3. **Results for trading retracements in downtrending stocks can be improved by:**

    A. Trading during bullish market conditions.

    B. Trading during bearish market conditions.

    C. Trading during trading range market conditions.

    D. Trading without reference to market conditions.

4. **The system for trading retracements in downtrending stocks:**

    A. Produces roughly the same number of trading opportunities each day.

    B. Produces roughly the same number of trading opportunities each month.

    C. Produces more trading opportunities in bearish markets.

    D. Produces more trading opportunities in bullish markets.

5. **Results for trading retracements in downtrending stocks can be improved by:**

    A. Trading when the NASDAQ 5MA is above the NASDAQ 20MA.

    B. Trading when the NASDAQ 5MA is below the NASDAQ 20MA.

    C. Trading when the NASDAQ is below an ascending trend line.

    D. Trading without reference to the NASDAQ.

6. **An appropriate exit strategy for trading retracements in downtrending stocks is:**

    A. Hold for three days, then consider closing.

    B. Hold for two weeks, then consider closing.

    C. Close when you think it is time.

    D. Close when the news on CNBC is strongly negative.

7. **Factors to consider when prioritizing multiple trading opportunities:**

    A. Price of the stock

    B. Distance between entry point and initial stop loss

    C. Distance between entry point and next resistance area

    D. Distance between entry point and lower Bollinger band

    E. All of the above

    F. None of the above

FOR THE ANSWERS,
VISIT WWW.TRADERSLIBRARY.COM/TLECORNER.

CHAPTER 5

ACCUMULATION BOTTOMING PATTERNS

Most stocks do not stay in uptrends or downtrends forever. At some point they reverse direction and head the other way. In addition to having multiple tools for trading trending stocks, traders should have a few tools for trading stocks that may be bottoming. One technique to identify potential bottoming candidates is to look for stocks that have significant accumulation around the lows.

Accumulation occurs if the stock is up on volume larger than the previous day. Strong accumulation occurs if the volume bar is significantly above average on an accumulation day. Figure 5.1 shows a stock that has been in a clear downtrend. Around the lows on the chart, it is showing several significant accumulation days as marked by the arrows on the volume chart. My system colors volume days differently depending on whether the day is up or down; it is easier to recognize important volume patterns this way. I would recommend using a system that has this capability.

FIGURE 5.1:
EXAMPLE OF AN ACCUMULATION PATTERN

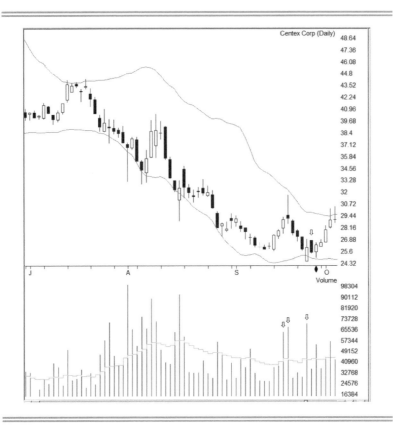

Courtesy of AIQ

Remember, volume is a measure of the interest in a stock. Interesting trading systems can be developed by looking for changes in the volume pattern. It is not the actual volume number that matters. It is more the change in the volume. A change in volume indicates a change in interest, and since stocks are sold at auction, a change in interest can lead to a change in price.

Figure 5.2 shows a price decline in ICF during May and June. The price decline came on relatively low volume with few large volume bar days. In the beginning of July, ICF started showing volume that was generally twice the volume of the previous two months. In mid-July, ICF started showing significant volume accumulation days, which were followed by a change in direction and a ten-point jump in the price.

The doubling of the volume in early July indicated that as the price of ICF came down, there was a lot more interest in ICF. By mid-June, the strong accumulation days indicated that a lot of people were willing to pick up shares at higher prices.

FIGURE 5.2:
CHANGE IN VOLUME PATTERN LEADS TO A CHANGE IN PRICE

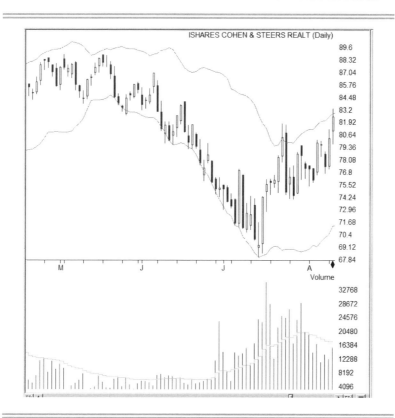

Courtesy of AIQ

AVBOTTOM DEFINITION

As we have seen in this book, a few examples and an explanation are interesting, but they prove nothing. Testing this concept will give us a better idea of how real it is, and whether or not it is practical to use as a trading tool. In order to test an accumulation pattern, we need to start with a clear definition, as outlined below. We will call this potential trading system AVBottom, and there are three parts to the system.

Strong accumulation occurs if:

- Today's close is greater than yesterday's close, and
- Today's volume is more than 150 percent of the 21-day simple moving average of the volume.

AVBottom occurs if:

- Today's close is greater than $5, and
- Average volume is greater than 200,000, and
- At least three of the last ten sessions have shown strong accumulation, and
- Today's close is less than the lowest value in the previous 200 days, starting five days ago.

Entry and Exit Strategy:

- When an AVBottom occurs, a position is entered at the next open, held for four days, and then sold at the following open. The entry is day one of the four-day holding period.

The first part of the AVBottom definition involves defining strong accumulation, which occurs if the stock is up on the day and the volume is more than 150 percent of the 21-day simple moving average of the volume. An example of strong accumulation is shown in Figure 5.3. The large volume bars marked by the arrows are days when the stock closed up for the day and the volume each day was at least 150 percent of the average volume.

Some people think that a stock has a certain intrinsic value. It reminds me of one of my neighbors who was always talking about what his house was worth. I told him the house, like a stock, is only worth what someone is willing to pay for it, and you do not know the value until you try to sell. He believed that real estate went up every year because it was just worth more. He had a different opinion by the middle of 2009 after the housing crash, when he found out no one was interested in buying the house and it did not matter much what he thought it was worth. Stocks, like houses, are only worth what someone is willing to pay for them; and volume measures the interest in the auction process.

FIGURE 5.3:
EXAMPLE OF STRONG ACCUMULATION

Courtesy of AIQ

The second part of the AVBottom system defines the occurrence of an AVBottom pattern as when three of the last ten sessions have shown strong accumulation, and the close is near a year low for the closing value, defined as being the lowest close in the previous 200 days, starting five days ago. A simple price/volume filter weeds out stocks with low prices and low volume as they may be difficult to enter and exit efficiently. An example of this AVBottom pattern is shown in Figure 5.4—the three large volume bars in December constitute strong accumulation and the closing price is the lowest value in a year.

Note that we are not looking for the lowest close in a calendar year, just the lowest close in the previous 200 trading sessions, which is a year period. Also the look-back period for the year starts five days previous to the current day, so the actual close may or may not be the actual low for the previous year. The five-day look-back period gives a little wiggle room for the stock. It will be near a year low but does not have to be exactly the year low.

The third part to the AVBottom system is the entry and exit strategy. The approach is simple and straight-forward. When an AVBottom pattern has occurred, a position is entered at the next session's open, held for four days, and then closed at the following day's open. The entry day counts as day one of the four-day holding period. An example of the entry and exit for an AVBottom pattern is shown in Figure 5.5.

In Figure 5.5, the AVBottom pattern is completed on October 23, which is marked by the down arrow on the price chart. The three days of strong volume accumulation that occurred in the ten days previous to October 23 are marked by down arrows on the volume chart. The day after the completion of the AVBottom pattern, a position is entered at the open, which is marked by the first up arrow on the price chart. The entry day is day one of the four-day holding period, which ends with the black candlestick. After the four-day holding period, the position is exited at the next session's open, which is marked by the right-most up arrow on the price chart of Figure 5.5. The entry price was about $9.15 and the exit price was about $10.48, which means a 14 percent gain in four days. Fourteen percent in four days is a nice gain!

Figure 5.6 shows another example of an AVBottom pattern with the three strong accumulation days marked by down arrows on the volume chart and

FIGURE 5.4:
STRONG ACCUMULATION NEAR A ONE-YEAR LOW

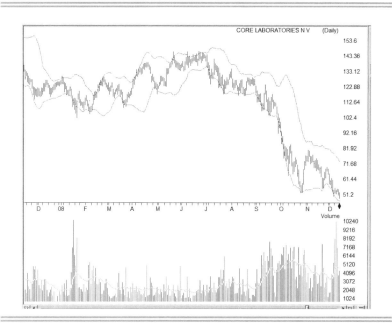

FIGURE 5.5:
AVBOTTOM PATTERN ENTRY AND EXIT

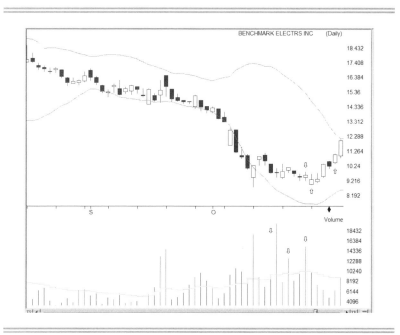

Courtesy of AIQ

the entry marked on the price chart. After the entry, KBH showed a strong move to the upper Bollinger band.

Courtesy of AIQ

INITIAL TESTING OF AVBOTTOM

Using the AVBottom definition and AIQ Systems Expert Design Studio, I ran an initial test of the AVBottom idea during calendar 2007 to see if the idea had merit. I picked 2007 for the initial test because it was a period that included both bullish and bearish runs. If the results are promising, then it is worth investing time in further testing. If the results are negative, then I will move on to other ideas. The results of testing the AVBottom scan during 2007 are shown in Figure 5.7.

The backtest found 250 trades during 2007. Taking all the trades resulted in an annualized ROI of 108 percent, which handily beat the overall market's return. Annualized ROI can be misleading for a variety of reasons. It is not the return you are most likely to see in the account. I use annualized ROI more as a figure of merit, and more is usually better. The key numbers I focus on are the percentage of winning trades and the difference between the average winning trade and the average losing trade. If I win more often than I lose, and I gain more on average with winning trades than I lose on average with losing trades, then the system has potential.

During 2007, AVBottom showed winning trades 61 percent of the time, and the average profit from winning trades was 5.4 percent compared to an average loss of 4.16 percent. These results are clearly interesting and indicate that it is worth investigating AVBottom further. I never trade a system based on one test, or a set of statistics. I am looking to fully examine a system until I clearly understand how it behaves. I want it to be a comfortable fit, like an old pair of jeans. I want to understand what the statistics mean and what to expect, and how different filters and changes in parameters affect the system before using it. Never trade something you do not fully understand.

FIGURE 5.7:
AVBOTTOM INITIAL TEST RESULTS DURING 2007

AVBottom		Winners	Losers	Neutral
Number of trades in test:	250	153	97	0
Average periods per trade:	5.66	5.68	5.64	0.00
Maximum Profit/Loss:		19.35%	(26.00)%	
Average Drawdown:	(2.79)%	(1.11)%	(5.45)%	
Average Profit/Loss:	1.69%	5.40%	(4.16)%	
Average SPX Profit/Loss	(0.31)%	0.27%	(1.23)%	
Probability:		61.20%	38.80%	
Average Annual ROI:	108.83%	346.95%	(269.48)%	
Annual SPX (Buy & Hold):	2.05%			
Reward/Risk Ratio:	2.05			
Start test date:	01/02/07			
End test date:	12/31/07			

Interval:Daily
Pricing Summary
　　　　Entry price: [Open]
　　　　Exit price: [Open]
Exit Summary
　　　　Hold for 4 periods

Courtesy of AIQ

AVBOTTOM PATTERN WITH STRONG DISTRIBUTION DAYS

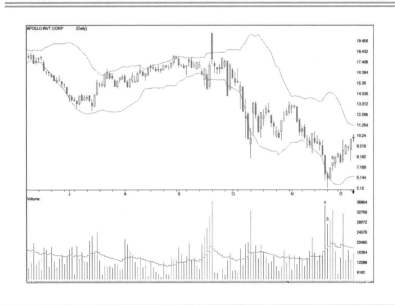

Courtesy of AIQ

EFFECT OF DISTRIBUTION DAYS ON AVBOTTOM RESULTS

The AVBottom scan looks for strong accumulation days and does not consider whether or not there is also strong distribution mixed in. One obvious question is, "Does the system perform better if strong distribution days are limited or eliminated?" A strong distribution day occurs when the stock is down on the day and the volume is larger than 150 percent of the average. An example of an AVBottom pattern with strong distribution days is shown in Figure 5.8. Note the large volume down days mixed in with the large volume up days during the past ten sessions.

Since volume measures the interest, or strength, of a move, it is logical to assume that moves with strong accumulation and without strong distribution may be more profitable. Remember, it is not what you think, or guess, or feel, or want, or need that counts. Trade what is real and proven. Rather than just filtering out AVBottom trades with strong distribution days because it sounded logical, I tested the idea. I always test new ideas, no matter how obvious they sound. This has saved me on many an occasion.

My oldest daughter is a mom with two young children. The kids often come to her with ideas that seem great to them. However, my daughter's experience helps her filter out ideas and activities that sound good to the kids but may not be appropriate for them. Her experience helps keep the kids out of trouble. Her willingness to use her experience to guide the kids keeps them from harm and helps them understand what is and is not appropriate. Like my daughter's experience and guidance, backtesting ideas before trading them helps keep traders from following paths that may not be appropriate for them.

Figure 5.9 shows the results of testing AVBottom during the 2007 initial test period with an added filter that limits strong distribution days to three or less in the last ten trading sessions. Limiting the strong distribution days increases the annualized ROI from 108 to 128 percent and also increases the percentage of winning trades from 61 percent to 63 percent. The results of limiting strong distribution days to three or less are interesting, but not dramatic. Given all the variables in trading, a two percent pop in the winning percentage rate could be washed out by other factors. Not that I would pass on an additional two percent; it is just that it is not yet exciting.

When testing a potential trading system, I want to use backtesting to gain an understanding of how the system performs and what filters and parameter changes affect the results most strongly. If a filter changes the percentage of winning trades by one or two percent, I will generally leave it out of the system because it reduces the number of potential trading opportunities, and the success of a trading pattern can be strongly influenced by market conditions and how close the next resistance level is. Rather than bump the winning percentage by just one or two percent with a filter, I want to see the additional trading opportunities and select the ones that have more room to run before they encounter a significant resistance area.

AVBOTTOM 2007 RESULTS AFTER
ELIMINATING STRONG DISTRIBUTION DAYS

AVBottom		Winners	Losers	Neutral
Number of trades in test:	197	124	73	0
Average periods per trade:	5.63	5.65	5.60	0.00
Maximum Profit/Loss:		19.35%	(30.53)%	
Average Drawdown:	(2.60)%	(1.00)%	(5.33)%	
Average Profit/Loss:	1.98%	5.67%	(4.27)%	
Average SPX Profit/Loss	0.01%	0.63%	(1.04)%	
Probability:		62.94%	37.06%	
Average Annual ROI:	128.58%	365.83%	(278.05)%	
Annual SPX (Buy & Hold):	2.05%			
Reward/Risk Ratio:	2.26			
Start test date:	01/02/07			
End test date:	12/31/07			

Interval:Daily
Pricing Summary
       Entry price: [Open]
       Exit price: [Open]
Exit Summary
       Hold for 4 periods

Courtesy of AIQ

There is nothing magic about limiting the number of strong distribution days to three or less. I am more interested in general principles than just rote statistics. At this point we know that the AVBottom system has promise and that restricting the number of strong distribution days to three or less helps the test results in our initial test period. That is a statistic. What I want to know is whether or not there is a general principle that I can apply when looking at potential trades. For example, if reducing the number of strong distribution days improves results, and fewer strong distribution days yield better results, then I have a general principle that I can use to prioritize multiple trading opportunities.

EFFECT OF "ROOM TO RUN" ON
AVBOTTOM TEST RESULTS

For obvious reasons, topping and bottoming pattern trading opportunities tend to be more available when the market is turning from bullish to bearish, or bearish to bullish. There are generally fewer trading opportunities for these patterns when the market is in a trading range.

When the market conditions are changing, this means more opportunities than I may be willing to trade, so I need proven ways to prioritize. I use the general principles developed from backtesting, along with data from testing different filters, as part of the prioritization process. I also look at the distance between my entry point and the next resistance level for the stock, which is one measure of potential profit. I also consider the risk in the trade, which is the difference between my entry price and the placement of my initial stop loss order.

Figure 5.10 shows an AVBottom pattern that occurred in TCO in late November. When the pattern was fully formed on November 24, 2008, the stock had retraced a bit and was just under horizontal resistance from the recent lows of November 12 and October 28. TCO meets all the conditions of the AVBottom scan, but I passed on the trade because it formed just under horizontal resistance (as shown by the line in Figure 5.10). In this case, the TCO trade lost money because the stock bumped into the horizontal resistance area marked on the chart and then followed the normal pattern and retraced.

FIGURE 5.10:
AVBOTTOM PATTERN IN TCO WITH LITTLE ROOM TO RUN

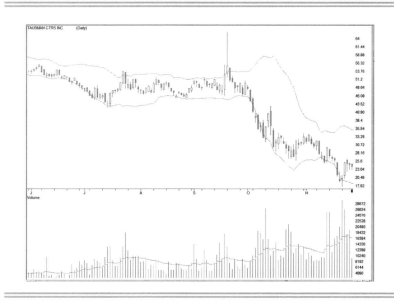

Courtesy of AIQ

Figure 5.11 shows an AVBottom pattern that occurred in MOV in mid-December of 2008. In this case, the AVBottom in MOV formed well below horizontal resistance from the recent low in late November. From the place where the AVBottom pattern formed, there was room for MOV to run up about 20 percent before hitting the horizontal resistance area, as marked on the chart.

When I run the AVBottom scan and I see patterns forming close to resistance, like TCO in Figure 5.10, I pass on the opportunity. I look for substantial opportunity like the kind seen in Figure 5.11.

FIGURE 5.11:
AVBOTTOM PATTERN IN MOV WITH SIGNIFICANT ROOM TO RUN

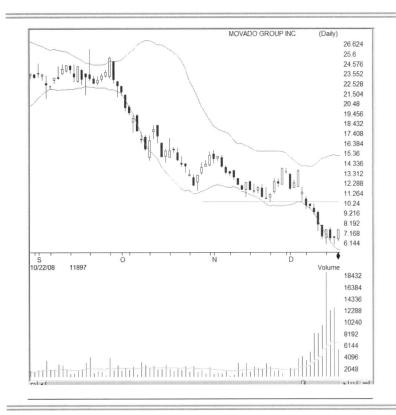

Courtesy of AIQ

I do not take trades just because they come up on a scan; I look at the overall picture including market conditions and room to run before deciding whether or not to take a position.

Limiting the strong distribution days to three or less during the formation of the AVBottom pattern improved results. Is our general principle that less distribution equals better results? I ran the test once more during the 2007 initial test period with a filter limiting the strong distribution days to two or less. The results are shown in Figure 5.12.

Limiting the strong distribution days to two or less during the formation of the AVBottom pattern significantly improved results, not only from the unfiltered scan, but as compared to the filter that limited strong distribution to three days or less. As shown in Figure 5.12, the annualized ROI increased from 108 to 188 and the percentage of winning trades increased from 61 percent to 69 percent. Fewer strong distribution days seem to yield better results. It sounds logical, but now there are test results to back it up.

Myth: Limiting strong distribution days during the formation of the AVBottom will significantly improve results.

Fact: While it sounds logical, we can't know for sure until we test it. In this case, our second test did indeed prove that the myth was true—limiting strong distribution days to two or less significantly improved the results of the AVBottom pattern.

AVBOTTOM PATTERN WITH TWO OR FEWER
STRONG DISTRIBUTION DAYS

AVBottom

		Winners	Losers	Neutral
Number of trades in test:	167	116	51	0
Average periods per trade:	5.58	5.59	5.57	0.00
Maximum Profit/Loss:		19.35%	(13.44)%	
Average Drawdown:	(2.26)%	(0.97)%	(5.18)%	
Average Profit/Loss:	2.89%	5.86%	(3.88)%	
Average SPX Profit/Loss	0.14%	0.64%	(0.98)%	
Probability:		69.46%	30.54%	
Average Annual ROI:	188.77%	383.11%	(254.64)%	
Annual SPX (Buy & Hold):	2.05%			
Reward/Risk Ratio:	3.43			
Start test date:	01/02/07			
End test date:	12/31/07			

Interval:Daily
Pricing Summary
        Entry price: [Open]
        Exit price: [Open]
Exit Summary
        Hold for 4 periods

TEST RESULTS FOR REDUCING THE DISTRIBUTION DAY VOLUME
REQUIREMENT TO 120 PERCENT OF AVERAGE

AVBottom

		Winners	Losers	Neutral
Number of trades in test:	920	533	383	4
Average periods per trade:	5.70	5.70	5.70	5.50
Maximum Profit/Loss:		33.77%	(29.48)%	
Average Drawdown:	(2.64)%	(1.00)%	(4.96)%	
Average Profit/Loss:	1.07%	4.78%	(4.08)%	
Average SPX Profit/Loss	(0.10)%	0.45%	(0.86)%	
Probability:		57.93%	41.63%	
Average Annual ROI:	68.51%	305.85%	(260.90)%	
Annual SPX (Buy & Hold):	2.05%			
Reward/Risk Ratio:	1.63			
Start test date:	01/02/07			
End test date:	12/31/07			

Interval:Daily
Pricing Summary
        Entry price: [Open]
        Exit price: [Open]
Exit Summary
        Hold for 4 periods

Courtesy of AIQ

TESTING THE DEFINITION OF STRONG ACCUMULATION

The testing to this point has used the definition of strong accumulation as a pattern having volume of at least 150 percent of the average volume. Nothing should be taken for granted, so this definition also needs to be tested. If the definition of strong accumulation is relaxed to be an up day that occurs on volume of at least 120 percent of the 21-day simple moving average of the volume, we get the results shown in Figure 5.13. The annualized ROI is reduced from 108 to 68 and the percentage of winning trades drops from 61 percent to 58 percent.

Since volume measures the interest in a stock, it is not surprising that lower volume accumulation days yield lower profits. Strong volume patterns show significant interest in a stock, and lots of interest often leads to good trading results.

Experienced traders learn to pay as much or more attention to the volume pattern as they do the price patterns. It is often not the absolute magnitude of the volume that is helpful, but the change in the volume pattern that is important. Some stocks trade at much higher average volume levels than others. This does not imply that they will be the best trades. We are looking for when the pattern changes because that's when something new or interesting is going on. In the case of the AVBottom pattern, the large up days on volume one and a half times average indicate that there is increasing interest in the stock at higher prices. More people are willing to pay more for the stock. This indicates that there is increasing demand as prices rise, and that is usually a good thing.

We learned that reducing the volume requirement for strong accumulation decreased results. We need to see what the effect is when we increase the volume requirement in the definition of strong accumulation. Figure 5.14 shows the results of running the AVBottom backtest again, only this time we increased the strong accumulation volume requirement from 150 percent of average to 170 percent of average.

Let's apply this model to the housing crash of 2008. It was driven in part by the government programs and regulations that required banks to lend to poor credit risks. Over the years a lot of bad loans were made and the banks moved to derivatives to hedge the bad loans.

Congress was warned about this for years. Yet, when the system collapsed, Congress blamed it on "too little regulation" when it was their regulations that contributed to the problem in the first place. If traders act like congressmen and put the blame for their decisions on someone else, they too will fail. Traders need to be truth seekers. They need to be responsible for their decisions and learn from them. They need to research techniques and find out what really works and not trade on fantasies of how they would like things to work.

The increased volume requirement improved the annualized ROI from 108 to 111 and increased the percentage of winning trades from 61 percent to 63 percent. The results are interesting, but not dramatic. Based on these results, I will use the original 150 percent definition, but when presented with more trading opportunities than I can take, I will look toward the ones with the stronger volume bars.

EFFECT OF STOCK PRICE ON AVBOTTOM TEST RESULTS

Another part of the AVBottom pattern that needs to be tested is the $5 minimum stock price. I typically start testing a new system using a filter for a $5 minimum stock price and a 200,000 share minimum average daily trading volume. These filters come from experience and generally keep me out of stock positions that can be hard to close effectively when things are moving rapidly. Some trading systems, however, are sensitive to price or average volume, so we need to look at whether or not this is the case with AVBottom.

EFFECT OF INCREASING STRONG ACCUMULATION VOLUME
REQUIREMENT TO 170 PERCENT OF AVERAGE

AVBottom		Winners	Losers	Neutral
Number of trades in test:	110	69	41	0
Average periods per trade:	5.72	5.84	5.51	0.00
Maximum Profit/Loss:		16.61%	(26.00)%	
Average Drawdown:	(3.02)%	(1.40)%	(5.76)%	
Average Profit/Loss:	1.74%	5.51%	(4.60)%	
Average SPX Profit/Loss	(0.60)%	(0.29)%	(1.11)%	
Probability:		62.73%	37.27%	
Average Annual ROI:	111.16%	344.18%	(304.35)%	
Annual SPX (Buy & Hold):	2.05%			
Reward/Risk Ratio:	2.02			
Start test date:	01/02/07			
End test date:	12/31/07			

Interval:Daily
Pricing Summary
        Entry price: [Open]
        Exit price: [Open]
Exit Summary
        Hold for 4 periods

Courtesy of AIQ

Figure 5.15 shows the effect of increasing the minimum stock price requirement in the AVBottom scan from $5 to $25. During the 2007 initial test period, the annualized ROI increased from 108 to 129 and the percentage of winning trades increases from 61 percent to 65 percent. These improvements come at the cost of reducing the number of trades from 250 to 115.

At a recent trading conference, I was discussing these results with a group of traders and one of them asked, "Why does the AVBottom pattern work better on the higher-priced stocks?" It is an interesting question and I could have come up with several good theories as to why. It may be that higher-dollar stocks are ones that have more interest from the fund managers and so when they start them moving, they keep going. When I mentioned this idea, the trader was quite happy and felt he better understood the system.

The interesting thing is that backtesting can give you an understanding of what has worked, but the statistics provide no insight into the specific

EFFECT OF INCREASING MINIMUM STOCK PRICE TO $25

AVBottom

		Winners	Losers	Neutral
Number of trades in test:	115	75	40	0
Average periods per trade:	5.64	5.64	5.65	0.00
Maximum Profit/Loss:		17.29%	(14.11)%	
Average Drawdown:	(2.11)%	(0.94)%	(4.31)%	
Average Profit/Loss:	2.01%	4.86%	(3.34)%	
Average SPX Profit/Loss	(0.29)%	0.42%	(1.61)%	
Probability:		65.22%	34.78%	
Average Annual ROI:	129.81%	314.30%	(215.51)%	
Annual SPX (Buy & Hold):	2.05%			
Reward/Risk Ratio:	2.73			
Start test date:	01/02/07			
End test date:	12/31/07			

Interval:Daily
Pricing Summary
       Entry price: [Open]
       Exit price: [Open]
Exit Summary
       Hold for 4 periods

Courtesy of AIQ

reasons why. To an experienced trader, the reason really does not matter. We are looking at what works, whether or not it is repeatable, how often it works, and in what market conditions it works best. The trader at the conference was reassured by a reason for the results that made sense to him. He was not reassured by the test data; he needed something else that made him feel better.

I have seen traders at trading seminars listen to a presentation of a carefully analyzed trading system and then get really interested in trading it. A few hours later, they hear a presentation promising fantastic returns, no losses, and the path to quick riches, without any solid data other than good presentation skills. The inexperienced trader is then excited about the new fantastic system because he wants to believe it, not because there is any evidence that it really works. In the trading business, greed can get you killed.

This approach to trading often leads to trouble because when someone else comes along with a different opinion or a new system that sounds good, the trader is likely to follow it since he is seeking something that "sounds good." Trading is not about trying to feel good. The market really does not care about our feelings. Traders need to focus on understanding what works and how it works and leave the philosophical stuff to others. Traders need to be data driven and make decisions based on what usually happens. Why it happens may be interesting, but you need to focus on the "what," not the "why."

I trade systems that have been shown to be clearly effective in the past. This does not guarantee any future profits whatsoever, but I would much rather trade something that backtested well over something with no data and lots of hype. It is interesting, though, that many people prefer the hype. It is amazing to me how many people will work most of their life to get some savings put together and then either invest it with a money manager who has a great commercial or a trading system that sounds fantastic. The money represents your time. It represents your life. No one cares more about your money than you do. Do your own research and fully and completely understand the method before trading it.

The other time I see this intense desire to try the magic trading system is with people who have not planned for retirement and all of a sudden realize that they only have five years to build a nest egg. They then want to invest using the magic trading system they saw advertised. Two wrong decisions do not make a right one. I have seen presentations and advertisements for systems that promise 200 percent, 300 percent, and even 500 percent returns on most trades with few losing trades. People line up because they like what they hear. Reality is another matter.

Think about it! Start with a $50,000 account and make a trade a week with a 200 percent return. At the end of the first week, you made $100,000 profit and still have the original $50,000 for a balance of $150,000. At the end of the second week, the balance is $450,000. At the end of the third week the balance is $1,350,000. At the end of the first month, the balance is four million dollars. At the end of the second month, the balance is over $300 million! At the end of the fourth month, the account has grown to over $26 billion. If that system were true, you would go from Joe Average to Bill Gates in just four months. I have seen people actually get excited about this and start thinking about yachts! There are no examples of someone actually doing this, so please don't fall for the hype. Focus on understanding how trading really works and do not trade until you clearly understand your system and the risks.

EFFECT OF MINIMUM AVERAGE VOLUME ON AVBOTTOM RESULTS

There are some systems that work better on large volume stocks than small volume ones. I checked to see if AVBottom was one of them by running the test again with a filter that increased the minimum average volume requirement from 200,000 to 500,000. The results of running the test in the 2007 initial test period are shown in Figure 5.16.

FIGURE 5.16:
EFFECT OF INCREASING MINIMUM AVERAGE VOLUME TO 500,000

AVBottom		Winners	Losers	Neutral
Number of trades in test:	161	100	60	1
Average periods per trade:	5.59	5.64	5.53	4.00
Maximum Profit/Loss:		19.35%	(26.00)%	
Average Drawdown:	(2.67)%	(1.19)%	(5.17)%	
Average Profit/Loss:	1.90%	5.40%	(3.90)%	
Average SPX Profit/Loss	(0.24)%	0.30%	(1.14)%	
Probability:		62.11%	37.27%	
Average Annual ROI:	123.99%	349.38%	(257.42)%	
Annual SPX (Buy & Hold):	2.05%			
Reward/Risk Ratio:	2.31			
Start test date:	01/02/07			
End test date:	12/31/07			

Interval:Daily
Pricing Summary
        Entry price: [Open]
        Exit price: [Open]
Exit Summary
        Hold for 4 periods

Courtesy of AIQ

As shown in Figure 5.16, increasing the minimum average volume requirement produces marginal improvements. The annualized ROI increases from 108 to 123 and the percentage of winning trades increases from 61 percent to 62 percent. This is not enough of an improvement to be worth incorporating into the system, or to use in prioritizing among multiple trading opportunities. Increasing the minimum stock price from $5 to $25 yielded better results than increasing the accumulation volume requirement from 150 percent to 170 percent or increasing the minimum average volume requirement from 200,000 to 500,000. Based on this data, I will use the stock price as one of the factors to help prioritize among multiple trading opportunities and will not pay attention to the other factors noted above.

AVBOTTOM TEST RESULTS SUMMARY

A summary of the results of testing different filters is outlined below. This information helps me to determine what to look for when selecting AVBottom trades.

AVBottom results are improved if:

- Minimum stock price is increased from $5 to $25.
- Strong distribution days are limited to two or less in the last ten days.

AVBottom results are reduced if:

- Strong accumulation volume drops from 150 percent to 120 percent of average volume.

AVBottom results are marginally affected by:

- Increasing minimum average volume requirement.
- Increasing strong accumulation volume above 150 percent.
- Limiting strong distribution days to three or less.

AVBOTTOM PERFORMANCE IN THREE-YEAR TEST

AVBottom

		Winners	Losers	Neutral
Number of trades in test:	374	223	149	2
Average periods per trade:	5.67	5.68	5.65	6.00
Maximum Profit/Loss:		19.82%	(26.00)%	
Average Drawdown:	(2.62)%	(0.93)%	(5.19)%	
Average Profit/Loss:	1.22%	4.78%	(4.08)%	
Average SPX Profit/Loss	(0.11)%	0.43%	(0.91)%	
Probability:		59.63%	39.84%	
Average Annual ROI:	78.84%	306.92%	(263.25)%	
Annual SPX (Buy & Hold):	7.26%			
Reward/Risk Ratio:	1.75			
Start test date:	01/03/05			
End test date:	12/28/07			

Interval:Daily
Pricing Summary
       Entry price: [Open]
       Exit price: [Open]
Exit Summary
       Hold for 4 periods

Courtesy of AIQ

AVBOTTOM LONGER TIME PERIOD TEST RESULTS

Before considering a trading system, I need to have a clear idea of how it performs in longer time periods. I need to test the system in longer time periods to see if there was something special about the initial test period. We don't want a system that works great in just 2007, because we cannot trade in 2007! I ran a test of AVBottom during the three-year period from the beginning of January 2005 through the end of December in 2007, and the results are shown in Figure 5.17.

Tripling the testing time period increased the number of trades. If it didn't, then we may have found a system that was based on some specific events during 2007. Tripling the time period also resulted in an annualized ROI of 78 instead of the 108 we saw for the 2007 test. Again, I use annualized ROI as a figure of merit, and the number for both tests is better than buy and hold, which is what I am looking for more than any specific number. The three-year test period shows that the percentage of winning trades dropped by one percentage point as compared to the 2007 test. This indicates that even in two different time periods, we are seeing about the same percentage of winning trades.

Some people continue this process by testing in a five-year period and then a ten-year period. There is nothing wrong with that but it does not say much for using the system. Are the next three years going to be like the last three years? Take a look at a 20-year chart of the NASDAQ and it is tough to find similar consecutive five-year periods. The market is changing, and one time period is not like the next. I know that mutual funds quote returns in one-, five-, and ten-year periods and so many people think it is important. Why?

Ten-year returns can easily mask a couple of trying down years. Five-year returns can easily mask a couple of down years that may have caused investors to change strategies. The advice to "hold for the long run" generally comes from people taking a percentage of your account every quarter! Of course they want you to stay invested and hold on during bear markets.

While time periods may not repeat in the future, whatever the market decides to do, it will consist of bullish, bearish, and trading range periods. Because of my methodology, I know by looking at the current market conditions whether or not I should use a particular system.

When I go to trading conferences, there are always people who want to know how I did last year, or how one of my trading systems did last year. Every once in awhile I meet a trader who wants to know how I did during the last bullish environment or how I handled the recent trading range. When I meet the guy or girl talking about market environments, I know I have found a real trader, and it is worth spending some time talking about tools and techniques. When I meet the traders focused on annual returns, I generally make polite small talk and move on.

AVBOTTOM MARKET CONDITION TEST RESULTS

Table 5.1 shows the results of testing AVBottom in six different bullish market periods. The percentage of winning trades is above 54 percent in five of the six bullish periods tested, and the average winning percentage of the six bull market periods is 58 percent. The annualized ROI is positive in all six bullish periods and above 100 in half of the periods tested. AVBottom looks like an interesting tool for consideration during bullish market periods.

Note that the percentage of winning trades varies from 48 to 64 percent. This helps traders understand what to expect when using AVBottom. Neither AVBottom nor any other trading system gives the same winning percentage every week, every month, every year, and in every bullish market. The winning percentage varies between markets, but over the long run it looks interesting. This testing tells us nothing about what will happen with any particular trade, or any group of trades.

TABLE 5.1
AVBOTTOM TEST RESULTS IN BULLISH MARKET PERIODS

TEST PERIOD TRADES	MARKET TYPE	WINNING %	ANNUALIZED ROI	# OF TRADES
08/13/04-12/31/04	Bull	47.6%	79%	21
07/21/06-11/24/06	Bull	64.54	109	31
03/14/07-07/20/07	Bull	60.0	20	15
08/17/07-10/09/07	Bull	61.2	178	31
03/17/08-06/05/08	Bull	54.5	117	44
07/16/08-08/18/08	Bull	61.5	40	26

Some traders are obsessed with finding out why a trade did not work; they think they did something wrong, or that there is another indicator that will filter out bad trades. Don't be this type of trader. Trading is a statistical business in which there is no way to know if any particular trade will be profit-

TABLE 5.2
AVBOTTOM TEST RESULTS IN BEARISH MARKET PERIODS

TEST PERIOD TRADES	MARKET TYPE	WINNING %	ANNUALIZED ROI	# OF TRADES
01/04/02-10/04/02	Bear	64.2%	165%	67
01/23/04-08/13/04	Bear	29.2	112	24
01/07/05-04/22/05	Bear	58.3	20	12
05/11/06-07/21/06	Bear	50.0	-109	14
07/20/07-08/17/07	Bear	53.8	54	104
06/06/08-07/15/08	Bear	23.4	-239	47

able. Traders use techniques that have shown favorable statistics, and then they focus on money management techniques to protect them from the times when a trading system shows a string of losses, as they all do. Searching for the next magic indicator will not change this. Traders must accept and understand the risks and be willing to take them.

Table 5.2 shows the results of testing AVBottom in six different bearish periods. The percentage of winning trades is 50 percent or less in half of the periods tested. Two of the bearish periods show significant losses. There are also two bearish periods in which the percentage of winning trades was 58 percent or better. It is nice that AVBottom seems to work in about a third of the bearish periods tested, but I am looking for systems that show more consistent results during the market conditions in which they will be used.

AVBottom shows poor winning percentages half of the time and that data keeps me from using the system during bearish market environments. It is not so much that AVBottom is really bad during bearish markets because it shows mixed results; it is more that there are better choices available for bearish market conditions. Again, the perfect system does not exist. What I am looking for is a tool box with tools that are the best choice for each of the three basic market conditions.

Someone usually asks how you can have a good annualized ROI when you only have winning trades 29 percent of the time, as shown on the second line. Remember, there are multiple aspects that work together to determine whether or not a trading system is profitable. The percentage of winning trades and the difference between the average winning trade and the average losing trade tell you a lot about whether or not a system may show profits.

During the first part of 2004 AVBottom only won 29 percent of the time, but the average winning trade showed significantly more profit than the average losing trade lost. If you gain on average $10 when you win and on average only lose $1 when you lose, then you can be profitable with a percentage of winning trades well under 50 percent. Looking at any one statistic can be misleading. There are some trading systems I use where I may only win a third of the time, but I can make profits because the winners on average are much larger than the losers.

Table 5.3 shows the results of testing AVBottom during five different trading range market conditions. AVBottom loses money in three of the five trading range periods tested, even though the percentage of winning trades is greater than 50 percent in all but one of the trading range periods. Once again, it is not just one statistic that defines a trading system. In this case, even though the system generally wins more often than it loses, the losses are larger than the gains on average, so the results are not favorable.

TABLE 5.3
AVBOTTOM TEST RESULTS IN TRADING RANGE MARKET PERIODS

TEST PERIOD TRADES	MARKET TYPE	WINNING %	ANNUALIZED ROI	# OF TRADES
11/25/05-05/05/06	Trading Range	53.8%	-52	13
01/05/06-05/11/06	Trading Range	53.8	-116	13
11/24/06-02/26/07	Trading Range	66.7	66	9
10/09/07-11/06/07	Trading Range	40	-170	15
01/24/08-02/28/08	Trading Range	51.0	5.6	49

AVBottom performs well in bullish markets, and poorly in bearish or trading range markets. One of the reasons for this may be that as stocks come off a bottom, they do better if the market is strong and helps to push the stocks up. It may be harder, or take more time, to come off a bottom during a trading range market when conditions are not as strong. One way to test this theory is to run the test in all the trading range market condition periods again with a longer holding time and see if the results improve.

All the AVBottom tests up to this point have used a simple four-day holding time. The results in Table 5.4 show what happens when the test is run again using an increased holding time of six days during the trading range market periods. The longer six-day holding time improves the percentage of winning trades in three of the five trading range markets and results in only one losing period instead of the three losing periods seen with the four-day holding time. Giving bottoming patterns a little more time to develop during trading range markets seems to make sense.

TABLE 5.4
AVBOTTOM RESULTS IN TRADING RANGE MARKET PERIODS, SIX-DAY HOLDING PERIOD

TEST PERIOD TRADES	MARKET TYPE	WINNING %	ANNUALIZED ROI	# OF TRADES
11/25/05-05/05/06	Trading Range	76.9%	63	13
01/05/06-05/11/06	Trading Range	60.0	17.6	10
11/24/06-02/26/07	Trading Range	55.5	52	9
10/09/07-11/06/07	Trading Range	30	-94	10
01/24/08-02/28/08	Trading Range	80.4	158	46

At this point, someone is saying, "of course the longer holding period just improves results in all three market conditions—it seems logical." As we've mentioned many times here, winning traders want to make decisions on data, not feelings, so I ran the test again and lengthened the holding time from the standard four days to six days, and then re-ran the test in each of the six bullish market periods that were used to obtain the data in Table 5.1. The results of re-testing AVBottom during the six bullish periods with the longer six-day holding time are shown in Table 5.5.

TABLE 5.5
AVBOTTOM TEST RESULTS IN BULLISH MARKET PERIODS, SIX-DAY HOLDING PERIOD

TEST PERIOD TRADES	MARKET TYPE	WINNING %	ANNUALIZED ROI
08/13/04-12/31/04	Bull	61.9%	65%
07/21/06-11/24/06	Bull	58.6	72
03/14/07-07/20/07	Bull	57.1	-9
08/17/07-10/09/07	Bull	46.7	71
03/17/08-06/05/08	Bull	56.8	19
07/16/08-08/18/08	Bull	50.0	-64

The results shown in Table 5.5 are interesting. The percentage of winning trades decreased in four of the six bullish market periods when the holding time was increased from the initial standard of four days to six days. The annualized ROI decreased in all six bullish periods tested and turned from positive to negative in two of them. Lengthening the holding time during bullish market conditions from four to six days did not help results. Lengthening the holding time during trading range markets conditions did help results.

The market is a very powerful force, and trading systems behave differently in different market conditions. We have seen that it is best to observe the current market conditions and then select a trading system appropriate for those conditions. We have also seen that the market conditions can affect the exit strategy of a trading system.

Once again, successful traders must adapt to the market.

Myth: Lengthening the holding time for a system will increase results.

Fact: For AVBottom, lengthening the holding time helped in a trading range market, but actually hurt trading results in bullish markets.

If you are interested in seeing how I adapt to current market conditions, you can request a sample of the Timely Trades Letter by sending an email to sample@daisydogger.com.

AVBOTTOM SUMMARY

The AVBottom pattern is one of the tools that I have in my trading tool box. An example of the pattern is shown in Figure 5.18, and the pattern and exit strategy are defined below.

FIGURE 5.18:
EXAMPLE AVBOTTOM PATTERN

Courtesy of AIQ

Strong accumulation occurs if:

- Today's close is greater than yesterday's close, and
- Today's volume is more than 150 percent of the 21-day simple moving average of the volume.

AVBottom occurs if:

- Today's close is greater than $5, and
- Average volume is greater than 200,000, and

- At least three of the last ten sessions have shown strong accumulation, and
- Today's close is less than the lowest value in the previous 200 days, starting five days ago.

Entry and Exit Strategy:

- When an AVBottom occurs, a position is entered at the next open, held for four days, and then sold at the following open. The entry is day one of the four-day holding period.

I consider using AVBottom during bullish markets and use the test results summarized below to help prioritize potential trades.

AVBottom results are improved if:

- Minimum stock price is increased from $5 to $25.
- Strong distribution days are limited to two or less in the last ten days.

AVBottom results are reduced if:

- Strong accumulation volume dropped from 150 percent to 120 percent of average volume.

AVBottom results are marginally affected by:

- Increasing minimum average volume requirement.
- Increasing strong accumulation volume above 150 percent.
- Limiting strong distribution days to three or less.

CHAPTER 5 SELF-TEST

1. Effective accumulation bottoming patterns involve:

    A. Two days of 150 percent of average volume in the last five sessions.

    B. Three days of 150 percent of average volume in the last five sessions.

    C. Two days of 150 percent of average volume in the last ten sessions.

    D. Three days of 150 percent of average volume in the last ten sessions.

2. Effective accumulation bottoming patterns involve:

    A. A stock near its monthly low.

    B. A stock near its annual low.

    C. A stock lower than it was 23 days ago and higher than it was five days ago.

    D. A stock setting two consecutive weekly lows.

3. The results for trading accumulation bottoming patterns can be significantly improved by:

    A. Limiting distribution days to four or more during the last ten sessions.

    B. Reducing the strong accumulation definition to 120 percent of average volume.

    C. Increasing the strong accumulation definition to 170 percent of average volume.

    D. Limiting strong distribution days to two or less during the last ten sessions.

4. What is the effect of stock price on accumulation bottom trading results?

    A. Results are best for stocks under $5.

    B. Results are best for stocks above $5.

    C. Results are best for stocks above $25.

    D. Results are best for stocks under $25.

5. What is the effect of minimum average volume on accumulation bottom trading results?

   A. Trading higher average volume stocks significantly improves results.

   B. Trading higher average volume stocks moderately improves results.

   C. Trading higher average volume stocks does not strongly improve results.

   D. Trading lower average volume stocks improves results.

FOR THE ANSWERS,
VISIT WWW.TRADERSLIBRARY.COM/TLECORNER.

DISTRIBUTION TOPPING PATTERNS

Traders need a variety of different tools in order to deal with all aspects of market behavior. Trending markets or stocks tend to run a bit, pull back, and then run some more. This type of environment often results in a number of setups for the DVpullback scan discussed in Chapter 3. Eventually runs end and the stock, or market, shows more than just a brief pullback. When the run is over, we often see distribution patterns, which can be useful in determining when it is time to exit a long position or take a short position in stocks that are topping out.

Distribution occurs when the stock is down for the day and the volume is larger than the previous day's volume. An example illustrating several distribution days is shown in Figure 6.1. The volume bar marked "1" is larger than the previous day's volume and occurred on a day when the stock was down. Similarly, the volume bars marked "2" and "3" also represent distribution days because the stock was down on those days and the volume was larger than the previous day's volume.

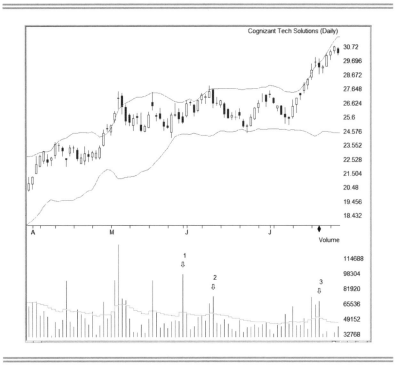

Courtesy of AIQ

In general, a day or two of distribution is not very predictive of the short-term behavior of prices. In Figure 6.1 the stock moved up following the distribution day marked "1." After the distribution day "2," the stock moved down, and then moved back up following distribution day "3." There is no direct correlation between a typical distribution day and whether or not the stock will most likely move up or down. Most single distribution days are not particularly interesting.

Multiple, strong distribution days on the other hand can indicate that fund managers are exiting the stock and hence the run may be over. A strong distribution day occurs when the stock closes down for the day and the volume is more than 150 percent of the 21-day simple moving average of the volume. It does not matter whether or not the volume is larger or smaller than the previous day; we are just looking for a down day on very strong volume.

Strong volume bars do not come from you and me trading. Our position sizes hardly make note in the volume bars. Significantly above average volume comes from either a lot more people than usual making trades or from fund managers adjusting large positions. If you are running a fund with a billion in assets and decide to take a $50 million position in a stock, it often shows up as increased volume.

AVTOP PATTERN DEFINITION

Distribution topping patterns occur when stocks have run up and then, near their highs, start showing multiple strong distribution days. The strong distribution days may indicate that funds are taking profits. Their positions are so large that their activity shows up in the volume pattern. A strong distribution pattern near a recent high is shown in Figure 6.2 where several strong distribution days, marked by the down arrows on the volume chart, occur after the stock ran up and traded around recent highs.

FIGURE 6.2:
MULTIPLE STRONG DISTRIBUTION DAYS AFTER A RUN-UP

Courtesy of AIQ

The idea of finding stocks that are topping by looking for strong distribution sounds promising, but a lot of things sound promising and do not pan out. In order to see if the idea has merit, and better understand what the key parameters are and how to trade it, we need to carefully examine the potential system using backtesting techniques.

In order to backtest a potential trading idea, we need to have a clear and specific definition of the system. Have you ever noticed how politicians will speak in generalities rather than specifics? Generalities can and will be interpreted differently by different people. By not committing to specifics, the politician can appeal to a broader base. In trading, your poll numbers will not increase with generalities. Traders need to seek the truth and a clear understanding of how things really work. In order to do this, you need to start with a clear and specific definition of a trading idea.

I call this system AVtop, and the definition is outlined below. The trading system includes not only the definition of the pattern, but the entry and exit rules as well. The first two lines in the AVTop definition limit the stocks traded to those with a current close above $5 and an average volume greater than 200,000 shares. These filters eliminate many thinly traded stocks that often have wide bid/ask spreads and may be difficult to enter or exit in a timely manner when things are moving quickly. There is no point in having a good pattern and then not being able to get in or out efficiently.

Strong distribution occurs if:

- Today's close is less than yesterday's close, and
- Today's volume is more than 150 percent of the 21-day simple moving average of the volume.

AVtop occurs if:

- Today's close is greater than $5,
- Average volume is greater than 200,000,
- At least three of the last ten sessions have shown strong distribution, and,

- Today's close is higher than the highest value in the previous 200 days, starting five days ago.

Entry and Exit Strategy:

- When an AVTop occurs, a short position is entered at the next open,
- Held for four days, then
- Sold at the following open.
- The entry is day one of the four-day holding period.

An AVtop requires that the stock has closed at the highest value in the previous 200 trading sessions (basically the last year) and that it has shown three or more strong distribution days in the last ten sessions. A strong distribution day is defined as a day in which the stock closed down on volume at least 150 percent above the average.

When an AVtop occurs, a short position is entered at the next day's open, held for four days, and then closed at the following open. The day the short position is entered is counted as day one of the four-day holding period. The system uses end-of-day data and does not require the trader to be at the computer watching charts all day.

An example AVtop pattern is shown in Figure 6.3. The strong distribution days are marked by the down arrows on the volume chart. After the third strong distribution day, a short position is entered at the next day's open (marked by the first arrow on the price chart). The position is held for four days and then closed (as marked by the second arrow on the price chart). The short position was entered on October 12, 2007 at $34.25 and closed on October 18, 2007 at $29.29 for a net profit of $4.96, or 13 percent in four days.

FIGURE 6.3:
EXAMPLE AVTOP PATTERN IN OSTK

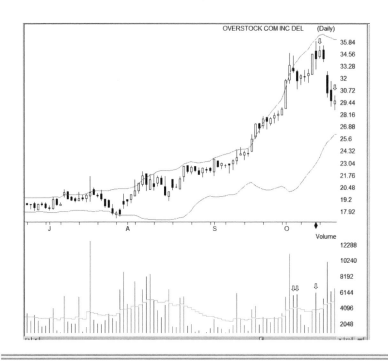

Courtesy of AIQ

INITIAL TEST RESULTS FOR AVTOP

If shorting topping patterns that show strong distribution are effective, they should work in bearish markets. They may also work in other market environments, but if they don't work in bearish markets, then we may not want to waste effort on further investigation. The market was bearish in 2008, so I ran the initial test of AVtop, using the above definition, during calendar 2008 using Trading Expert Pro from AIQ systems. The results of this initial test period are shown in Figure 6.4.

The test results for AVtop during 2008 show an interesting annualized ROI of 257 percent, which is an improvement over the market's loss of 36 percent during the same period. Sixty-nine percent of the trades were profitable, which is also an interesting sign. The average winning trade returned over seven percent and the average losing trade lost about three and a half percent.

INITIAL TEST RESULTS OF AVTOP DURING 2008

AVTop		Winners	Losers	Neutral
Number of trades in test:	97	67	30	0
Average periods per trade:	5.79	5.73	5.93	0.00
Maximum Profit/Loss:		25.00%	(11.08)%	
Average Drawdown:	(1.90)%	(0.99)%	(3.91)%	
Average Profit/Loss:	4.09%	7.49%	(3.52)%	
Average SPX Profit/Loss	1.12%	1.47%	0.34%	
Probability:		69.07%	30.93%	
Average Annual ROI:	257.39%	477.00%	(216.38)%	
Annual SPX (Buy & Hold):	(36.32)%			
Reward/Risk Ratio:	4.76			
Start test date:	01/02/08			
End test date:	12/31/08			

Interval:Daily
Pricing Summary
      Entry price: [Open]
      Exit price: [Open]
Exit Summary
      Hold for 4 periods

Courtesy of AIQ

EFFECT OF DISTRIBUTION VOLUME ON RESULTS

When testing a system, I do not rely on data from just one time period, but these initial results indicate that the AVtop system is worth further investigation.

The definition of strong distribution used in the AVtop system requires volume at least 150 percent of the average on a day that the stock closes down. It is important to look at each part of the definition of a system, and determine how variations or changes in that definition affect the results. I do not want to find a system that depends on specific numbers and only works in a few cases. I am looking for general principles as to what affects the results.

If I test different definitions of strong distribution and find that the general relationship is: "the larger the distribution day volume is compared to the average volume, then the better the results," then I have a general principle that can be used to prioritize trading setups when multiple opportunities are available. This is useful because AVtop showed 97 trades during the initial 2008 test period, and many traders will not take that many trades from a single system. If we are going to choose a subset of the trading opportunities, then by understanding how changes in the parameters affect results, we will have a logical way to select among multiple opportunities.

Figure 6.5 shows the results of running the AVtop scan during the initial 2008 test period after changing the definition of strong distribution to be a down day that occurs on 130 percent of average volume instead of 150 percent. When the volume requirement for strong distribution is relaxed, the system generates almost three times as many trades during the 2008 test period. These extra trades come at little expense since the annualized ROI is still over 200 and the percentage of winning trades is more than 66 percent. When a change to a trading system shows more trading opportunities with about the same results, I want to incorporate the change into the system because I want the additional trading opportunities.

From this point forward, we will be using the AVtop system with strong volume, defined as 130 percent of the average volume.

When running a trading scan in the evening, I look at all the opportunities that show up on the scan and then prioritize them using information gleaned from the test results, along with information about the risk and potential reward of the trade.

If I am taking a short trade, like AVtop, I want to take profits as the stock approaches support. Stocks that have more distance between the entry point and support have more room to run and can generate more profits. Having more trading candidates gives me more chances to find trades with plenty of room to run.

EFFECT OF STOCK PRICE ON AVTOP RESULTS

The next test is to determine if increasing the minimum stock price will affect results. The initial AVtop definition looks at stocks that have a closing price of $5 or more. I ran the test again during the 2008 initial test period and raised the minimum stock price requirement to $25. The results of that test are shown in Figure 6.6. These results also include the revised definition

AVTOP RESULTS DURING 2008, WITH LOWER VOLUME REQUIREMENT FOR STRONG DISTRIBUTION

AVTop		Winners	Losers	Neutral
Number of trades in test:	271	180	91	0
Average periods per trade:	5.77	5.73	5.84	0.00
Maximum Profit/Loss:		31.73%	(17.98)%	
Average Drawdown:	(2.44)%	(1.10)%	(5.10)%	
Average Profit/Loss:	3.36%	7.23%	(4.30)%	
Average SPX Profit/Loss	1.12%	1.53%	0.33%	
Probability:		66.42%	33.58%	
Average Annual ROI:	212.34%	460.13%	(269.23)%	
Annual SPX (Buy & Hold):	(36.32)%			
Reward/Risk Ratio:	3.32			
Start test date:	01/02/08			
End test date:	12/31/08			

Interval:Daily
Pricing Summary
       Entry price: [Open]
       Exit price: [Open]
Exit Summary
       Hold for 4 periods

RESULTS DURING 2008, WITH MINIMUM $25 CLOSE AND 130 PERCENT OF AVERAGE VOLUME

AVTop		Winners	Losers	Neutral
Number of trades in test:	197	142	55	0
Average periods per trade:	5.83	5.78	5.96	0.00
Maximum Profit/Loss:		31.73%	(17.98)%	
Average Drawdown:	(2.25)%	(1.12)%	(5.18)%	
Average Profit/Loss:	3.80%	6.96%	(4.37)%	
Average SPX Profit/Loss	1.31%	1.19%	0.85%	
Probability:		72.08%	27.92%	
Average Annual ROI:	237.54%	439.34%	(267.57)%	
Annual SPX (Buy & Hold):	(36.32)%			
Reward/Risk Ratio:	4.11			
Start test date:	01/02/08			
End test date:	12/31/08			

Interval:Daily
Pricing Summary
       Entry price: [Open]
       Exit price: [Open]
Exit Summary
       Hold for 4 periods

Courtesy of AIQ

of strong distribution (at least 130 percent of average volume), which is now a standard part of the AVtop definition.

Increasing the minimum stock price to $25 reduced the number of trades during 2008 from 271 to 197. We would expect to see fewer trades, but this is still a significant number. The annualized ROI increased from 212 to 237 and the percentage of winning trades increased from 66 percent to 72 percent. The system clearly performs better when trading the higher-dollar stocks.

Based on this data, I made the price change a standard part of the AVtop definition and will use the $25 minimum stock price in all subsequent testing.

FIGURE 6.7:
AVTOP PATTERN USING MODIFIED DEFINITION

Courtesy of AIQ

Figure 6.7 shows an AVtop pattern in Peabody Energy using the new definition. The arrows on the volume chart show the three strong distribution days when the stock was down and the volume was at least 130 percent of the 21-day simple moving average of the volume. The arrow on the price chart shows the entry point where a short position was taken. Note that

Peabody energy moved up for two days after the entry (creating a paper loss for the short position) and then fell quickly for the next two days, resulting in a profitable trade.

In a situation like this, I look at the volume pattern when the stock is moving against me. Peabody moved up on volume that was much less than the volume it was moving down on. This indicates that when the price rose, there was less interest, and when the price fell, there were a lot of people getting out. This type of volume pattern indicates a weak stock, so the position was held even though it was going the wrong way for two days.

AVTOP RESULTS IN DIFFERENT MARKET CONDITIONS

The testing up to this point has all been during the 2008 initial test period. I would never trade something that tested well in just one period. There is no way to know the future (testing does not guarantee future results), but I would rather be trading something that consistently tests well than something with unknown behavior. We do this all the time: in relationships, business forecasting, and budgeting. Testing a trading system is the same; we are looking at past results to make an educated assessment of what the future might bring.

Figure 6.8 shows a recent five-year period of activity on the NASDAQ. What are the odds that the next five years will look similar? The 2008 bear market was one of those strong markets that only come around every few decades.

Making decisions about your trading systems based on unusual market conditions like those seen in Figure 6.8 does not make much sense, yet that is what people are doing when they compare five-year performance histories. Rather than look at a variety of time period performance histories of a trading system, I simply want to know how it performs in multiple bullish markets, multiple bearish markets, and multiple trading range markets.

Carpenters, doctors, and plumbers do not use the same tool all the time. They have a variety of different tools for different aspects of the job. Suc-

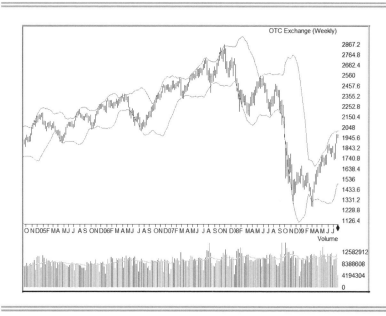

Courtesy of AIQ

cessful traders are the same way. They have several tools that are suitable for bullish environments, several for bearish environments, and several trading tools for trading range environments. They then look at the current market environment and use the most appropriate tools.

Remember, trading will always present risks, and good traders must learn how to manage those risks through careful analysis of the market conditions and adjustments to exit strategies, number of trading positions, and position sizes.

Table 6.1 shows the results of testing AVtop during six different bullish market conditions. The percentage of winning trades is below 50 percent in four of the six bullish market periods. AVtop lost money during the majority of the bullish periods tested. The system did well during the summer run of 2008, with 66 percent winning trades, but the overall picture for bullish market periods is negative. Based on the data in Table 6.1, I would not use AVtop during bullish market periods.

My son started his career in the marketing department of a large company. He enjoyed the work but he could see what people who had been there for awhile were making and realized that following that path would not get him where he wanted to be. He looked at current and past conditions to make a reasonable assessment of the future and based on that information, he changed companies, moving to something with more potential.

During the 2008 economic downturn, his business slowed way down. Based on the data available, he realized that the situation was going to last long enough to have a significant impact on him. He used this analysis of the recent past to determine that he and his wife should start a part-time business to supplement their income. He was using past data to make an informed decision about future events, and then acted in a way that improved his quality of life. Backtesting does not guarantee future performance, but it allows traders to make more informed decisions to prepare for the future, just as my son did.

TABLE 6.1
RESULTS OF TESTING AVTOP DURING SIX DIFFERENT BULLISH MARKET PERIODS

TEST PERIOD TRADES	MARKET TYPE	WINNING %	ANNUALIZED ROI	# OF TRADES
08/13/04-12/31/04	Bull	37.6%	-46%	101
07/21/06-11/24/06	Bull	37.9	-48	87
03/14/07-07/20/07	Bull	44.3	-11	158
08/17/07-10/09/07	Bull	44.0	-68	25
03/17/08-06/05/08	Bull	54.0	6	37
07/16/08-08/18/08	Bull	66.7	89	6

The fact that the summer of 2008 bounce showed an interesting annualized ROI and a strong percentage of winning trades is interesting. It illustrates the point that traders cannot rely on a single test. If the only bullish period tested was the summer bounce, then an inexperienced trader may conclude that using AVtop during bullish periods is fine. When I test a system, I want to function like a jury and look for the preponderance of the evidence. One piece of data proves nothing. I draw a reasonable conclusion based on a number of different tests.

The other thing I am interested in is how AVtop performs in the other market conditions. I am looking at AVtop as potentially one of the tools in my trading tool box. I do not expect any trading system to work well in all market conditions; I am looking for the market conditions where each system appears to work best. That is no guarantee that it will always work in the selected market condition; during any given period traders may experience losses. I am trying to build a picture of when to use each tool in my trading tool box and to see if, over the long haul, they have profit potential.

Table 6.2 shows the results of testing AVtop during six different bearish market conditions. The data indicates that AVtop is a more promising tool during bear market periods than it is during bullish markets. AVtop is profitable in five of the six bearish periods tested, and the one loss of 12 percent was a much smaller magnitude than all the other gains.

TABLE 6.2
RESULTS OF TESTING AVTOP DURING SIX DIFFERENT BEARISH MARKET PERIODS

TEST PERIOD TRADES	MARKET TYPE	WINNING %	ANNUALIZED ROI	# OF TRADES
01/04/02-10/04/02	Bear	58.3%	20%	36
01/23/04-08/13/04	Bear	58.4	21	89
01/07/05-04/22/05	Bear	47.1	-12	70
05/11/06-07/21/06	Bear	60.0	94	25
07/20/07-08/17/07	Bear	75.2	180	97
06/06/08-07/15/08	Bear	62.0	75	29

Again, I do not expect a trading system to be 100 percent effective; each trading system will have losing stretches, which is why money management is a key part of trading. We do not risk the entire account on just a few trades from a single system.

The interesting thing here is that the magnitude of the single losing period is about half the magnitude of the smallest of the five winning periods. If I expect to see the occasional losing period, it would be nice if it was a small loss.

Table 6.3 shows the results of testing AVtop during six different trading range market conditions. The system lost money in four of the five trading range environments, and the single winning period was essentially breakeven. AVtop is not a suitable trading system for trading range market periods.

Based on these test results, AVtop is one of the tools I consider during bearish market environments. When the market is bearish, I run this scan looking for trading opportunities.

TABLE 6.3
**RESULTS OF TESTING AVTOP DURING SIX DIFFERENT TRADING RANGE
MARKET PERIODS**

TEST PERIOD TRADES	MARKET TYPE	WINNING %	ANNUALIZED ROI	# OF TRADES
11/25/05-05/05/06	Trading Range	48.9%	-41	182
01/05/06-05/11/06	Trading Range	46.4	-57	183
11/24/06-02/26/07	Trading Range	46.4	-18	112
10/09/07-11/06/07	Trading Range	52.5	-27	73
01/24/08-02/28/08	Trading Range	53.3	1	15

AVTOP TRADE MANAGEMENT

I also ran tests to determine if the four-day holding time was the most appropriate. In one series of tests during the 2008 period, I found that increasing holding time from four to five days resulted in 70 percent winning trades. Further increasing the holding time to six days resulted in 72 percent winning trades. AVtop did not show a strong sensitivity to holding times between four and seven days. This allows me to manage positions using distance to the next support level and volume patterns in addition to using just the fixed time period exit strategy.

If I am in a position that is dropping on increasing volume (which generates paper profits for short positions), I will often hold the position longer than four days. If it is dropping on light or declining volume, I will often exit the position after three or four days. If the stock moves quickly to a support area, I will take profits whether or not it has been four days. The most likely thing for a stock to do at support is bounce, so I do not want to be slavishly holding on for four days no matter what. I want to use all the chart information, trading skills, and experience to improve my odds.

Testing also indicates that more distribution days around the topping pattern may improve results. I ran a test during the 2008 period looking for four strong distribution days instead of three and found that the annualized ROI and the percentage of winning trades increased. The issue is that the number of trades dropped from about 200 to about 50. I stick with the definition of three strong distribution days when running the scan, but if the evening scan shows more trades than I am interested in taking, I can use the number of distribution days as another factor in prioritizing the available trades.

Trading is about the odds. We have no idea whether or not any specific trade will be profitable. Testing may indicate that over a large number of trades in specific market conditions we will see profitable trades more often than losing trades, but it tells us nothing about what to expect from any specific trade. Traders are not smart when the trade works, and they may not have missed something when the trade fails—it is just about the odds.

AVTOP SUMMARY

A summary of the final definition of AVtop is below and another example of the pattern is shown in Figure 6.9.

FIGURE 6.9:
EXAMPLE AVTOP TRADE

Courtesy of AIQ

Strong distribution occurs if:

- Today's close is less than yesterday's close, and
- Today's volume is more than 130 percent of the 21-day simple moving average of the volume.

AVtop occurs if:

- Today's close is greater than $25,
- Average volume is greater than 200,000,
- At least three of the last ten sessions have shown strong distribution, and

- Today's close is higher than the highest value in the previous 200 days, starting five days ago.

Entry and Exit Strategy:

- When an AVtop occurs, a position is entered at the next open, held for four days, and then sold at the following open. The entry is day one of the four-day holding period.

CHAPTER 6 SELF-TEST

1. Trading distribution tops:

    A. Requires a knowledge of only ten different rules.

    B. Results do not depend on market conditions.

    C. Involves four basic rules for selecting entries.

    D. Is for intermediate term traders.

2. Trading distribution tops:

    A. Works significantly better when strong distributions days are 150 percent of average volume instead of 130 percent.

    B. Requires one or more strong distribution days in the last ten sessions.

    C. Requires three or more strong distribution days in the last ten sessions.

    D. Is not dependent on current market conditions.

3. Trading distribution tops:

    A. Results are best for stocks under $5.

    B. Results are best for stocks above $5.

    C. Results are best for stocks above $25.

    D. Results are best for stocks under $25.

4. Trading distribution tops:

    A. Showed strong test results in a number of bullish market conditions.

    B. Showed strong test results in trading range and bearish market conditions.

    C. Showed strong results in a number of bearish market conditions.

    D. Showed a rather small difference in test results in different market conditions.

5. **Trading distribution tops:**

    A. Shows stronger results with a few accumulation days mixed into the pattern.

    B. Shows stronger results when a trading range market is moving to a bullish environment.

    C. Shows stronger results with four distribution days as compared to three.

    D. Shows little difference between stocks with two or three distribution days.

FOR THE ANSWERS,
VISIT WWW.TRADERSLIBRARY.COM/TLECORNER.

CHAPTER 7

MARKET ADAPTIVE TRADING

Trading is about being positioned to make profits if a stock, or the market, does the usual thing in a given situation. If we find that a specific price or volume pattern is most often followed by price increases in bullish markets, then we focus on taking long positions when we see the pattern form during a bullish environment. If we find that another pattern is most often followed by price declines during a bearish environment, then we focus on taking short positions when we identify the pattern in bearish market conditions. There is no way to predict the future and know what the outcome of any particular trade will be. We can, however, discover what the most likely outcome of a trading pattern is over hundreds of trades in similar market conditions, and thus have a reasonable expectation that over a number of trades, in similar conditions, profits may be realized.

The market has three basic modes: bullish, bearish, and trading range. It really can not do anything else. There is no way of knowing what the market will do next year, or over the next five years, and it is odd that so many people gamble their life savings based on some stranger's prediction of future market direction. Listening to market forecasters is basically "hold and hope."

> Hope is not a trading strategy.

As we've learned throughout this book, whatever the market does over the next year, or five years, or ten years, it will be made up of a series of bullish, bearish, and trading range movements. The market has to be either moving up, down, or sideways. This fact led me to develop my Market Adaptive Trading strategy, or MAT.

WHY TRADE WITH MAT?

In order to adapt to the market, you need to have identified and developed several tools that have been shown to be effective in each market environment. You must then select the most appropriate ones to use based on the current market conditions. You will not earn money sitting in front of real time charts all day entering trades; you can earn money by carefully analyzing potential trading systems and finding ones that show profitable trades more often than not during specific market conditions. This is the premise of Market Adaptive Trading (MAT).

Identifying and developing trading systems with an edge is a lot of work. Making the trades is the easy part. Once you have your trader's tool box, making the trades can be emotionless and statistically in your favor. This is exactly what you want.

In order to have an edge (or to develop your own MAT tool box), you need to know what the usual outcome of a particular trading pattern is in each of the three basic market environments. Beginning traders often look for the magic indicator that shows winning trades all the time. Those perfect indicators do not exist. Trading is a statistical business; it is about knowing the odds and being positioned to profit from the usual or normal course of action in a given situation. You are not insightful when you have a winning trade, and wrong when you lose. Winning and losing are just part of the natural statistics of a trading system.

To trade according to MAT, you are looking for systems that win more often than they lose and have a larger average winning trade than average losing trade. Trading systems that meet these criteria have a good chance of showing profits over the long run. Any particular trade, or group of trades, may or may not be profitable; but, over the longer run, if you win more often than you lose and the average winning trade is larger than the average losing trade, then you can expect profits. As a trader, you want tools that have favorable statistics and then you want to be positioned to profit when the normal or usual thing happens. When the unusual happens, you will lose money, but by definition, the unusual is less statistically likely to happen.

In this book (and also in my first book, *Money-Making Candlestick Patterns*), we have extensively tested several trading systems. The testing process helps us understand how stocks usually behave after forming a specific pattern such as moving outside the Bollinger bands, showing strong distribution or accumulation, or pulling back or retracing during a trend.

Now, none of our testing has indicated that a stock always moves a certain way when one of these patterns forms, but it has shown that the stock has a probable path in a specific market condition after the formation of the pattern. Understanding what a stock is most likely to do is the beginning of a trading strategy. We take positions based on what is most probable based on the current conditions—we adapt to the market. Our job is to find systems with an edge in each market condition and then make trades without worrying about what happens on each individual trade.

The market adaptive trading approach focuses on selecting and using appropriate tools for the current market conditions. Traders do not try to predict or forecast the market, they observe the current market conditions and adapt to them.

We have investigated six potential trading strategies in this book and summarized the results. These six trading tools are ones that I use in my own trading. But, as you should have learned by now, this is just the beginning. You should begin your own investigation of these and other trading tools. It is critical for you to fully understand how a system performs and its potential risks before using it. Once a trading system is fully analyzed, and its behavior is like an old friend, then you can consider adding it to your trading tool box. When you have multiple tools for each market condition in your tool box, then you are ready to go to work.

We have developed and tested six trading tools in this book, and they fall into three different categories. The pullback and retracement systems are some of my "bread and butter" tools. They generate plenty of trading opportunities in a variety of market conditions. The two Bollinger band systems look for overbought and oversold stocks and are specialty tools to generate trading candidates after extended runs. Because of this, the selections from these scans tend to come in bunches rather than spread evenly over time. The accumulation and distribution patterns look for top and bottoming patterns, which tend to form after the market has been trending for awhile. The six tools together provide a basic set of techniques for most market conditions.

TRADING PULLBACKS AND RETRACEMENTS IN TRENDING STOCKS

The DVpullback and DVretrace systems look for pullbacks in uptrending stocks and retracements in downtrending stocks. The DVpullback system is an interesting trading system in bullish market conditions and may be used with reduced position sizes in trading range markets. The definition of the DVpullback system is outlined below.

A DVpullback occurs if:

- The stock shows three consecutive lower highs, and
- The stock has three consecutive days of lower volume than the previous day, and
- The stock is in an uptrend, which is defined as the highest high of the last two weeks is higher than the highest high of the previous two weeks, and the lowest low of the last two weeks is higher than the lowest low of the previous two weeks.

A price trigger occurs if:

- Today's high is greater than yesterday's high, and
- The close is greater than $5, and
- The 21-day simple average of the volume is greater than 200,000, and
- The stock has "room to run," which is defined as when the stock is at least two daily ranges below the upper Bollinger band on the price trigger.

The entry strategy is:

- If a DVpullback occurred yesterday, and
- A trigger occurs today, then
- Buy at the open tomorrow.

The exit strategy is:

- Hold for three days (the entry day, the next day, and the following day) and then
- Sell at the following day's open.

When using DVpullback, traders should be more aggressive and exit more quickly when the market is in a trading range. Consider exiting if the stock approaches resistance, the upper Bollinger band, or a trend line.

Results are improved by only taking trades that have volume on the trigger day above the volume of the previous day. As a general rule, I pay close attention to this rule when using DVpullback in trading range markets and have a little more flexibility in strongly trending markets.

Traders can use their own observation of the market to determine if conditions are suitable for DVpullback. They can also use the moving average filter to identify bullish and trading range markets for using DVpullback. Finally, traders can use market trend lines to determine if bullish conditions exist, and then use DVpullback when the market is trading above an ascending trend line.

The DVretrace system is an interesting trading system in bearish market conditions and should not be used in bullish or trading range markets. The definition of the DVretrace system is outlined below.

A DVretrace occurs if:

- The stock is in a downtrend, defined as the highest close in the last two weeks is lower than the lowest close of the previous month,
- There are three consecutive days of higher lows,
- Three consecutive days of lower volume,
- The close is greater than $5, and
- The 21-day simple average of the volume is greater than 200,000.

A trigger occurs if:

- Today's low is less than yesterday's low.

The DVretrace entry strategy is:

- If a DVretrace occurred yesterday, and
- A trigger occurs today, then
- Short at the open tomorrow.

The DVretrace exit strategy is:

- Hold for three days then cover.
- Day one is the entry day; then hold two more days, and
- Buy to cover at the next open.

I use the three-day holding period as a guideline and consider exiting if the position approaches support, the lower Bollinger band, or a trend line.

Results are improved by only taking trades that have a stock price above $25 on the trigger day. I use this information to help prioritize potential trades when the scan presents multiple opportunities on the same day. Other factors that should be considered in prioritizing trades include the distance between the entry point and the initial stop loss, the distance to the lower Bollinger band, the distance to the recent low, and the distance the market has to its next support area.

Traders can use their own observation of the market to determine if conditions are suitable for DVretrace. They can also use the 5 x 20 moving average filter developed above to identify bearish markets for using DVretrace. Finally, traders can use market trend lines to determine if bearish conditions exist and then use DVretrace when the market is trading below a descending trend line.

TRADING ACCUMULATION TOPS AND DISTRIBUTION BOTTOMS

Most stocks do not stay trending forever. At some point they reverse direction and head the other way. In addition to having multiple tools for trading trending stocks, traders should have a few tools for trading stocks that may be bottoming. One technique to identify potential bottoming candidates is to look for stocks that have significant accumulation around the lows. The definition of the AVbottom scan is shown below. The AVbottom pattern performs well in bullish markets, and poorly in bearish or trading range markets. AVbottom results are improved if the minimum stock price is increased from $5 to $25, or strong distribution days are limited to two or less in the last ten days.

Increasing the holding time to six days improves the percentage of winning trades in three of the five trading range markets, and results in only one losing period instead of the three losing periods, as seen with the four-day holding time. Giving bottoming patterns a little more time to develop during trading range markets seems to make sense.

Strong accumulation occurs if:

- Today's close is greater than yesterday's close, and
- Today's volume is more than 150 percent of the 21-day simple moving average of the volume.

AVbottom occurs if:

- Today's close is greater than $5, and
- Average volume is greater than 200,000, and

- At least three of the last ten sessions have shown strong accumulation, and
- Today's close is less than the lowest value in the previous 200 days, starting five days ago.

AVbottom Entry:

- When an AVbottom occurs, a position is entered at the next open.

AVbottom Exit:

- The position is held for four days, and then sold at the following open.
- The entry is day one of the four-day holding period.

The AVtop scan looks for topping patterns showing strong distribution. The idea behind distribution-topping patterns is to look for stocks that have run up and then, near the highs, start showing multiple strong distribution days. The strong distribution days may indicate that hedge funds are taking profits, and their positions are so large that their activity shows up in the volume pattern.

The definition of AVtop is provided below. If the evening scan shows more trades than I want, I can use the number of distribution days as another factor in prioritizing. AVtop did not show a strong sensitivity to holding times between four and seven days, which allows me to manage positions using distance to the next support level and volume patterns in addition to the fixed time period exit strategy. AVtop is one of the tools I consider using during bearish market environments.

Strong distribution occurs if:

- Today's close is less than yesterday's close, and
- Today's volume is more than 130 percent of the 21-day simple moving average of the volume.

AVtop occurs if:

- Today's close is greater than $25,
- Average volume is greater than 200,000,
- At least three of the last ten sessions have shown strong distribution, and

- Today's close is higher than the highest value in the previous 200 days, starting five days ago.

Entry Strategy:

- When an AVtop occurs, a position is entered at the next open.

Exit Strategy:

- The position is held for four days, and then sold at the following open.
- The entry is day one of the four-day holding period.

When running a trading scan in the evening, I look at all the opportunities that show up on the scan and then prioritize them using information gleaned from the test results, along with information about the risk and potential reward of the trade. If I want to take a short trade, like AVtop, I want to take profits as the stock approaches support. Stocks that have more distance between the entry point and support have more "room to run" and can generate more profits. Having more trading candidates gives me more chances to find trades with plenty of room to run.

If my position is dropping on increasing volume, I will often hold the position longer than four days. If it is dropping on light or declining volume, I will often exit the position after three or four days. If the stock moves quickly to a support area, I will take profits whether or not it has been four days. The most likely thing for a stock to do at support is bounce, so I do not want to be slavishly holding on for four days no matter what. I want to use all the chart information, trading skills, and experience to improve my odds.

Testing also indicates that more distribution days around the topping pattern may improve results. I ran a test during the 2008 period looking for four strong distribution days instead of three and found that the annualized ROI and the percentage of winning trades increased. The issue is that the number of trades dropped from about 200 to about 50. I stick with the definition of three strong distribution days when running the scan, but if the evening scan shows more trades than I want, I can use the number of distribution days as another factor in prioritizing the available trades.

TRADING EXTENSIONS BEYOND THE BOLLINGER BANDS

As we have learned in this book, it is unusual for prices to move outside the Bollinger bands, which is the basis for the AboveBB and BelowBB systems. The AboveBB system works best in bearish market conditions and should be avoided in bullish or trading range markets. This can be accomplished by only trading AboveBB when the NASDAQ's five-period exponential moving average is below its 20-period exponential moving average.

The rules defining the AboveBB system are shown below.

- If today's high was more than four percent above the upper band, and
- The volume is less than the 21-day simple moving average, and
- The close is greater than $10, and
- The average volume is at least 300,000 shares, then
- Enter a short position at the opening tomorrow, then
- Hold the position for three days, then
- Close the position on the next open.

This system is not something I would use during trading range market periods because during the testing process, it showed a negative annualized return during three of the five trading range periods tested, and the percentage of winning trades was not strongly favorable in any of the trading range periods tested.

I would not use this trading technique during bull market periods since it showed widely varying results, with a negative annualized return, in five of the bullish periods tested. It had a great run during the first bullish bounce in 2008, but remember, one example proves nothing. I need some consistency over similar market conditions and this technique shows reasonable performance during all of the bearish market periods tested, and poor performance during other market periods.

Good win loss ratios and annualized returns were shown in most of the bearish market periods; however, one period showed breakeven returns. Traders have to be willing to experience some periods when a system will not produce strong results. If you make a few trades and they do not work out, don't immediately move on to another technique because you may miss the times when the system performs well. Traders need to use money management techniques to ensure that they can ride out slow times when a system is not running strongly.

Volume relationships play a role in selecting the most appropriate candidates in many different trading systems. In the case of AboveBB, we only take trades when the volume on the day the stock extends at least four percent above the upper band is less than the 21-day moving average of the volume. Even lower volume on the day of the extension above the upper band improves the percentage of winning trades from 62 to more than 65 percent. If I do not want to take all of the trades presented in the AboveBB scan on any particular day, I will take the trade(s) with the lowest volume.

If I am trading shorts using AboveBB, or one of my other systems, and the market is approaching support, I become cautious. The reason is that the market often bounces or bases near support and thus shorts would be less attractive. When the market is clearly trending and well away from support, I will use larger position sizes in my trades. I cannot influence what the market does, but I can react to it and reduce my risks by taking smaller position sizes when the market is approaching a support level.

Stocks are sold at auction based on supply and demand. Sometimes this process results in stocks moving too far too fast, and an inevitable correction results. One way to measure whether or not a stock is oversold is by examining its relationship to the lower Bollinger band. The Bollinger bands measure the volatility of a stock around a simple moving average. Stock prices are contained within the bands about 95 percent of the time. Moves outside the bands are unusual and typically do not last long.

I want to have a variety of different trading tools in my trading tool box so that I can adapt my trading approach to different market conditions. Since strong movements below the band do not happen very often, I do not expect to see a system like this generate trades every day, but a technique for picking up oversold stocks can be very useful after the market has made an extended decline.

We tested a system for taking long positions when a stock closes more than four percent below the lower Bollinger band and found interesting results using the definition outlined below.

- If today's close was more than five percent below the lower band, and
- The close is greater than $5, and
- The average volume is at least 300,000 shares, and
- The close is in the bottom 20 percent of the day's range, and
- The open is greater than or equal to yesterday's close, then
- Enter a long position at the opening tomorrow, then
- Hold the position for three days, then
- Close the position on the next open.

The amount of extension below the lower Bollinger band has an effect on trading results. We found that adding a requirement to only take trades when the closing price for the stock occurs within the bottom 20 percent of the day's trading range improves results. The annualized ROI increases from 68 to 133 and the percentage of winning trades increases from 53 to 56 percent.

It appears that when stock prices move below the lower band, it is like stretching a rubber band which causes them to snap back inside. Closing below the band instead of just briefly moving below it stretches the rubber band more. Closing in the bottom 20 percent of the day's trading range and being below the band stretches the rubber band even farther, resulting in better moves. This knowledge is not only useful for the BelowBB system, but can be used in trade management when using other systems. If excursions below the lower band do not last long, and are the basis for a trading system taking longs, then it would not make much sense to hold short positions in declining stocks when they move below the lower band. I use this information to help manage my short trades and frequently take profits when short positions approach the lower band.

By focusing BelowBB on stocks that do not gap down on the day the pattern forms, the annualized ROI increases from 133 to 232 and the percentage of winning trades increases from 56 percent to nearly 59 percent. The spread between the average winning trade and the average losing trade also improves. Stocks that do not open with a gap on the day they make the move below the lower band tend to bounce back more in the short term than stocks that gap down.

If a long setup forms a point under strong resistance, I am not nearly as interested in it as a setup that forms three points under weak resistance. The most likely thing for stocks to do at resistance is stall or bounce, so I want to pick the trades with more room to run. Using the five percent number instead of the seven percent number showed about twice as many trades, which allows more opportunity to consider other factors such as support and resistance areas before making trades. Trading systems are not magic boxes that lead to wealth, they are just one of the tools that the trader uses along with market conditions and risk management techniques.

I also use the time stop (sell after three days) as a guideline, rather than a hard and fast rule. When one of my positions approaches resistance, I take the profits and move on, especially if the market is in a trading range environment. When the position moves into resistance, I close it and take my profits to another trade whether it has been one, two, three, or four days. The most likely thing for a stock to do at resistance is retrace, by definition. If the stock is likely to retrace, then I want to have my profits and move on, not blindly hold on for three days. Trading systems are not magic formulas to be blindly followed; traders must use all their knowledge and skills regarding how stocks and the market perform to manage trades.

Volume patterns are another important trade management tool. When I have a long position (from any of my trading systems) that starts going up on declining volume, I generally take profits and close the position, whether or not I have held it for the amount of time used in the testing. Stocks moving up on declining volume are generally weak; fewer people are willing to pay higher prices for the stock, so I want to take my money and put it to work in another trade.

The Bollinger band systems are looking for overbought and oversold stocks. These conditions generally occur when the market has been running for awhile and occur less often when the market is indecisive or basing in a tight range. I do not expect to see a number of setups for overbought and over-sold stocks every day. Pullback and retracement systems tend to generate trading candidates more frequently than either of the Bollinger band systems because the natural rhythm of stock movement is frequently showing runs and pullbacks. The Bollinger band systems are more specialized tools that look for stocks that have run too far in one direction, and this happens less often than either pullbacks or retracements in trending stocks.

PRACTICAL ASPECTS OF TRADING

Successful traders examine the current market conditions to determine if the market is bullish, bearish, or in a trading range environment. In most cases, you can tell the market conditions just by looking at a daily chart of the market action over the last year. We also showed in previous chapters how to use the 5 x 20 moving average filter and trend line analysis to determine the market environment.

After this, you can select the tool from your trading tool box that performs best in the current conditions. When the market conditions change, then you need to adapt to the new market environment by selecting new tools that are most appropriate for the new conditions.

In addition to using the market adaptive trading tool strategy, there are several practical aspects of trading that you need to master in order to be successful in the markets.

Tips from Steve

- Never enter a position without having a plan for exiting the position. If you do not know where to get out of a position, you should not enter it in the first place. In swing trading time frames, stocks often run to the next resistance or support level and then stall. We have seen that stocks rarely remain outside the Bollinger bands for long, so when a position reaches the bands, it is often a good place to look at taking profits, especially in trading range environments.

- I have seen traders enter a swing trading position and then when it goes against them decide, "I really wanted it for a long-term position anyway, so I will hold on to it for awhile and see what happens." This is generally not a winning strategy. If you want to trade long term, then use proven long-term trading techniques. Do not assume that a position that was entered on a swing trading basis will eventually work out if you hold long enough. There are new trading opportunities every day; there is no need to "ride a dead horse."

- There is usually no need to rush in when the market's trend changes. Any trend worth trading does not require you to be in on the first day. It is usually better to make sure the trend change is real and then react rather than assuming that the first day of a potential change is something that is going to continue.

- Stocks generally have a rhythm. They move up, pull back, then move some more. When a stock moves very rapidly for a few days, it is generally not sustainable. Regression to the mean is normal, so I look at taking profits and then putting them to work in another trade. I have seen people in a stock that moves a few dollars a day get very excited when it makes a $15 move in a couple of days. Some have actually told me that, "After a few more weeks of this I can pay off the car." Amazing! By definition, unusual events do not continue for long. When a position has an unusual run, I take my profits and move on.

- There are a lot of jobs where people get paid every Friday. Trading is not one of them. There will be profitable weeks and losing weeks as the normal statistics work out. Remember that if you trade enough, there is a reasonable probability of seeing ten losing trades at some point, even with good trading systems. This is part of trading, and traders need to allow for it when they work out position sizing and money management techniques.

- You do not have to trade every day or take trades just because they are on the evening scan. Carefully consider the recent price and volume action in the market before taking positions. Look for the best trades; consider long trades that have not shown a lot of recent distribution and have room to run before hitting the next resistance area or the upper Bollinger band.

- Make sure that your position sizing is such that if all your current positions were stopped out, the total loss would still be comfortable. This happens from time to time and wishing that it did not will not change it. Be prepared by using sensible position sizes.

- Look at the daily market chart every evening and determine what the current market conditions are: bullish, bearish, or trading range. What are the next support and resistance levels? If the market is within a typical day's range of support or resistance, consider taking at least some profits on positions since the market is most likely to stall around those levels.

- Run through all the setups generated by your scans and pick out the ten best ones. These are the ones with good volume patterns, "room to run," and the smallest distance between your entry point and a chart-based initial stop. You do not have to trade every setup. If you have a suitable trading tool box, there usually will be more setups than positions you want. Pick the best of what is available based on risk (the difference between the entry and the chart-based initial stop loss) and potential reward (the distance between the entry and the next support or resistance area).

- Review your positions every evening and determine if each is something you still want to hold based on the recent market action and the price and volume patterns of the position. Longs moving up on declining volume are showing weakness, and I generally close out those positions and put the money to work in something stronger. You are hiring a stock to do a job for you; if it is not doing the job, fire it and hire another.

- Do not get caught up in forecasting where the market is going or listening to those who do. Focus on determining the current market environment and selecting the best tools.

- Market conditions determine risk, and risk should determine position sizing and the number of trading positions used. When the market is strongly trending, I will trade more positions and use larger position sizes than when it is in a trading range environment.

- Stocks tend to "pop and drop" when the market is in a trading range. If they all moved out of a setup and kept going, then the market, which is the sum of a large number of stocks, could not be in a trading range. When the market is in a trading range, it is telling you that the typical stock is not going to run far. This indicates that profits should be taken more quickly than in a trending market.

- In trading range market environments, the Bollinger bands often act as support or resistance and so I take profits when a position approaches these areas. In a strongly trending market, stocks may "ride the bands" by moving along them. In these situations, do not use the bands as profit-taking opportunities. As always, adapt to the current market conditions.

- During trending market conditions, I use the three- to five-day holding period as a guideline. After this "time stop" period, I examine the position to determine if there is a good reason to continue holding. Stocks showing accumulation are bullish, so I consider holding longer. Stocks moving up on strong volume and retracing on light volume are strong, and I will often manage the exit using trend lines during bullish market conditions. Stocks approaching strong resistance are likely to stall, so I take profits before they get there. When in doubt, take profits—it is hard to go broke taking profits.

- Narrow trading ranges, ones where the distance between support and resistance is small enough for the market to cover the distance in two or three days, do not happen often, but when they do, they are best left alone. By the time you get confirmation of a move, the market reverses. These conditions do not happen often, and the good news is that they frequently lead to strong moves. Narrow trading ranges are the market's way of telling traders to take a few days off.

- When the market is in a wide trading range, I try to concentrate my trades during times when the market is bouncing off support or retracing from resistance. Trading in the middle of the trading range carries additional risk since the market has the least distance to go either way. Increased risk implies smaller position sizes and fewer trading positions to compensate for the risk.

- Trading is about managing risk, not eliminating it. Be positioned to profit if the market does the usual or normal thing.

- Ignore the talking heads on financial television and in the internet chat rooms. No one cares more about your money than you do. Focus on extensive testing, and then trade what you know and understand.

- Get a trading partner; work with someone who has significant experience. Doctors, pilots, engineers, and most professionals learn from someone with experience after they get out of school. I publish the Timely Trades Letter twice a week, which is my trading plan for my account. I also share trading tips and answer subscribers' questions. If you want to see more about what I am doing in the current market and learn from my experience, go to www.daisydogger.com or send a request to sample@daisydogger.com.

Finally, remember that this book is the beginning of your journey, not the end!

CHAPTER 7 SELF-TEST

1. Trading is about:

    A. Being lucky.

    B. Having good instincts.

    C. Being positioned to profit if the stock or market does the normal thing.

    D. Understanding how economic patterns affect the market.

2. Why does a trader need multiple tools in their trading toolbox?

    A. So they can make more money.

    B. So they can trade different types of stocks.

    C. So they can pick the best ones for the current market conditions.

    D. So they can correlate results between them.

3. When do the Bollinger band systems generally show significant trading opportunities?

    A. When the market is in a trading range

    B. When the market is approaching support

    C. When the market is approaching resistance

    D. When the market has had an extended run

4. How should traders trade pullbacks in trading ranges?

    A. They shouldn't, trading ranges should be avoided.

    B. They should be more aggressive and exit more quickly.

    C. They should hold longer to give the pattern more time to work.

    D. They should take larger position sizes.

5. How should traders use the three-day holding time for trading retracements in declining stocks?

    A. It is always the exit strategy for this pattern.

    B. It should be a guideline and they should consider other factors.

    C. It should be shortened in bearish markets and lengthened in trading range markets.

    D. It should be lengthened in bullish markets and shortened in trading range markets.

6. Using the accumulation topping pattern in trading range markets shows better results if:

    A. Holding times are below three days.

    B. Holding times are lengthened from three to six days.

    C. Holding times are shortened and lower priced stocks are picked.

    D. Holding times are lengthened and the pattern is close to the lower Bollinger band.

7. Never enter a trade without:

    A. Knowing it will work.

    B. Having seen a similar trade work.

    C. Having an exit plan.

    D. Checking its PE ratio.

8. For more information on effective trading techniques you can:

A. Read *Money-Making Candlestick Patterns*, available through Traders' Library.

B. Read *How to Take Money from the Markets*, available through Traders' Library.

C. Visit www.daisydogger.com.

D. All of the above

FOR THE ANSWERS, VISIT WWW.TRADERSLIBRARY.COM/TLECORNER.

STOCHASTIC INDICATOR STRATEGIES

STOCHASTIC BUY SIGNAL

The Stochastic indicator relates the current stock price to the price range over the previous 21 days. The range is the difference between the highest and lowest prices in the last 21 days. The Stochastic indicator is expressed as a percentage, and plotted on a scale of 1 to 100. A buy signal is indicated when the signal moves from below 20 to above 20, and a sell signal is indicated when the Stochastic moves from above 80 to below 80.

An example of the Stochastic indicator and its use is shown in Figure A.1. As shown, in late September the Stochastic moved below 80, indicating a sell signal, and BEBE started dropping in price. In late October, the Stochastic moved up above 20, indicating a buy signal, after which BEBE began a rapid price rise. The Stochastic moved below 80 five days later, indicating a sell signal. The next buy signal came in late November and was followed by a sell signal in late December. There was another buy signal in mid-January. All of these trades, which were triggered by the Stochastic indicator moving above 20 or below 80, would have been profitable. If you saw five good examples like this in a magazine article, you might develop an interest in the Stochastic indicator.

Figure A.2 shows the Stochastic indicator for CSH during late 2008 and early 2009. The Stochastic moved above 20 in early October, indicating that CSH was a buy. The stock subsequently moved down until mid-December when the Stochastic indicated a sell signal. The next buy signal came in early 2009 and the stock subsequently dropped about 28 percent. The Stochastic, like any indicator, does not work all the time.

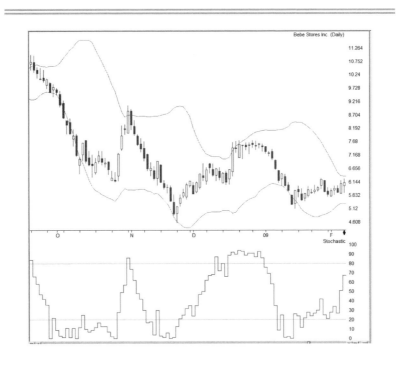

Courtesy of AIQ

Courtesy of AIQ

The questions of course are, "how often does this work?" and "should I risk my money based on these signals?" In order to answer these questions, I looked at all the trades made during calendar year 2008 using the following three rules:

- Only consider stocks for which the 21-day simple moving average of the volume is greater than 200,000.

- Buy at the open tomorrow if the stochastic was below 20 yesterday and is above 20 today.

- Hold for five days, then sell at the open the following day.

If the movement of the Stochastic indicator from below 20 to above 20 indicates that the stock is beginning a run, then a reasonable check on this is to buy on this signal and see if the stock is up or down five days later. We

Courtesy of AIQ

can use backtesting techniques to examine a large number of stochastic buy signals in order to determine the effectiveness of this indicator.

An example trade using the rules shown above is illustrated in Figure A.3. The Stochastic signal for CF moved from below 20 to above 20 on July 27, 2008, which is marked by the up arrows. The trading rules called for an entry at the open on the next day, which resulted in buying CF near $140.99. CF was held for a total of five days and then sold the following day at the open, as marked by the down arrow, at a price near $165.14. Following the Stochastic trading rules resulted in a net profit of about $24 in five days.

Figure A.3 also shows that CF made a Stochastic cross in late May that would have been profitable using these trading rules. A third profitable trade resulted from another Stochastic signal in early July. Three profitable trades in

BASIC STOCHASTIC TEST FOR CALENDAR 2008

StoMovesAbove20		Winners	Losers	Neutral
Number of trades in test:	26154	10871	15164	119
Average periods per trade:	7.18	7.22	7.16	7.25
Maximum Profit/Loss:		185.71%	(72.41)%	
Average Drawdown:	(6.46)%	(1.71)%	(9.91)%	
Average Profit/Loss:	(1.97)%	7.03%	(8.43)%	
Average SPX Profit/Loss	(1.70)%	0.64%	(3.39)%	
Probability:		41.57%	57.98%	
Average Annual ROI:	(99.86)%	355.34%	(429.63)%	
Annual SPX (Buy & Hold):	(36.32)%			
Reward/Risk Ratio:	0.60			
Start test date:	01/02/08			
End test date:	12/31/08			

Interval:Daily
Pricing Summary
    Entry price: [Open]
    Exit price: [Open]
Exit Summary
    Hold for 5 periods

Courtesy of AIQ

a two-month period are interesting; however, a few examples prove nothing, so I looked at every Stochastic signal that occurred in all the stocks in my database during calendar year 2008. The results are summarized in Figure A.4.

INITIAL TEST RESULTS FOR STOCHASTIC BUY

My database consists of about 2,500 stocks with average daily volume above 200,000 shares a day. I use this database for testing because it is the same one I use for trading. I like to trade stocks with at least 200,000 shares average volume because the low volume stocks may have wide bid/ask spreads, making them hard to get into or out of when the stock is moving. The 2,500-stock database provides plenty of trading opportunities, so there is no need to deal with the additional issues of low volume stocks.

Figure A.4 shows that during 2008, there were more than 26,000 signals on stocks in the database from the Stochastic indicator system noted above. That is more trades than anyone is likely to take. The key information is that after seeing a Stochastic buy signal, only 41 percent of the trades were profitable after five days. Trading a system that shows losing trades nearly 60 percent of the time and demonstrates an annualized loss more than double just buying and holding the SPX does not make much sense.

The year 2008 was tough on stocks, and market conditions can affect most trading systems, so I looked at all the Stochastic buy signals during calendar 2007. The results of the Stochastic trades during calendar 2007 are shown in Figure A.5. There were more than 20,000 Stochastic buy signals during calendar 2007, but only half of them were winning trades and the annualized return of all the trades was negative. I also looked at the 16,000 Stochastic buy signals that occurred during 2006 and found that 51 percent of them were winning trades. A slight annualized profit was realized, but it was less than the return for buying and holding the SPX.

FIGURE A.5:
BASIC STOCHASTIC TEST FOR CALENDAR 2007

StoMovesAbove20		Winners	Losers	Neutral
Number of trades in test:	20224	10181	9917	126
Average periods per trade:	7.23	7.26	7.2	7.37
Maximum Profit/Loss:		74.51%	(50.47)%	
Average Drawdown:	(2.79)%	(0.98)%	(4.68)%	
Average Profit/Loss:	(0.07)%	3.76%	(4.00)%	
Average SPX Profit/Loss	0.16%	0.84%	(0.53)%	
Probability:		50.34%	49.04%	
Average Annual ROI:	(3.55)%	188.90%	(202.74)%	
Annual SPX (Buy & Hold):	2.05%			
Reward/Risk Ratio:	0.96			
Start test date:	01/02/07			
End test date:	12/31/07			

Interval:Daily
Pricing Summary
      Entry price: [Open]
      Exit price: [Open]
Exit Summary
      Hold for 5 periods

Courtesy of AIQ

In all three years, the Stochastic buy signals resulted in poor returns, with the odds of a winning trade being equal to or less than a coin flip. I tested the effects of the holding period by running the tests using holding periods of three, five, and seven days. The results of varying the holding period during each of the three years tested are summarized in Table A.1.

TABLE A.1
EFFECT OF HOLDING TIME ON STOCHASTIC BUYS

HOLDING PERIOD	TEST YEAR	% WINNING TRADES	ANNUALIZED ROI	SPX ROI
3 Days	2006	48%	-4.0%	13%
5 Days	2006	51	11	13
7 Days	2006	51	8.7	13
3 Days	2007	50	4.6	2
5 Days	2007	50	-3.5	2
7 Days	2007	51	-1.0	2
3 Days	2008	41	-116	-36
5 Days	2008	41	-100	-36
7 Days	2008	40	-104	-36

The results shown indicate that, for the three years tested, varying the holding time of the Stochastic buy system did not have a significant effect on results. There are a number of trading systems that show much better results than simply buying a stock when the stochastic moves from below 20 to above 20. A lot of traders use this technique because they have seen examples of times when it works. Of course, even a stopped clock is right twice a day. It is possible to make a few trades and get lucky by hitting several winners in a row using this technique. The tests run during 2008 show a number of trades with over 30 percent profit in just a few days, but if the system was traded regularly, it was quite likely that traders using the "Stochastic buy" would have lost money.

TRADING IS A STATISTICAL BUSINESS

Remember that trading is a statistical business. Even when the odds are just 50-50, there will be some people who are big winners. Imagine 64 traders in a room and all are using the "buy when the Stochastic moves above 20, hold for five days, and then sell" system. All 64 traders pick one of the many Stochastic signals on a given day and enter positions. A week later, we would expect to see about 32 traders with winning trades and the same number with losing trades. If everyone takes another trade at the end of the second week, we would expect about half of the 32 first-week winners to have winning trades in the second week. Thus, after two weeks, about 16 traders have two winners in a row and everyone else has at least one loser. After the third week, about eight traders would have three winners in a row, with everyone else having at least one loser. After the fourth week, about four traders would have four winners in a row.

If we interview traders about the system at the end of four weeks, we will find that a few have seen every trade lose money. They probably feel it is a bad system. Most of the traders have seen mixed results, and they might be willing to try it awhile longer. The four traders who have seen all profitable trades are likely to speak highly of the system and start making larger trades. They probably will tell all their friends what a great system it is!

The "strong results" of the four traders who had four profitable trades in a row is due to random chance, not the strength of the trading system. Of course, some of them will tell their friends it is because they have "a feel for the market" or something along those lines. If you are going to trade just using the stochastic for a long time, and make a large number of trades over a few years, you are highly likely to see results along the lines of our analysis; about half will be winners and half losers. In the long run, you are likely to just churn the account.

Of course, there will be periods where you see a number of winners in a row, just like it is possible to see four or five heads in a row when you flip a coin. Knowing what the odds of winning trades are over a large number of trades is important in understanding whether or not a trading technique is worth using. There are trading techniques that give traders an edge; the basic stochastic signal just isn't one of them. If you trade a system that has not been fully analyzed, you are driving with your eyes closed. You may not crash right away, but eventually you will.

Myth: The popular Stochastic indicator provides an easy system for buying stocks; just buy when the Stochastic moves from below 20 to above 20.

Fact: The Stochastic buy system, when tested over thousands of trades and different years, shows (on average) about a 50-50 chance of success. No better than a coin flip.

MODIFIED STOCHASTIC BUY SIGNAL

One of the advantages of backtesting is that you can try out different modifications and filters and see how they have affected trading results. After scanning through a number of the trades made by the simple Stochastic buy system, I noticed that many stocks showed a number of buy signals (the Stochastic moved from below 20 to above 20) that were relatively close together and resulted in losing trades.

An example of this characteristic is shown in Figure A.6. There were five Stochastic buy signals relatively close together as marked by the down arrows, and each one would have resulted in a losing trade. Since there were a number of charts with these occurrences, I wanted to see what the effect on the "simple Stochastic buy system" would be if I required that the system only trade Stochastic buy signals (a move from below 20 to above 20) when the stochastic had been below 20 for at least three weeks (15 consecutive days).

Figure A.7 shows an example of a stock where the Stochastic was below 20 for at least 15 days and then moved above 20. The stochastic buy signal is marked by the down arrow. After the buy signal, VMC makes a quick nine-point run. The example illustrates the type of signal I am looking for, but to find out if it improves results, we need to look at a large number of trades over several time periods.

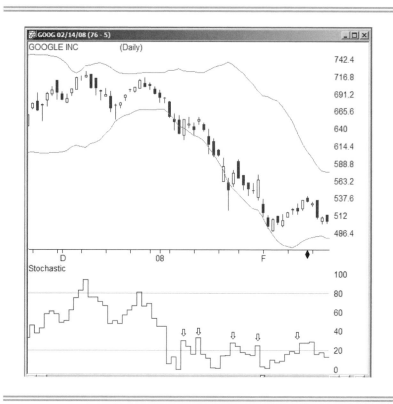

Courtesy of AIQ

The four rules for the modified Stochastic buy system are:

- Only consider stocks for which the stochastic indicator has been below 20 for each of the last 15 days.

- Only consider stocks for which the 21-day simple moving average of the volume is greater than 200,000.

- Buy at the open tomorrow if the stochastic was below 20 yesterday and above 20 today.

- Hold for five days, then sell at the opening the following day.

Courtesy of AIQ

During 2008, this "modified Stochastic buy system" showed better results than the basic system we first tested. As shown in Figure A.8, the percentage of losing trades dropped from about 58 percent (as shown in Figure A.4) to slightly over 50 percent. The annualized loss of the basic Stochastic buy turned into a slight annualized profit. These numbers are a significant improvement over the basic Stochastic buy system. Buying and holding the SPX showed a significant loss during 2008 and the modified Stochastic buy system showed a slight annualized profit.

StoMovesAbove20

		Winners	Losers	Neutral
Number of trades in test:	1140	554	577	9
Average periods per trade:	7.12	7.12	7.12	7.00
Maximum Profit/Loss:		101.07%	(71.43)%	
Average Drawdown:	(6.50)%	(1.92)%	(11.00)%	
Average Profit/Loss:	0.11%	9.99%	(9.38)%	
Average SPX Profit/Loss	(1.12)%	0.46%	(2.66)%	
Probability:		48.60%	50.61%	
Average Annual ROI:	5.47%	511.79%	(480.57)%	
Annual SPX (Buy & Hold):	(40.80)%			
Reward/Risk Ratio:	1.02			
Start test date:	01/02/08			
End test date:	12/26/08			

Interval:Daily
Pricing Summary
      Entry price: [Open]
      Exit price: [Open]
Exit Summary
      Hold for 5 periods

Courtesy of AIQ

In order to get a better understanding of how the modified Stochastic system performs, I ran it in three different time frames using three different holding periods in each time period. The results of this testing are shown in Table A.2.

Comparing the results shown in Table A.2, which uses the modified Stochastic buy system, with the results shown previously for the basic system indicates that adding the requirement that the Stochastic be below 20 for at least 15 days significantly improves the results for the 2008 test period. However, it decreases the results during both the 2006 and 2007 test periods.

TESTING PERIODS OF THE STOCHASTIC SYSTEM

Figure A.9 shows the 2006 through 2008 market period during which the previous testing had been done. Looking at Figure A.9, you can see that the market started in a trading range environment. After the first week in May,

TABLE A.2
MODIFIED STOCHASTIC BUY SYSTEM TEST RESULTS

HOLDING PERIOD	TEST YEAR	% WINNING TRADES	ANNUALIZED ROI	SPX ROI
3 Days	2006	43.6%	-10.1%	13%
5 Days	2006	47.5	8.1	13
7 Days	2006	49	-6.38	13
3 Days	2007	44	-16.2	2
5 Days	2007	44	-38	2
7 Days	2007	48	-15.8	2
3 Days	2008	48	26.0	-36
5 Days	2008	48	0.5	-36
7 Days	2008	50	8.12	-36

the market transitioned to a bear market environment, and declined until the end of July. From the end of July through November, the market was in a bullish mode and then went back into a trading range environment. During this three-year period, the market showed four bearish periods, five bullish periods, and three trading range periods. The periods varied in length, but the market was always either up, down, or sideways.

Table A.3 shows the results of testing the basic Stochastic buy indicator in different market conditions. Trades were taken using the basic system. If the Stochastic indicator was below 20 yesterday and above 20 today, then long positions were entered at the open the next day, held for five days, and then sold. Trades were only taken in stocks with a 21-day average volume of at least 200,000 shares.

The data in Table A.3 gives a much clearer picture of how the basic Stochastic buy system performs over the calendar time frame testing. It shows the results of more than 79,000 trades, and indicates that the basic Stochastic

BULL, BEAR, AND TRADING RANGE MARKET PERIODS

Courtesy of AIQ

buy performs dramatically better during bullish market periods than it does during bearish market periods. During bullish market periods, the percentage of winning trades was well above random chance, and it showed an attractive annualized ROI in each of the seven bullish periods tested.

During every one of the bear market periods tested in Table A.3, the basic Stochastic buy system showed a percentage of winning trades less than random chance, and a negative annualized ROI. Clearly, the basic Stochastic buy system is not an effective trading strategy in bear market conditions.

Table A.3 also shows that the basic Stochastic buy system performed fairly well during trading range periods. The results were not as strong as the results during bullish market conditions, but in four of the five trading ranges, the results showed a percentage of winning trades that was above random chance.

BASIC STOCHASTIC BUY TEST RESULTS BY MARKET CONDITION

TEST PERIOD	MARKET TYPE	WINNING %	ANNUALIZED ROI	# OF TRADES
03/07/03-01/23/04	Bull	63%	86%	6955
08/13/04-12/31/04	Bull	65	82	3903
07/21/06-11/24/06	Bull	56	38	4791
03/17/07-07/20/07	Bull	56	32	6037
08/17/07-10/09/07	Bull	63	85	2079
03/17/08-06/05/08	Bull	58	60	3869
07/16/08-08/18/08	Bull	61	153	2065
01/04/02-10/04/02	Bear	43	-49	8589
01/23/04-08/13/04	Bear	47	-12	8291
01/07/05-04/24/05	Bear	48	-10	4852
05/11/06-07/21/06	Bear	43	-30	4468
07/20/07-08/17/07	Bear	34	-106	2417
06/06/08-07/15/08	Bear	25	-190	2970
11/25/05-05/05/06	Trading Range	55	34	5978
01/05/06-05/11/06	Trading Range	53	23	4848
11/24/06-02/26/07	Trading Range	57	29	3458
10/09/07-11/06/07	Trading Range	44	-56	1194
01/24/08-02/28/08	Trading Range	52	26	1193

Traders who do not test trading systems, or just test them in calendar periods, are missing out on valuable information that is necessary in order to use the Stochastic buy system effectively. Traders using the system consistently during all calendar periods would be quite likely to see significant drawdowns during bearish market conditions. These losses may be avoided by traders who understand that the basic Stochastic buy system is sensitive to market conditions. Effective traders always test an indicator or trading system before using it.

STOCHASTIC INDICATOR TESTING SUMMARY

The Stochastic indicator relates the current stock price to the price range over the previous 21 days. The range is the difference between the highest and lowest prices in the last 21 days. The Stochastic indicator is expressed as a percentage, and plotted on a scale of 1 to 100. A buy signal is indicated when the signal moves from below 20 to above 20, and a sell signal is indicated when the Stochastic moves from above 80 to below 80.

The tests run during 2008 show a number of trades with over 30 percent profit in just a few days, but if the system was traded regularly, it was quite likely that traders using the stochastic buy would have lost money during 2008. There were more than 20,000 stochastic buy signals during calendar 2007, but only half of them were winning trades and the annualized return of all the trades was negative. I also looked at the 16,000 stochastic buy signals that occurred during 2006 and found that 51 percent of them were winning trades. A slight annualized profit was realized, but it was less than the return for buying and holding the SPX.

Many traders are interested in knowing how a trading system did last year, or the year before. If they see these numbers it makes them happy, and they feel that it is what they should expect going forward. When some people evaluate mutual funds' or money managers' performance, they want to know how the performance was in each of the last few years. While this seems to make people happy, it does not mean much, or give a realistic impression of what to expect going forward. The reason is that the market is not the same from one year to the next. How the market, or a trading system, performed last year may have little to do with how it will perform next year. Looking at annual returns may be interesting, but it does not tell you how and when to use a trading tool.

Rather than look just at annual results, I want to know how a trading system performs in bull and bear markets. No one knows what the market will do next year. Even the "expert" economists have predicted ten of the last three recessions; they are usually all over the financial channels telling you we are in a recession or a boom period after they have started. Few, if any, consistently predict them in advance. Driving while looking in the rear view mirror can be problematic.

After testing the Stochastic buy signal in a number of different bullish, bearish, and trading range markets, the results of more than 79,000 trades indicate that the basic stochastic buy performs dramatically better during bullish market periods than it does during bearish market periods. During bullish market periods, the percentage of winning trades was well above random chance and it showed an attractive annualized ROI in each of the seven bullish periods tested. Knowing when to use a system or indicator and when to avoid it and pick another tool from the trader's tool box is one of the keys to successful trading. If you would like to see my analysis of the current market and the tools I am currently using, you can request a sample of my Timely Trades Letter by sending an email to sample@daisydogger.com.

ABOUT THE AUTHOR

STEVE PALMQUIST is a trader with more than 25 years of market experience who puts his own money to work in the market every day. He has pioneered the development of Market Adaptive Trading techniques in which specific trading tools are developed for different market conditions. Steve has shared a variety of trading systems (along with illustrating how they were designed, tested, and analyzed) at seminars across the country. He has presented trading techniques at the Traders' Expo, at the annual AIQ Tahoe seminars, and at the Traders' Library Trading Forums. He has published trading articles in *Stocks & Commodities*, *Traders Journal*, *The Opening Bell*, and *Working Money*.

Steve is the author of *Money-Making Candlestick Patterns: Backtested for Proven Results*, in which he analyzes the performance of popular candlestick patterns in different market conditions and shows specific techniques for significantly improving trading results. Steve's techniques for ETF trading were featured in the book, *ETF Trading Strategies Revealed*, by David Vomund.

Steve is the founder of www.daisydogger.com, which provides trading tips and techniques. He is also the publisher of the Timely Trades Letter in which he shares his market analysis, trading setups, and trading tips twice a week.

Steve holds a BSEE from Washington State University, and a Masters in Electrical Engineering from the University of Illinois. Steve has been involved in the management and development of communications systems, high speed computers, test equipment, infrared vision systems, and color printers at companies such as Bell Laboratories, Integrated Measurement Systems, Flir Systems, and Tektronix. He holds ten US patents. Steve is a father of four, and has a private pilot license with an instrument rating.

INDEX

NOTE: Page numbers in *italics* indicate figures or tables.

CSH (Cash America International Inc.), 252, *253*

CTSH (Cognizant Technology Solutions Corp.), 208

CTX (Centex Corp.), 171, *172*

D

data interpretation variables, 12–14

data sorting methods, 9, 75–77

declining stocks, 141. *See also* DVretrace system

declining volume, 16–18, 86–87. *See also* DVpullback system

descending trend lines, 27, 134

distribution, 207–8

distribution days, 180–82, 185, *186*, 208–9, 210, 214, 236

distribution of trades, 159–63

distribution patterns, 207–11, *212. See also* AVtop system

distribution volume, 213–14, *215*

double bottom pattern, 84–85, *86*

drawdowns, 6, 19, 124, 135, 265–66. *See also* risk management

DVpullback system

    and Bollinger band test data, 105–7

    holding times, 110–12

    initial test results, 98–101

    and market conditions, 111–18, 125–35

    overview, 69–70, 93–98, 98–101, 135–37, 232–33

    pullback depth, 119–25

    and room to run, 106–7, 108–10

    and trend lines, 132–35

    uptrend and uptrend filter, 101–5

    using BB systems data, 105–10

    utilization of, 108, 110

    volume, 118–20

See also bear markets; bull markets; trading range markets; trending markets

mechanical moving average filter, 133

MET (MetLife Inc.), 94–95

milkers vs. trading professionals, 38, 117, 195

minimum average volume, 192–93

modified Stochastic buy signal, 259–62

morning star patterns

AboveBB system, 20–30

MOV (Movado Group Inc.), 184

moving averages

and AboveBB system, 31–36, 44–46

and DVretrace system, 164–65

as filters for determining market conditions, 29–30, 41, 129–32, 164–65

holding period, volume, and, 37–38

mechanical moving average filter, 133

and trend of the price movement, 29

See also entries beginning with "five-" *and entries beginning with* "20-" *or* "21-"

multiple trading candidates, 48–52. *See also* prioritizing trades

MYGN (Myriad Genetics), *57*

O

OMG (OM Group, Inc.), 49, *50*

OSTK (Overstock.com), 211, *212*

OTC Exchange, *4, 21, 22, 24, 28, 30, 35, 42, 53, 80, 81, 84, 85, 86, 99, 112, 133, 134, 165, 218, 264*

oversold stocks, 61, 78–79, 87–89, 239, 242. *See also* BelowBB system

P

position-sizing strategies

and abnormal activity in the market, 78

overview, 19, 244

trend lines

    20-period exponential moving average as, 29

and bearish conditions, 21, *22*, 23, 167

    and bullish patterns, 22, 233, 245

    for determining market conditions, 27–30, 132–35

    and DVretrace system, 234

    for stock chart analysis, 33, 242

    and taking profits, 136

trigger day volume, 146–49

20-period exponential moving average, 29, 31, 33, 39, 56, 81, 164, 238

20-period moving average

and AboveBB in bearish markets, 31–34, *35*, 37

    for determining market conditions, 129–35

and DVretrace system, 158–59, 164, *165*

and intermediate-term trend, 80–83, 122, *123*

    similarity to trend line, 29–30, 31

    and support areas, 53–54

20-period simple moving average, 31, 39

21-day moving average, 15, 48, 239, 263

21-day simple moving average

    and AboveBB system, 15–17, 56

    and AVbottom, 174, 187, 202

    and BelowBB system, 63–64

    and distribution, 208–9, 210, 216–17, 224, 235–36

    and DVretrace, 143, 150, 166, 234

    and extensions beyond Bollinger bands, 238

    and Market Adaptive Trading, 233, 234

    and pullbacks, 97, 136

    and Stochastic indicators, 253, 260

overview, 15, 142, 172, 241–42

price of stock vs., 49

W

winning percentage

TRADING RESOURCE GUIDE

RECOMMENDED READING

MONEY-MAKING CANDLESTICK PATTERNS: BACKTESTED FOR PROVEN RESULTS

by Steve Palmquist

Candlesticks are one of the most widely used technical tools in trading. Designed to provide detailed, at-a-glance information, these charts are integrated into almost every web site and charting software solution. But, despite their popularity, the definitions of these candlestick patterns are often vague and misleading. Now, for the first time ever, Steve Palmquist hands you the secrets for effectively using candlestick patterns in all market conditions. Data that would take years to compile and years to interpret is now at your fingertips. Based on intensive back testing and research, Money-Making Candlestick Patterns shows how to appropriately use the most popular candlestick patterns in bull, bear, and sideways trends.

Item # 5510567 • List Price: $99.00

NEW MONEY-MAKING TRADING SYSTEMS: ADVANCED RESULTS FROM SIX SIMPLE, PROVEN STRATEGIES

by Steve Palmquist

In this brand-new, six-hour DVD course, Steve reveals the results of his tests on Bollinger bands, declining volume pullbacks and retracements, as well as volume accumulation and distribution to bring you six proven trading strategies. Each system was developed, tested, and analyzed for maximum profits. Steve will provide you with complete rules and exit strategies that have been backtested in various market conditions and time frames. Steve will also show you how to analyze the current market conditions and select the trading strategy that will make you the most money in a bear, bull, or trading range market.

Item # 6379227 • List Price: $995.00

PROVEN CANDLESTICK PATTERNS

by Steve Palmquist

Candles are an effective tool for extracting profits from the market. But there are hundreds of candles, and thousands of strategies for you to consider. How do you know which ones will work for you?

This 90-minute course arms you with what you need to know about candlestick patterns. It shows you the candlesticks you should be using and which ones you should avoid. Most traders spend years collecting this powerful information, and you'll have access to it all at once! Don't let another day go by without knowing these proven candlestick patterns!

Item # 5197576 • List Price: $99.00

PRECISE EXITS & ENTRIES:
THE GUIDE TO AVERAGE TRUE RANGE

by Chuck LeBeau

In this two-disk DVD, LeBeau is ready to teach you the secrets that he has seen stand the test of time and that he still uses to increase his winning percentage in today's market.

The key is to be adaptive in your trading; to have multiple strategies available in order to tackle any challenge the market throws at you. But how do you define these strategies and how do you optimize them for your trading style?

Enter LeBeau's two weapons of choice: Average Directional Index (ADX) and Average True Range (ATR). With in-depth analysis and step-by-step instruction, LeBeau will teach you how these two tools will reinvent how you trade.

Item # 5705109 • List Price: $299.00

TRADING FULL CIRCLE:
THE COMPLETE UNDERGROUNDTRADER SYSTEM FOR TIMING AND PROFITING IN ALL FINANCIAL MARKETS

by Jea Yu

Have you ever felt that could make more in the markets? Has the success you know you are capable of been just within your grasp, only to slip away before you can lock in the profit? Profitable trading is a combination of strategy, analysis, psychology, and determination and until now, it took years to find the perfect balance of each. Never before has a master outlined how to put the pieces together in a guide that is so easy to understand and interesting to read. The key to gaining control of your trading and collecting the payouts you know the market holds is finally available.

In *Trading Full Circle*, Yu gives you complete explanations of the tools he uses to trade, along with his personal playbook of powerful techniques using these tools to trade nearly any situation the market presents you.

Item # 8006857 • List Price: $199.00

SHORT-TERM PROFIT HUNTER:
STOCHASTICS, MOVING AVERAGES AND THE MINDSET TO MAKE YOU A WINNING TRADER

by Jea Yu

Traders are always on the hunt—for the right market environment, the strongest setup, the greatest odds. What if you had a way to narrow that search?

It's as simple as using the best weapons in your search. With this new course, you will find out how to sharpen those tools and make them even more potent. Let Jea Yu, founder of UndergroundTrader.com and market veteran, show you how to create explosive profit-making opportunities by combining the strength of his top trading tools.

Item # 9644618 • List Price: $199.00

▲ ▲ ▲ ▲ ▲ ▲

To get the current lowest price on any item listed
Go to www.traderslibrary.com

Marketplace Books is the preeminent publisher of trading, investing, and finance educational material. We produce professional books, DVDs, courses, and electronic books (ebooks) that showcase the exceptional talent working in the investment world today. Started in 1993, Marketplace Books grew out of the realization that mainstream publishers were not meeting the demand of the trading and investment community. Capitalizing on the access we had through our distribution partner Traders' Library, Marketplace Books was launched, and today publishes the top authors in the industry — household names like Jack Schwager, Oliver Velez, Larry McMillan, Sheldon Natenberg, Jim Bittman, Martin Pring, and Jeff Cooper are just the beginning. We are actively acquiring some of the brightest new minds in the industry including technician Jeff Greenblatt and programmers Jean Folger and Lee Leibfarth.

From the beginning student to the professional trader, our goal is to continually provide the highest quality resources for those who want an active role in the world of finance. Our products focus on strategic information and cutting edge research to give our readers the best education possible. We are at the forefront of digital publishing and are actively pursuing innovative ways to deliver content. At our Traders' Forum events, our readers get the chance to learn and mingle with our top authors in a way unprecedented in the industry. Our titles have been translated in most major world languages and can be shipped all over the globe thanks to our preferred online bookstore, TradersLibrary.com.

Visit us today at:

www.marketplacebooks.com & www.traderslibrary.com

This book, and other great products, are available at significantly discounted prices. They make great gifts for your customers, clients, and staff. For more information on these long-lasting, cost-effective premiums, please call (800) 272-2855, or email us at sales@traderslibrary.com.